# SILENCE, LOVE, AND DEATH:

## SAYING "YES" TO GOD

# IN THE THEOLOGY OF KARL RAHNER

# SILENCE, LOVE, AND DEATH:

## SAYING "YES" TO GOD

## IN THE THEOLOGY OF KARL RAHNER

### SHANNON CRAIGO-SNELL

MARQUETTE
UNIVERSITY
PRESS

MARQUETTE STUDIES IN THEOLOGY

NO. 56

ANDREW TALLON, SERIES EDITOR

LIBRARY OF CONGRESS CATALOGING-IN-PUBLICATION DATA

Craigo-Snell, Shannon Nichole.
  Silence, love, and death : saying "yes" to God in the theology of Karl Rahner /
Shannon Craigo-Snell.
    p. cm. — (Marquette studies in theology ; no. 56)
  Includes bibliographical references (p.    ) and index.
  ISBN-13: 978-0-87462-733-6 (pbk. : alk. paper)
  ISBN-10: 0-87462-733-8 (pbk. : alk. paper)
  1. Rahner, Karl, 1904-1984. 2. Spirituality—Catholic Church. 3. Silence—Religious
aspects—Catholic Church. 4. Love—Religious aspects—Catholic Church. 5.
Death—Religious aspects—Catholic Church. 6. Catholic Church—Doctrines. I.
Title.
  BX2350.65.C73 2008
  230'.2092--dc22

                                         2008017238

COVER ART © BY CHRISTINA CRAIGO
"THE PASSERSBY"
PRIVATE COLLECTION, CONNECTICUT
INK ON PAPER
1995
23 X 21"
http://christinacraigo.com/

♾ The paper used in this publication meets the minimum requirements of the
American National Standard for Information Sciences—
Permanence of Paper for Printed Library Materials, ANSI Z39.48-1992.

MARQUETTE UNIVERSITY PRESS
MILWAUKEE

The Association of Jesuit University Presses

# TABLE OF CONTENTS

Chapter 1: Saying "Yes" .................................................. 9
    Introduction ........................................................ 9
    Reading Rahner ................................................. 13
    Rahner's Theological Anthropology .................. 19
    Saying "Yes" ...................................................... 35

Chapter 2: Silence ..................................................... 39
    Introduction ...................................................... 39
    Images of Silence .............................................. 40
    Divine/Human Dialogue ................................... 42
    God in Language ............................................... 54
    Language and Experience ................................. 59
    Rahner's Use of Silence .................................... 75

Chapter 3: Love ........................................................ 79
    Introduction ...................................................... 79
    The Love of God and The Love of Neighbor ...... 82
    Anonymous Christians ...................................... 96
    Lonely Decision in Community ......................... 110
    Spirituality and Theology of Love .................... 119

Chapter 4: Death ...................................................... 121
    Introduction ...................................................... 121
    Death as Act ...................................................... 124
    Dying in Sin and Dying in Christ ...................... 128
    Sanctified Humanity ......................................... 136
    An All-Cosmic Soul? .......................................... 144
    Silence, Love, and Death ................................... 150

Chapter 5: A Modern Medieval in Postmodern Times ........ 155
    Introduction ...................................................... 155

Modernity, Postmodernity, and Human Knowing.............156
Being .................................................................................158
Language ............................................................................161
Being and Language ..........................................................163
Postmodern Questions Regarding Rahner's Theology......166
Reading Rahner in a New Key ...........................................175
Turn to the Other...............................................................200
Self-Evident Mystery .........................................................202
Continuing Constructive Vitality......................................208

Coda .......................................................................................211
Introduction .......................................................................211
Silence, Love, and Death....................................................211
Silence and Love ................................................................214
Love and Death..................................................................224
Conclusion .........................................................................232

Works Cited ...........................................................................233

Index.......................................................................................247

# ACKNOWLEDGEMENTS

This book has been several years in the making and I have accrued multiple debts of gratitude. Many people I have known through Yale—as professors, colleagues, and students—have contributed to the progress of these pages. With patience, generosity, and care, Margaret Farley and David Kelsey advised the dissertation in which I first wrote of Karl Rahner. Serene Jones is a supportive mentor who deeply shaped my theological questioning. During my graduate studies, Cyril O'Regan and Nicholas Wolterstorff encouraged and guided my constructive theological pursuits. Marilyn and Bob Adams have offered rigorous criticism, wise counsel, and gracious friendship. My fellow students in the graduate program at Yale encouraged this work through sustained, and sustaining, theological conversation. My thanks to Jennifer Beste, Wendy Boring, Stephen Edmondson, Amy Laura Hall, Jeff Hensley, Cyndi Hess, Ruthanna Hooke, Aimee Light, Stephen Wray, Warren Smith, Tracy Swan Tuite, John Utz, and Madhuri Yadlapati. Since I began teaching at Yale, my colleagues have also helped me bring this book into being. I am grateful for comments from Miroslav Volf and conversation with Denys Turner; for advice from Dale Martin, Skip Stout, and Emilie Townes; for support from Terri Boustead. Ludger Viefhues-Bailey and Siobhán Garrigan have helped me hone my arguments, refine my prose, and keep my sanity. Three students—Scott Larson, Luke Moorhead, and Ed Waggoner—helped me prepare the manuscript and provided challenging and clarifying conversation. Christopher Doucot gave helpful comments on the final chapter and Camille Lizarribar provided a keen eye for grammatical detail.

Beth and Mel Keiser, with whom I first studied theology, have continued to teach and mentor me, including reading drafts of this text and discussing many of its central themes. Roger Haight graciously read a prior version of this manuscript and offered insightful comments. Andrew Tallon gave me knowledgeable comments, challenging suggestions, and welcome encouragement.

Others have contributed to this project through their life-giving friendship. I give thanks to Leslie Callahan, Chris Carr, the Farris family, Emily Flaherty, Sheri Garzelli, Scott Gordon, Jen Ho, Mike Hopkins, Susannah Mozley, Shawnthea Monroe Mueller, Anna Parr, Janet Redmiles, Karen Seto, Cynthia Terry, Mimi Walters, and Shirley Woodall.

Several communities have also sustained this work. Hartford Meeting of the Religious Society of Friends, and in particular Jeannette Smith, taught me much about silence, community, and grace. First Congregational Church in Albuquerque, New Mexico, was an oasis in the desert. I am grateful for the Thursday night Bible study and especially to Colleen Miller. Since returning to New Haven, my family has found an unexpected home at First Presbyterian Church. The years during which I have written this coincide with the early years of my children's lives. This was made possible and joyful by the extraordinary community of Abiyoyo, and by the enormous blessing of Kathy and Jack McMurray.

I also thank my family, including Blaine Parkins, Arnie and Naomi Craigo, and Easil Martin. Betty and Darrell Haslacker, Paul and Polly Iman, and all the Snells have patiently supported this odd endeavor. My sisters—Sabrina, Chris, and Desirée—demanded articulate argument at an early age and continue to challenge me through speed-Scrabble and fiercely competitive Botticelli. My parents, Oshel and Joanna Craigo, have enabled me, through their effort and encouragement, to make a career out of work that I love. This is an immeasurable gift. My children have also been part of this project. Jacob came home from kindergarten and wrote books at the kitchen table with me, in solidarity. Elias learned to crack an imaginary whip, sending me off to work with laughter. I am grateful to and for them. I also thank my husband, Seth, who has been my partner in the writing of this book in countless practical ways. He has sustained, inspired, and challenged me throughout years of school, work, and parenting. This book has been written both with and for him.

Finally, as a theologian, a feminist, a teacher, and a Christian, Letty Russell has been a profound influence on my life. She died after this manuscript was written, but before it was printed. Always generous and demanding, she gave me comments on the final chapter in our last meeting before her death. I have not altered the text of the book to reflect her passing, but here I must note that the embarrassing length of these acknowledgements is, in itself, a witness to Letty's mentoring. She taught me that feminist theology is done in community, and modeled a praxis of community-building that inspires hope for the Household of God.

# CHAPTER I
## SAYING "YES"

### INTRODUCTION

One of the central elements of Karl Rahner's theology is the affirmation that God offers salvation to every human being and, in so doing, empowers each of us to say "yes" to this holy vocation. This divine-human dialogue of offer and response is the heart of Rahner's understanding of Christian faith. In this book, I explore what it means to say "yes" to God in Rahner's theology. In keeping with Rahner's own commitment to bring theology and spirituality together, I address this issue from these two, interrelated angles. What are the theological groundings and implications of Rahner's portrayal of this dialogue? Can Rahner continue to be relevant for constructive Christian theology?

As with any work on Rahner, this exploration must begin with an analysis and assessment of his view of the human person. Rahner's distinctive theological anthropology paints a picture of the human person as deeply connected to the mystery of God on an ontological level and within her everyday experiences of life. Is Rahner's complex and subtle theological anthropology compelling in the twenty-first century? It can seem outdated—based on a philosophical methodology that appears obsolete, uncritical of the dangers of universalizing, individualistic and essentialist accounts of humanity, and permeated with a grand narrative that cannot address the fragmented reality of a postmodern world. Yet seen from another perspective, Rahner's view of the self is particularly well suited to present concerns. His description of the human person both acknowledges the many ways that she is embedded in a social location that shapes her deeply and yet claims there is something more to each of us than the interconnections of myriad external events and influences. Who we are is profoundly influenced by our cultures, families, and histories. At the same time, we are more than the sum of our parts, no matter how minutely and extensively our parts are described.

Similarly, current philosophical and theoretical writings on freedom help us to understand the many ways in which our freedom is limited, restricted, dependent, and constrained. And yet we must continue to make choices, to live our lives in ways that create and sustain a sense of who we are over time. We cannot be unburdened of ourselves. After analyzing Rahner's work in the context of modern philosophy and theology, I argue that his anthropology cannot be simply equated with modern views of the self. His vision of human community is not solely based on a modern model of free interrelation among autonomous selves; it is held within a view of the mystical interrelation of persons grounded in the mystery of God. Thus Rahner's theology and spirituality can provide useful resources in navigating current debates about the self.

Saying "yes" is so central to Rahner's theology and spirituality that he describes it again and again, both in the language of a systematic theologian and in the words of a priest offering spiritual care and guidance to laypersons. Thus to fully explore what it means to say "yes," it is important both to analyze Rahner's sophisticated academic accounts and to pay close attention to the images and examples he uses in more pastoral moments. In this book I draw on a variety of Rahner's writings and focus on three moments in human freedom that he repeatedly points to in describing how we say "yes" to God: silence, love, and death.

Rahner frequently uses the image of silence in his descriptions of God and of the proper human response to God, yet this has received relatively little sustained attention in publications on his work. I examine silence in relation to the self, the mystery of God, and the supernatural existential. This analysis provides insight into his view of the human person, the spiritual possibilities of human relationships, and the fundamental character of Christian faith. In Rahner's writings, silence marks the distinction and difference between persons that make relationships possible, as well as the discipline of accepting that difference, of choosing to take up a risky posture of openness to the mysterious and unmanipulable other. This posture of openness—to both the human other and the divine Other—is an intrinsic element of faith.

In such silent openness a person risks the reconfiguration of herself through encounter with mystery. Understanding what it means to say "yes" through the image of silence highlights the apophatic, mystical, and individualistic aspects of Rahner's thought.

Love is the act of freedom that Rahner most explicitly connects to accepting God's offer of salvation. Given Rahner's Christocentric theological anthropology, in each act of loving the neighbor, people love God. Furthermore, one cannot love God without loving one's neighbor. Rahner understands love not as a sentiment or emotion, but rather as the free act of risking one's own benefit or sense of safety for the sake of the other. In every moment that a person is loyal when disloyalty would not be condemned, kind when unkindness would be overlooked, honest when deceit would be rewarded, or refuses to use the other for her own self-advantage, that person is saying "yes" to God. In continuity with his use of the image of silence, Rahner portrays Christian love of neighbor as opening oneself to encounter with the other who is too finite and flawed to be worthy of unconditional love. Rahner claims that Jesus, who stands as surety for both parties in such an encounter, empowers Christians to love extravagantly. Exploring how we say "yes" to God in loving emphasizes the social, political, and communal aspects of Rahner's view of salvation. In this context, I address Rahner's theory of anonymous Christians, his relation to political and liberation theologies, and his rejection of the modern division between the secular and the religious.

Rahner's understanding of death weaves together his existentialist influences and his deep roots in the mystical traditions of Christianity. The specter of death, threatening to negate us, demands that we take up a stance in response—either to accept that death is the limit of human life or to trust that human life is held within a reality stronger than death and greater than finitude. Death, then, demands our "yes" or "no" to God. Death also confronts us with the limits of human knowledge. In stripping away all finite structures of meaning, death both makes it difficult to trust in God and more possible to trust in the God of mystery instead of a human creation. Furthermore, death marks the culmination of human freedom, when the "yes" or "no" spoken throughout an individual human life becomes valid for all eternity.

All of Rahner's discussions of death are shaped by the cross as the Christological climax of the dialogue between God and humanity and influenced by a Thomistic understanding of the relationship between spirit and matter. Rahner attempts to articulate a contemporary vision of the communion of the saints, in which the relations between spirit and matter, individual and community, are neither oppositional nor dualistic. In this discussion I explore the implications of an eschatology focused on a communally sanctified humanity, in contrast to the notion of the immortality of the individual human soul. In addressing saying "yes" to God in death, the Christological and mystical elements of Rahner's thought are revisited in the context of a radical inter-communion of persons.

Looking closely at these three moments in which human persons say "yes" to God in succession builds a cumulative argument concerning Rahner's theological anthropology. The openness to the other marked by the theme of silence is fundamental to how Rahner views the person. This openness is concretely realized in love and is fully actualized in an eternal inter-communion.

Bringing Rahner's theology into conversation with feminist and postmodern concerns regarding the nature of the self, I address interpretations of Rahner's work that suggest his anthropological starting point determines his theology to a large degree, such that his view of the human person is just one more rendition of the modern self. In this view, Rahner's theology falls prey to the criticisms of modernity leveled by feminist and postmodern thinkers. Evaluating Rahner's work on key issues such as language, individualism, and the social construction of the self, I find resources for an alternative reading that fits neatly into neither modern nor postmodern molds.

Attending to silence, love, and death in Rahner's work reveals three correlative, significant ways in which his thought departs from mainstream modernity. First, in contrast to modern anthropologies, Rahner portrays openness to the mysterious other as a primary characteristic of what it is to be human. This emphasis on openness, otherness, and mystery connects with an epistemology that sees the summit of human knowledge not in the intellectual transparency of geometry or mathematics, but rather in the mystical encounter of love. Second, Rahner's description of love as the way humans actualize this openness to the other presents human identity as both gift received and task accomplished. Furthermore, it rejects modern compartmentalization of the secular and the sacred. No part of human reality is untouched by the offer of grace; no moment of human life is free from the demands of sanctification. Third, Rahner's writing about death is not a Cartesian affirmation of the immortality of the individual soul. Rather, it is a portrait of a communally sanctified humanity, in which the relationship between individual and community cannot be understood in oppositional terms. Concluding that Rahner's thought eludes easy categorization as either modern or postmodern, I then offer a constructive theological coda, suggesting three particular ways that Rahner's theology could be useful for contemporary feminist theology.

## READING RAHNER

This book offers a new approach to Rahner's theology by adopting a particular manner of reading his work and by focusing on the themes of silence, love, and death. The rationale for focusing on these themes is straightforward: they figure consistently in Rahner's descriptions of saying "yes" to God. My manner of reading Rahner requires more explanation.

There are two prominent strands of traditional Rahner interpretation. One sees Rahner as offering, in his early writings (*Spirit in the World* and *Hearer of the Word*), a philosophical account of the human person that is the starting point and guiding logic of his later theology.[1] In this light, Rahner's large corpus is significantly unified by an underlying philosophy, which falls squarely within the traditions and trajectories of modern German philosophy. Rahner's theology begins with the self-reflection of the knowing subject, asks about the *a priori* conditions for the possibility of human knowledge, and generates an account of Christianity upon this basis. Such readings often view Rahner as appropriating Thomas Aquinas after Immanuel Kant, and look closely at the influence of Joseph Maréchal.[2] Many such read-

1 Kilby also notes these two types, described somewhat differently (Kilby 2004, 9, 10).

2 For a brief description of such readings, see Vorgrimler (Vorgrimler 1966, 52-55).

ings understand Rahner as, to some degree or another, a philosophical foundationalist. That is, they view his early works as constructing
a foundation—rationally derived and external to Christian claims of
faith—upon which his claims about Christianity are built. There is
much to support such interpretations of Rahner, both within Rahner's texts and in the insight garnered by this method of understanding them.[3]

However, this approach to Rahner is also problematic. Its assumption of unity in Rahner's writings overlooks the occasional and ad hoc
manner of their production that has been noted by many scholars,[4]
and renders a view of Rahner with a number of significant inconsistencies. Specifically, Rahner's statements about the corporate nature
of humanity and the importance of interpersonal relations seem in-
congruous and secondary within a theology built up from individual
self-reflection. At the same time, the importance of Rahner's spiritual
writings is greatly diminished by such an approach.

The second prominent strand of Rahner interpretation has several
similarities to the first, even though it begins with different assumptions. This approach focuses on Rahner's spirituality and highlights
the experience of God as the unifying element of Rahner's work.[5]
Some readings in this vein understand all of Rahner's theology as the
explication of his own experience of God. This can be seen as a different kind of foundationalism, one which identifies a firm ground
for Christian claims not in rationally derived statements, but rather
in religious experience. Both views seek to locate a firm, indubitable
touchstone upon which faith can rest, although they locate such a
touchstone somewhat differently. While this approach to Rahner also
has textual support and insightful benefits, it has difficulties as well.
Particularly, as Philip Endean notes, it undermines the intellectual

---

3 For example, see Burke (2002). Burke states: "Rahner's theology is rightly
recognized as a theological system because of the fundamental unity that
runs throughout his writings. The key to this unity of approach lies in a foundational structure of thought that is revealed in the philosophical works with
which he began his intellectual career" (Burke 2002, vii).

4 This will be discussed more below. Here I note that the term "ad hoc" is
applied to Rahner's apologetics by Healy (1992).

5 See, for example, Egan (1998).

achievement of Rahner's theology and can appear to use the notion of religious experience to shelter his ideas from critical debate (Endean 2001, 142).

Both of these views are susceptible to contemporary criticisms of foundationalism (of any sort) that builds upon insights, essences, or experiences that are abstracted from cultural, social, and historical contexts. In other words, both ways of reading Rahner portray him as locating a basis for Christian faith outside of the language and practices of Christian communities. There are at least two problems with this. First, it seems inadequate to the realities of how human beings know the world around them. Many current theories, including several that fall within the umbrella term "postmodernism," describe human knowledge as so profoundly shaped by language and culture that it is impossible to know something apart from that. If there is some pure touchstone—of reason or experience—the minute we try to understand it and talk about it, we do so through lenses that have been formed in culture. Therefore attempts to build upon such a foundation always fail, as they are always bound up with unrecognized cultural assumptions. Second, basing Christian faith on something outside the life of Christian faith—either through reason or through a universally-available experience of God—subjugates Christian revelation to another form of knowledge. Christian truth, on this view, appears as a subset of some other form of truth, be it philosophical or revealed in a general religious experience. This undercuts both the authority and the distinctiveness of the Christian faith. These two criticisms, applied to traditional readings of Rahner, depict his work either as an unsuccessful attempt to ground Christianity on secular philosophy, or as failing to understand the ways in which communal language and practice shape how Christians experience God.[6]

There are many places in which Rahner's texts strain against either of the forms of foundationalism discussed above. Consider, for example, *Foundations of Christian Faith*, the most systematic presentation of Rahner's theology. The title of the book suggests that it will, indeed, provide the foundations of Christian faith. However, in the

---

6 This small typology, like most others, oversimplifies the picture, since many readers of Rahner combine these two approaches or stray from both of them.

introduction to the book Rahner criticizes traditional understandings of fundamental theologies that aim to establish such foundations on non-theological grounds, and declares his own intentions to offer an alternative. He writes:

> As fundamental theology is in fact usually understood, it does not consider any particular theological data or any individual dogmas, except when it becomes dogmatic ecclesiology. But that brings it into a noteworthy difficulty, at least from the viewpoint of the purpose of this foundational course. The point of our foundational course in theology is precisely this, to give people confidence from the very *content* of Christian dogma itself that they can believe with intellectual honesty. (Rahner 1982, 11, 12.[7])

He describes his own aim in relation to Thomas Aquinas, as "a justification of faith by faith" (12, 13).[8]

Rahner thus rejects the idea of grounding theology on a non-theological foundation, and discusses Christianity within the framework of a commitment to Christian faith and life. He introduces another text by stating, "The following reflexions are written by one who is not 'neutral' but 'committed,' by one in other words who hopes he is a Christian to the best of his ability. The ultimate questions of life can in fact be expressed only by a committed person, because, in so far as they are questions embracing everything as a totality, they have no standpoint outside themselves" (Rahner 1975a, 21).

In recent years, many scholars have moved towards new ways of reading Rahner that appreciate his apologetic stance, his spiritual convictions, the unsystematic production of his work in several genres, and the historical debates and concerns to which he spoke. Peter C. Phan discusses Rahner's "new and valuable apologetical approach," in which the resurrection grounds faith from within (Phan 1988, 177).[9] Russell Reno describes Rahner's method in relation to the particular debates

---

7  Except where otherwise noted, within quotations I replicate the emphasis of the author.

8  See also Rahner (1968, 120, 121) for related comments.

9  This is particularly interesting in relation to Rahner's comments about Christian faith as integral to the resurrection, discussed in later chapters. Note also Rahner's similar comments about martyrdom as both content and motive of faith in Rahner (1964, 123).

of his day on the relationship between nature and grace (Reno 1995). William Dych argues that Rahner always begins with theological conviction and then picks up available and useful philosophical tools to elaborate that theology. Dych uses Rahner's development of the concept of the supernatural existential as a response to the nature/grace debate to illustrate this point (Dych 1992, 32-39). Nicholas Healy looks closely at Rahner's apologetic commitments and refers to him as an "ad hoc apologist" (Healy 1992). Geffrey Kelly points out the inadequacy of the various labels that are attached to Rahner's theology (Kelly 1992, 62). While Endean is primarily in conversation with the second type of interpretation, centered on Rahner's spirituality, his work addresses difficulties with both approaches (Endean 2001, 7). Michael J. Scanlon sees in Rahner not an epistemological foundationalism, but a "theological foundationalism" (Scanlon 1999, 226). Even Fergus Kerr, who once dismissed Rahner as irredeemably Cartesian, sees in the work of contemporary Rahner scholars the possibility of reading Rahner in new, even "postmodern," ways (Kerr 1997b, 180). Clearly many of these scholars do not read Rahner as a philosophical foundationalist.

It can be challenging to persuade readers that Rahner eludes this classification. Several elements of his theological method lend themselves to a foundationalist interpretation. In teaching Rahner's theology, often to students who are immersed in the methodological struggles of modern theology and who have recently read Karl Barth, I try to communicate that Rahner's theology moves in an unexpected pattern. Barth argues brilliantly that the starting point of a theology will be its endpoint as well: that beginning with humanity can lead only to the human and not to the divine. Thus his discussions of theology always begin with God, more specifically, with Jesus Christ. Having been persuaded by Barth, many of my students (especially those from Protestant churches) assume that Rahner's anthropological starting point reveals his priorities and his limitations. He chooses to write about humanity and can never legitimately make his way to talk about the God of Christianity. Students have valid reasons for such suspicions and their worries are echoed in many pages of Rahner scholarship and criticism.

However, I explain to my classes that, with Rahner, the punchline comes at the end of the story. It is only in the conclusions of his narratives that one finds the driving force and centering logic of Rahner's argument. Rahner begins with humanity not to spin out the truth of Christianity from human cognition, but to invite the reader on a journey, one that begins exactly where the reader is already standing. Following Rahner along the path he lays out in his theology, the reader is introduced to the content of Christian faith, the mystery of God, and the love of Jesus Christ. From this vantage point, the reader can look back at her original standpoint—as well as the one she now inhabits—and experience it in a new way. I suggest to my students that Rahner's theological method is not an attempt to reach God by human means or build Christianity on reasonable foundations, but rather a discursive strategy aimed at altering self-understanding, such that by the end of Rahner's journey, the reader can only locate her own starting point in reference to the God of Jesus Christ.[10]

Something similar to this pedagogical analogy has been argued for quite substantially by Karen Kilby in her recent book, *Karl Rahner: Theology and Philosophy*. Kilby contends that while many scholars understand Rahner to be a philosophical foundationalist, or semi-foundationalist, one can legitimately interpret his theology in a nonfoundationalist way. Kilby does not argue that foundationalist readings are inaccurate, but rather that they are accompanied by a number of inconsistencies and difficulties that can be avoided by a nonfoundationalist view.[11] Reading Rahner as a nonfoundationalist, Kilby claims, allows one to see Rahner's theology in its strongest form. She thus construes the relationship between his theology and philosophy such that they are related without the theology being grounded in the philosophy. She states:

> On such a [nonfoundationalist] reading, though Rahner does make use of ideas developed in his philosophical writings, his theology is

---

10   See Rahner (1982, 307).

11   Kilby does argue that there is a significant problem in viewing Rahner's theology as being built upon his earlier philosophy, in that the argument in *Hearer of the Word* is incompatible with the supernatural existential, and that Rahner fails to establish a "philosophical demonstration of the existence of a *Vorgriff*" (2004, 63, 76).

not *logically dependent* on the arguments he offers for these ideas. The theology stands on its own. The same claims, on such a reading, may function differently in different parts of Rahner's corpus: what is at one point presented as the conclusion of a philosophical argument may elsewhere function as a theological hypothesis.... What must be denied, for the nonfoundationalist, is that Rahner's theology is dependent on a philosophy *formally* distinct from it, on an independently argued philosophy which makes no appeal to revelation. (Kilby 2004, 76)

In this book, I follow the authors who read Rahner in new ways, eschewing both types of interpretation discussed above (philosophically foundationalist or reflection on personal spiritual experience) and attending to the style and contexts of Rahner's work in several genres. Particularly, I follow Kilby in understanding the basis of Rahner's theology not as independent philosophy, but as theological claims made within the context of Christian tradition. Furthermore, I accept a distinction she makes at several points, namely, that Rahner makes theological claims about *truth* that transcends history and human culture, without thereby asserting that his own *claims* escape historical and cultural conditioning (97, 105).

## RAHNER'S THEOLOGICAL ANTHROPOLOGY

What it means to read Rahner in a nonfoundationalist manner, that is, to view his statements as theological claims related to, but not dependent upon, his philosophy, is perhaps best explained by describing such a view of Rahner's theological anthropology. Rahner explicates his theological anthropology in many different writings. For clarity, I rely primarily on *Foundations* in this brief introduction, and apply a nonfoundationalist reading to many diverse texts in the chapters to come.

The process Rahner uses to describe the human person is generally referred to as transcendental method, even though it is recognized that the label does not quite fit. The term is generally used, following Kant, to indicate an inquiry into the *a priori* structures of human knowing, the conditions of the possibility of knowledge. This is an ahistorical form of questioning that leads to universal traits of cognition. At the same time, Rahner aims to apply this general form of questioning to a decidedly historical matter. He asks about the conditions of the possibility of the hearing of the Christian message, seeking the structures within the human person that make faith possible. He asks, "What kind of hearer does Christianity anticipate so that its real and ultimate message can even be heard?" (Rahner 1982, 24). He writes of the presuppositions of the Christian message and the message itself as "interwoven." He states, "Christianity assumes that these presuppositions…are inescapably and necessarily present…and that at the same time the Christian message itself creates these presuppositions by its call" (24). Thus Rahner's method is a hybrid form of transcendental inquiry: it asks both an ahistorical question about the structures in the human person that make knowing possible and an historical question about the structures in the human person that make hearing the message of Christianity possible (Marmion 2003, 199).[12]

Rahner states that he is asking about the human person's "essential being as something which is always historically constituted," and acknowledges that the presuppositions of Christian hearing "belong to the content of a revealed theology which announces Christianity" to humanity (1982, 24-25). He is clearly moving away from transcendental inquiry in strictly philosophical terms, and, in fact, he rejects the terms of such philosophy that is done in isolation from theology. He states, "A philosophy that is absolutely free of theology is not even possible in our historical situation" (25). Thus Rahner's theology, while shaped by transcendental inquiry in philosophy, also departs from it in acknowledging the historical constitution of persons, in asking about the presuppositions of the reception of an historical religion, by announcing that the presuppositions it seeks are revealed in Christianity, and by rejecting the idea of a philosophy untainted by theology.

Having explained the hybrid method he uses to ask about the human person, Rahner then delves into the meaning of the fact that human persons can ask about themselves in their totality. Many different sciences and methods are used to try to explain who and what a human being is. Biology, psychology, anthropology, sociology—all of these are "quite legitimately trying to derive and explain man, to dissolve him, as it were, into his empirical causes which can be specified

---

12   See also Kelly (1992) for another discussion of Rahner's method as transcendental and historical.

and analyzed and isolated" (27). Our own experience confirms many of their findings as correct. We realize, with both relief and horror, that we are a product of things other than ourselves (27). So much of who we are, how we respond to the world around us, our dreams and difficulties, pains and patterns, can be ascribed to the causality of our cultural heritage, our genetic makeup, our upbringing and past experiences. Christianity addresses the whole person and thus rejects a dualism of matter and spirit that would allow us to separate out the part of ourselves that can be thus accounted for and declare our spirits to somehow remain untouched by these causal factors. We cannot avoid the claims of these regional anthropologies. And yet, regardless of how well our scientific knowledge unravels and explains us, we continue to experience ourselves as personal subjects, as people who cannot be truly unburdened of ourselves. We realize that none of these scientific approaches can account for the part of ourselves that instigates their investigations, the part of us that sees ourselves as whole individuals and asks who we are. Rahner writes:

> In the fact that man raises analytical questions about himself and opens himself to the unlimited horizons of such questioning, he has already transcended himself and every conceivable element of such an analysis or of an empirical reconstruction of himself. In doing this he is affirming himself as more than the sum of such analyzable components of his reality. Precisely this consciousness of himself, this confrontation with the totality of all his conditions, and this very being-conditioned show him to be more than the sum of his factors. For a finite system of individual, distinguishable elements cannot have the kind of relationship to itself which man has to himself in the experience of his multiple conditioning and his reducibility. A finite system cannot confront itself in its totality... It does not ask questions about itself. It is not a subject. The experience of radical questioning and man's ability to place himself in question are things which a finite system cannot accomplish. (29, 30)

Part of what personhood means, Rahner concludes, is "the self-possession of a subject as such in a conscious and free relationship to the totality of itself" (30). As persons and subjects, we are more than can be explained or derived from other causes and elements. Every attempt to objectify and analyze ourselves into a plurality of origins and explanations inadvertently affirms ourselves as subjects who are something more, prior, and more original than any combination of such origins and explanations (31). Our very recognition of our finitude indicates that we transcend it.

In experiencing our finitude, we reach beyond it, and thus experience ourselves as "transcendent being, as spirit" (32). Rahner writes, "Man is a transcendent being insofar as all of his knowledge and all of his conscious activity is grounded in a pre-apprehension (*Vorgriff*) of 'being' as such, in an unthematic but ever-present knowledge of the infinity of reality" (33). He explains, "[t]he movement of the mind to the individual object, with which it is occupied, always goes toward the particular object *precisely* by going beyond it. What is objectively known and named as individual is always grasped in a wider un-named, implicitly present horizon of possible knowledge and freedom as a whole" (1983c, 196).

Every human act of knowing, willing or love is directed to a particular, categorical object or person. Rahner claims there are two implicit elements of such acts. First, the human person experiences herself as actor—as the one who knows, wills, or love. Second, she experiences the infinite horizon of possibility that surrounds and enables her relations to self, to objects, and to other persons. These two experiences, subjective self-possession and the *a priori* openness to infinity, form the basis of Rahner's concept of transcendental experience. He writes:

> We shall call *transcendental experience* the subjective, unthematic, necessary and unfailing consciousness of the knowing subject that is co-present in every spiritual act of knowledge, and the subject's openness to the unlimited expanse of all possible reality. It is an *experience* because this knowledge, unthematic but ever-present, is a moment within and a condition of the possibility for every concrete experience of any and every object. This experience is called *transcendental* experience because it belongs to the necessary and inalienable structures of the knowing subject itself, and because it consists precisely in the transcendence beyond any particular group of possible objects or of categories. Transcendental experience is the experience of *transcendence*, in which experience the structure of the subject and therefore also the ultimate structure of every conceivable object of knowledge are present together and in identity. (1982, 20)

This self-presence and openness are *transcendental* experience because knowledge of them is deduced from asking about the conditions of the possibility of human knowing. Rahner also calls them, considered together, the experience of *transcendence*, because they form an element of all experience in which the human person both knows his own finitude and goes far beyond it in openness to the infinite.

Rahner's use of these two phrases—"transcendental experience" and "experience of transcendence"—dovetails with his hybridization of transcendental method. Rahner both wants to use a method of reasoning that deduces *a priori* structures of the human subject and he wants to talk about these structures as aspects of ourselves to which we are not entirely without experiential access. Transcendental inquiry in a traditional, purely philosophical form, would not result in something that could be understood as an experience. It would yield speculative knowledge of conditions of experience, not claims about another type of experience (Adams 2005, 217).[13] Rahner explains transcendental experience as a unique form of experience, but an experience nonetheless. It is "incommensurable with what we ordinarily describe as 'experience'…and does not signify an encounter with any sort of particular object that happens to come upon us from outside." Yet, he claims, "in addition to these individual experiences of certain individual realities, there is a quite different experience, not by any means given thematic expression in the ordinary routine of our experiences: the experience of the one subject as such, that has all these experiences as its own and has to answer for them, that is itself present in its original unity and totality" (1983c, 190).[14]

---

13  I have encountered readers of Rahner, including scholars of his work and professors who teach his texts, who understand Rahner as drawing his theology out of a philosophy situated within the trajectory of modern German thought to such a degree that they simply deny that Rahner intends "transcendental experience" to mean anything to which we have access, to be anything other than a speculative condition of experience. I find such a reading renders Rahner's theology untenable and his spirituality incoherent.

14  Rahner speaks of experiencing the Holy Spirit here, rather than simply transcendence. However, given that human transcendence is, in the present order of salvation, elevated into the supernatural existential, and given Rahner's description of experience of the Spirit as knowledge of self and openness, and as the "singular, original, primordial experience by the subject of

Transcendence is an element of all human experience, but is not the entirety of any particular experience: it is mediated categorically in knowing, willing, or loving objects and persons. Rahner refers to it as a "secret ingredient" of human experiences of the world (1982, 35; 1976a, 46). At times he describes transcendental experience as analogous to repressed memories—it is something we know but we do not exactly know that we know it (1991a, 119).[15] At the same time, it is possible with spiritual discipline to place oneself before this knowledge reflexively, although it will always continue to take place unthematically behind our backs (1986b, 141).

The centrality of transcendental experience for Rahner's theology becomes evident when he further describes it as an orientation to mystery. The infinite horizon of being is mystery, that which cannot fit within our matrix of understanding and yet makes human knowledge possible. Rahner calls this horizon Holy Mystery and, ultimately, God. Once he identifies the silent mystery that is the source and term of our transcendence with the word "God," he can further assert that, as a spiritual, transcendent being, the human person is oriented towards God. This picture contains a claim that every human subject has transcendental experience, and therefore knowledge, of God. This knowledge of God, which we have through our transcendence, is still *a posteriori* knowledge, as "every transcendental experience is mediated by a categorical encounter with concrete reality in our world, both the world of things and the world of persons" (1982, 52). All of our knowing, willing, loving, and experience of grace takes place in and through categorical experience. Even in our most intimate knowledge of God, with the possible exception of a few extraordinary mystics, we cannot bypass our worldly existence to somehow know God in a way that is not mediated in time and space, society and culture.

---

itself," it seems clear that these words apply to transcendence (1983c, 191).

On this topic, see Kilby (2004, 33-35). It would be interesting, given Rahner's understanding of mysticism, to bring his description of transcendence as a different kind of experience into conversation with Denys Turner's work on the concept of experience in mysticism. However, that is beyond the scope of this work. See Turner (1995).

15   See also Rahner (1983c, 192).

In our transcendence we do know God, yet we know God not as a categorical object or a finite existent that can be situated within our system of coordinates. Rahner writes:

> Hence the term of this transcendence is present only in the mode of otherness and distance. It can never be approached directly, never be grasped immediately. It gives itself only insofar as it points wordlessly to something else, to something finite as the object we see directly and as the immediate object of our action. (64-65)

In our transcendental experience, we have knowledge of God that is both unthematic and *a posteriori*. The term of our transcendence cannot be understood as an object among objects, but is revealed to us as the holy mystery that makes categorical knowledge of finite objects possible. Rahner writes of "mediation of immediacy with regard to God" in addressing how this God of otherness and distance is also present to us in every act of knowing, willing, and loving. Our immediate transcendental knowledge of God as the horizon of being is mediated by the finite existents we know, act in relation to, and love (83).

Describing the human person as transcendent leads Rahner directly to other characteristics of the human person, or existentials. Because the human person experiences herself in her totality—she is self-possessing—and she transcends her finite situations such that she can imagine many future possibilities, she is responsible and free. Freedom, for Rahner, is not a neutral capacity to choose between options in a stream of individual choices. Rather, it is the freedom to decide about oneself in one's totality and in relation to God. It is the freedom to accept or reject one's orientation to God. This freedom to actualize oneself in relation to God is, in Rahner's theology, a participation in one's own creation. Over the course of a lifetime, each person chooses to accept or reject her orientation to God. This choice, or fundamental option, is granted eternal validity by God.

While she is free and responsible, the human person is not an absolute subject. In the experience of self-transcendence the human subject is open to the unlimited expanse of being, of possibility, of infinity. At the same time, she is confronted by herself in her totality and finitude. She experiences herself as a question that she cannot answer. This simultaneous infinite openness and radical questioning points to the fact that the human subject does not create this horizon

against which she knows herself, but rather experiences being itself as
something that has been given to her. The human person experiences
herself as not at her own disposal. She is not entirely her own creation
nor is her freedom absolute. Her freedom is deeply conditioned by the
world around her, by an historical situation not of her own choosing
(42). Rahner writes, "man as a personal being of transcendence and
of freedom is also and at the same time a being in the world, in time
and in history. This assertion is fundamental in describing the presuppositions which the message of Christianity ascribes to man" (40).
Furthermore, historicity is not something that is merely also present
in the human subject, alongside freedom and transcendence. Nor is it
something that exists in struggle with transcendence and freedom as
an opposing force. Rather, "transcendentality and freedom are realized
in history" (40).

Of course, we experience our historicity as profoundly conditioning
us, and therefore as limiting our possibilities and shaping our freedom.
As historical beings constituted by our acts, we are deeply influenced
by the world in which we find ourselves, the circumstances that befall
us. At the same time, it is precisely these historical and worldly realities that mediate and create the possibility of our transcendentality
and freedom. As profoundly finite creatures open to infinity, we are
both dependent and free. Rahner asserts of the human subject, "insofar as he experiences his historical conditioning, he is already beyond
it in a certain sense, but nevertheless he cannot really leave it behind.
Being situated in this way between the finite and the infinite is what
constitutes man, and is shown by the fact that it is in his infinite transcendence and in his freedom that man experiences himself as dependent and historically conditioned" (42).

Given the description of the human person as transcendent, responsible and free, historical, and oriented to God, there inevitably arises
the possibility of sin. Rahner affirms, as an existential of humanity,
the possibility that persons, in their historical freedom, might deny
or reject their orientation to God. This is an important implication
of Rahner's understanding of human freedom, which, in turn, is an
important aspect of the difference he envisions between creature and
creator. Rahner asserts that the "difference separating God and the
created subject reaches its real essence and the essence of a subjective

existent precisely in the act of freedom" (105). While the difference
between God and the human person is affirmed more fully in a good
act than in sin, the possibility of sin is an integral part of the freedom
that is established by God as the essence of that difference.

As finite, dependent, and historical creatures, we experience our
freedom as already underway and in process, within a material and
social world. Our choices are always already being shaped by our categorical reality, our previous choices, and the choices of others. Thus
both our freedom and our reflection upon our freedom are affected
by the situation in which our freedom is actualized. This means that
we cannot know with any reflective certainty whether an objectively
guilty act is a free rejection of the orientation to God or "is more in the
nature of a manipulation which ... has about it the character of necessity" (104).[16] Furthermore, both our experience and the Christian
message inform us that sin is not just a possibility, but also a reality.
The situation in which we actualize our freedom is co-determined by
the guilt of others, such that even good acts always remain ambiguous.
Part of the material for our freedom is the objectification of the guilt
of others (109). This co-determination by guilt, when understood to
be universal and permanent, is how Rahner understands "original sin"
(109-113).

This view of sin, along with Rahner's explication of human transcendence, historicity, and dependence, all confirm one more existential discussed in *Foundations*, namely, the social nature of the human
person. In other texts, Rahner describes transcendence primarily in
terms of transcendence to other persons.[17]

In describing created human nature, Rahner asserts that each human being is a person and a subject, and as such experiences herself as
a question. She is also responsible and free, such that she constitutes
herself by her own acts. As historical and transcendent, she is finite
infinity. Each human being is freedom embodied, history and transcendence. As both responsible for ourselves and also not at our own
disposal, we are finite creatures oriented toward the infinity of being
that is God. Yet the term and source of our transcendence is a personal

---

16   Questions concerning how much our freedom is affected, not merely our
reflection upon it, will be addressed in Chapter Five.

17   See Rahner (1969d, 243).

God, not merely a silent horizon. This personal God relates to us not just as distant question but also as answer drawn near. In depicting how God draws near to humanity, Rahner asserts that the transcendence of the human person has been elevated by grace, becoming the "supernatural existential."

In *Foundations*, Rahner asserts that God makes Godself the "innermost constitutive element" of humanity, such that humanity "is the event of a free, unmerited and forgiving, and absolute self-communication of God" (1982, 116). He claims that there is an "ontological self-communication of God," whereby God makes an offer of God's own self an existential element of humanity without ceasing to be infinite mystery (116, 119).

This offer of the ontological communication of God is what Rahner calls the supernatural existential. Although it is not part of our created nature, neither is it a later addition: it is to be found always and everywhere. It is not an offer in the sense that God asks us if we want some and then does or does not give it to us according to our response. Rather, God gives God's very self to us and that in itself is the offer, an offer which bears its own acceptance. It exists in each human being, in the mode of antecedent offer, in the mode of acceptance, or in the mode of rejection (128). When we accept God's self-communication, God bears this acceptance so that it, too, is grace. "In order to be able to accept God without reducing him, as it were, in this acceptance to our finiteness, this acceptance must be borne by God himself" (128). God gives us grace to accept an ontological self-communication without reducing God to another element within our system of coordinates. When God, the infinite horizon that is always present to us in our transcendence as silent mystery, becomes immediate to us not as horizon but object, God does so precisely as infinite mystery—that which cannot be categorized and objectified. Christianity traditionally talks about this, in the mode of acceptance, as the communication of the Holy Spirit (120). Rahner does not shy away from the radical implications of any of this. He asserts boldly that this self-communication "has 'divinizing' effects" and that humanity "participates in God's being" (120).

Rahner develops the concept of the supernatural existential, as he did many of his ideas, in a number of different writings that addressed various issues and concerns. His understanding of the supernatural existential is often understood primarily in terms of an essay, "Concerning the Relationship of Nature and Grace," that spoke to a controversy among Roman Catholic theologians regarding how to understand the relationship between nature and grace. The specific issue contested was whether the desire for God is an inherent part of human nature.[18] If so, then it seems God's creation of such creatures obliges God to fulfill their inherent desire, and thus undermines the freedom of God and the gratuity of grace. If not, then the grace of God seems to be something that might be quite fine but is not, in any compelling way, necessarily connected to ordinary life.[19] Such a view sees eternal meaning as quite separate from mundane human existence. Rahner's uses the supernatural existential in his attempt to avoid both of these difficulties and chart out a third option. Given Rahner's overarching concern to explain how God is a part of ordinary life and how everyone experiences God, it is clear that he rejects making grace extrinsic to the human person. At the same time, he is committed (for both spiritual and theological reasons) to protecting the freedom of God and the otherness of grace. Therefore he is unwilling to elide nature and grace.

Addressing these concerns, Rahner attempts to make clear two unexacted gifts, the second more radically unexacted that the first (Rahner 1961a, 308, 309). In creation, God gives us ourselves. In grace, God gives us Godself. Yet these two must be so connected that God does not create us and then call us to something foreign to our created nature. Rahner addresses this by asserting that this disposition to grace is not natural but supernatural, a gift given always and everywhere but not part of our created nature. In this context, Rahner describes the supernatural existential as call, vocation, and offer. It is a "binding ordination to the supernatural end" (302). It is humanity's inner reference to God. It is possible to separate out two elements within this—that God has really transcendentally offered us this self-communication and that God has made it possible for us to receive it, has given us an unexacted receptivity for grace within ourselves (313).

---

18   For a nice summary of this controversy, see Dych (1992, 32–46).

19   See also Kerr (1997b, 179).

Endean points out that this essay is not Rahner's first articulation of the idea of the supernatural existential, and therefore it is best not to understand this concept primarily in relation to the nature/grace debate. The primary theological context for the development of this idea, he argues, is Christology. In order to understand the grace of the incarnation without imagining God as changing God's mind or intervening in chain of creaturely causality, Rahner claims that the extra grace beyond creation that Christ represents is present throughout the cosmos. Endean states, "It is this sense of how a doctrine of the incarnation implies a doctrine of grace, rather than the need to find a solution to the extrincisism-intrinsicism dilemma, that grounds Rahner's concept of the supernatural existential" (Endean 1996, 286, 287).[20]

Kilby notes that Rahner's presentation of the supernatural existential in *Foundations* differs significantly from the one in this essay, and is much stronger in its assertion of the communication of God to the human person (2004, 55, 56). For example, where Rahner refers to the supernatural existential as a "potency" in "Concerning the Relationship between Nature and Grace" (1961a), and distinguishes between the offer of grace and the receptivity for grace, in *Foundations* he says such separation is not helpful. He writes:

> Ontological self-communication must be understood as the condition which makes personal and immediate knowledge and love for God possible. But this very closeness to God in immediate knowledge and love, to God who remains absolute mystery, is not to be understood as a strange phenomenon which is added to another reality which is understood in a reified way. It is rather the real essence of what constitutes the ontological relationship between God and creatures. (1982, 122)

Both texts portray our spiritual nature as the obediential potency for the supernatural existential.[21] An obediential potency is a possibility that is not meaningless if it is not fulfilled. In *Foundations*, Rahner identifies the supernatural existential as an elevation or modification

---

20   Endean is here drawing on Schwerdtfeger (1982) who draws upon Tuomo Mannermaa.

21   I draw this conclusion from Rahner (1961a, 308, 309, 315), and its consistency with Rahner (1982).

of our transcendence (130, 133).[22] Furthermore, Rahner claims that the supernatural existential—like transcendence, of which it is an elevation—is experienced in that it is an aspect of all experience. While this transcendental experience is one that escapes precise conceptual comprehension, it is part of our lived reality. This experience "gives evidence of itself in human existence and is operative in that existence" (130).

The affirmation that we experience God in our everyday lives, especially when we say "yes" to God's offer of self-communication, is Rahner's primary understanding of Christian mysticism. Declan Marmion states: "In Rahner's view, every Christian is called to a mysticism of everyday faith, hope and love that differs only in degree, and not in kind, from the extraordinary experiences of recognized mystics" (1998, 62). Rahner acknowledges the possibility that some extraordinary persons (whom we usually connect with the term "mystic") might experience this more explicitly, perhaps such that it was not accompanied by the mediating concepts of mundane existence. Yet within Rahner's framework, such mysticism differs from the experience of God in everyday life because of the psychological propensities or contemplative practices of the mystics, not because it is a different kind of experience altogether.[23]

For all of humanity, there is an element of mysticism in our everyday experience that can find resonance and affirmation in Christian proclamation of God's grace. However, Rahner notes that the nature of this experience makes it such that it cannot "be recognized with unambiguous and reflexive certainty within an individual's experience" (1982, 130, 131).[24] Rahner therefore appeals to this experience not from a standpoint external to Christianity that seeks a certain touchstone upon which to build knowledge, but rather from within the doctrines of Christianity, hoping to evoke a recognition of experience through the lens of Christian interpretation. He writes:

---

22 For a survey of Rahner's descriptions of the supernatural existential, and an interpretive style quite different from my own, see Coffey (2004).

23 See Egan (1998, 75). See also Rahner (2005, 92). For a different take on this issue, see Caponi (2007, 211) and Rahner (1979b, 44-45).

24 I have removed Rahner's emphasis on "unambiguous."

> Even if by simple introspection and by making his original, tran-
> scendental experiences thematic individually a person could not
> discover such a transcendental experience of God's self-communi-
> cation in grace, or could not express it by himself with unambigu-
> ous certainty, nevertheless, if this theological and dogmatic inter-
> pretation of his transcendental experience is offered to him by the
> history of revelation and by Christianity, he can recognize his own
> experience in it. He can find in this interpretation the confidence to
> interpret what is ineffable in his own experience in accordance with
> it, and to accept the infinity of his own obscure experience without
> reservation and without limitation. (131)

The experience of transcendence and its elevation in the supernatural existential are often seen as the foundational elements of Rahner's
thought. However, many scholars note that it does not have to be interpreted as a stable, certain experience or concept, known apart from
Christianity. Indeed, readings that view the supernatural existential in
this way overlook many elements of Rahner's account. Endean argues
that Rahner's description of the human person "implies that human
experience of the spiritual and the 'transcendent' is shaped by language
and tradition" (2001, 182). He also notes that Rahner's affirmation
of the experience of God took place within a context in the Roman
Catholic church that denied both the accessibility and the theological
significance of an experience of grace. Read against this background
(instead of that of Descartes and modernism, as is often done in Eng-
land and America), Rahner's claim to have experienced God immediately is interpreted by Endean to mean: "I came to realize that the con-
ventional statements of a Christian culture are making claims about
me and about my experience" (226).[25]

Kilby's nonfoundationalist reading notes that in *Foundations*, Rahner "presents Christianity as...an interpretation of experience," and
the book itself aims to "make sense of Christianity as something which
can make sense of experience" (Kilby 2004, 81)[26]. He does not, Kilby

---

25   See also Adams (2005, 219).

26   See, in relation, Bell (2005), where she asks, "Couldn't Rahner be used
as the basis for Christianity in trying to understand its particular humanity,
not *anthropos* in some general and ultimate way, but Christianity's own way of
being in the world, which means of course its many ways of being Christian?"
(41)

contends, build Christian claims upon prior grounds, either philosophically deduced or individually experienced, but rather offers a
theological interpretation of experience that can then play a role in
evoking and shaping experience (113). On this reading, Rahner begins
squarely within the traditions and practices of Christian faith. Transcendental experience of God is not the starting point of Rahner's
theology, but one of its conclusions (10, 98). Having previously joined
the ranks of current scholars who view Rahner's work not as a unified,
single whole, but as a collection of ad hoc apologetic and occasional
writings, Kilby does not need to argue that every text of Rahner's supports this as the only legitimate reading. Instead, she claims that there
are enough texts that indicate this (*Foundations* among them) to make
a nonfoundationalist reading possible.

Given this, both Endean and Kilby disagree with views that see
Rahner's apologetics as simply building upon a prior, transcendental
experience. Endean states: "[t]he task of apologetics is not to justify the
truths of faith by the standards of some neutral reason, but to show
up the connections between Christian proclamation and everyday human existence" (2001, 230). Kilby asserts that in apologetics directed
towards non-Christians, Rahner's theology would not warrant a two-
step approach that first convinces the listener that he has a certain
experience and then interprets that experience in a Christian manner.
Instead, Rahner's apologetics attempt to make a Christian interpretation of experience compelling, to initiate the listener into Christianity in the very process of persuading him that he has "a certain kind
of experience" (Kilby 2004, 113).[27] Kilby further notes that Rahner
is primarily engaged in "internal apologetics," presenting Christianity
clearly to Christians in hopes of facilitating the further integration of
faith into their lives (107, 108).[28]

While Endean and Kilby argue from context and structure and
Rahner does not attempt to ground theology on a universally-available experience independent of Christianity, there are elements within
the content of this experience, as Rahner describes it, that also point
in this direction. However, the experience that Rahner describes is

27   See again Rahner (1982, 307).

28   She borrows the phrase "internal apologetics" from Nicholas Healy
(1992).

not the kind of experience that has been sought after as a foundation of knowledge in modernity. The supernatural existential is an experience of mystery, not the starting point of mastery. This mystery makes knowledge possible, while also radically undermining the pretensions of human certitude. Rahner writes:

> In the ultimate depths of his being man knows nothing more surely than that his knowledge, that is, what is called knowledge in everyday parlance, is only a small island in a vast sea that has not been traveled. It is a floating island, and it might be more familiar to us than the sea, but ultimately it is borne by the sea and only because it is can we be borne by it. Hence the existentiell question for the knower is this: Which does he love more, the small island of his so-called knowledge or the sea of infinite mystery? Is the little light with which he illuminates this island—we call it science and scholarship—to be an eternal light which will shine forever for him? That would surely be hell. (Rahner 1982, 22)[29]

While the experience of God in the supernatural existential need not be understood as the externally-derived foundation of his theology, it must be acknowledged as a central element of his portrayal of Christianity. Like transcendence, the supernatural existential cannot be clearly demarcated but rather is an element in all human experience. It is not beyond human access, even though it cannot be isolated. In certain circumstances, or limit situations, the experience of the Holy Spirit that takes place in the supernatural existential in the mode of acceptance is more easily brought into focus. Harvey Egan discusses several types of situations and experiences that evoke awareness of the experience of God in Rahner's theology. These include longing, joy, and emptiness, outrage, and love (Egan 1998, 57-70). Rahner asserts that humanity's inner reference to God is announced "more forcefully in certain situations" (Rahner 1983c, 199). While these include positive situations of goodness and beauty, Rahner often focuses on negative experiences in which the finite meanings established in our lives appear bankrupt and our patterns of understanding have been shattered by doubt, grief, or unintelligible tragedy. Often, he claims, our experience of God

---

29   See also Ochs (1969, 105) for a gloss on Rahner's description of transcendence that underlines this point.

is perceived most clearly where the definable limits of our everyday realities break down and are dissolved, where the decline of these realities is perceived, when lights shining over the tiny island of our ordinary life are extinguished and the question becomes inescapable, whether the night that surrounds us is the void of absurdity and death that engulfs us or the blessed holy night already shining within us is the promise of eternal day. (199, 200)

## SAYING "YES"

Precisely where human knowledge fails, we become aware that our existence is surrounded by mystery. Part of the questioning that defines the human person, for Rahner, is the quest to understand the self in its totality in relation to this mystery. Said differently, in questioning her own identity in relation to this mystery, the human person chooses either to despair that the darkness encompassing human life is the negation of meaning, or to affirm that this emptiness is somehow the embrace of a loving God. This choice is what Rahner means by freedom. Because Mystery has drawn near to us in the supernatural existential, human freedom is the decision to accept or reject God's offer of God's own self to humanity, a choice which is enabled by the offer itself. Given that God's self-communication is the fulfillment of humanity, this is also a "yes" or "no" to human actualization.

This choice is made over the course of a lifetime and its content is not immediately available for reflection. Our individual actions are always ambiguous and we can never know with certainty if our answer to the question of our lives is a "yes" or a "no" (Rahner 1982, 104, 109). Both answers are possible. Yet a "no" to God's offer "must never be understood as an existential-ontological parallel possibility of freedom alongside the possibility of a 'yes' to God" (102). If God is the horizon of being, the source and term of our transcendence, then we cannot exist and know and exercise freedom without affirming a "yes" of some sort to God. "Consequently, there is in the act in which freedom says 'no' a real and absolute contradiction by the fact that God is affirmed and denied at the same time" (99). We are free to say "yes" to God and actualize ourselves. We are free to attempt a contradictory "no." We cannot escape the question, which is the question of our existence.

For Rahner, the human person participates in her own creation. She is given an identity by God, as someone created by God and called into communion with God. However, she is also burdened with the freedom to participate in her own creation, either by accepting her ordination to a future with God or rejecting this vocation. In saying "yes," a person freely chooses to accept the identity granted her by God. In saying "no," she denies God's offer as well as God's determination of who she most truly is. Such a "no" is never entirely successful, since God's definition of the human person (as someone loved and called by God) cannot be undone. It is a failing, contradictory, contorting denial of the self, as well as a denial of God. It is a choice to "barricade ourselves against [God's offer] in a hell of freedom to which we condemn ourselves" (Rahner 1983c, 203).

Our human freedom, enacted in our temporal lives, bears eternal fruit. We are choosing to accept the offer of eternal life with God or to reject it, crafting ourselves as people in communion with God or people willfully denying grace. Rahner writes, "Freedom is the event of something eternal. But since we ourselves are still coming to be in freedom, we do not exist with and behold this eternity, but in our passage through the multiplicity of the temporal we are performing this event of freedom, we are forming the eternity which we ourselves are and are becoming" (1982, 96). Stated in somewhat more traditional terms, God offers each human being salvation, and in that offer enables us to respond in freedom. God's universal salvific will does not override human freedom, but rather demands that we make a choice. Rahner states, "There is never a salvific act of God on man which is not also and always a salvific act of man" (142). We cannot evade this decision: "God is the ground of man's act of freedom, and in his own act he burdens man with the grace and the responsibility for his own accountable acts" (142).

How do we say "yes" to God's offer of salvation? That question will be taken up in the rest of this book. In the following pages, I explore three themes that arise repeatedly in Rahner's explications of saying "yes" to God: silence, love, and death. I argue that Rahner, standing within a particular religious and historical location that he recognizes as one among many, articulates the gospel of Jesus Christ as the good news of God's universal love for humanity. While Rahner acknowl-

edges the many ways in which we are historically, culturally, and materially conditioned—indeed declares that the Christian affirmation
of the unity of body and soul means we must take all of these issues
quite seriously—he also recognizes that we make choices, that we
have a measure of freedom. He offers a Christian interpretation of
this freedom in which all our many temporal choices are part of the
one decision of human life, to accept or reject God's offer of salvation.
Through this decision, we shape who we are for all eternity. If we say
"yes," we craft our own identities in community over time, precisely by
accepting the identity that God has granted to us, by accepting who
we are called to be. Thus the choice of saying "yes" bears the shape
of the human person, as that person is presupposed by the message
of Christianity. It is the shape of self-possession and openness. These
two elements are critical to Rahner's explication of the structure of the
human person.[30] The choice to enact them, to freely accept our identity as created and called by God, also takes this form. A person says
"yes" to God, in Rahner's theology, when, within a sturdy individuality
granted by God and formed in community, she opens herself to the
unknown and mysterious other, both human and divine.

---

30   Bruno Brinkman uses the terms "eccentricity of being" in God and "cen-
tredness of 'being-in-the-world'" to refer to Rahner's description of the human person in her finite infinity (1984, 258). Brinkman's analysis of Rahner
is quite different from mine, but I appreciate his language for depicting this
central element of Rahner's thought.

# CHAPTER 2
# SILENCE

*[W]hat is more self-evident than the silent question which goes beyond everything which has already been mastered and controlled, than the unanswered question accepted in humble love, which along brings wisdom?* (Rahner 1982, 22)

## INTRODUCTION

"Silence" is mentioned frequently in Rahner's writings, although he does not address the subject of silence directly as an element of his systematic theology. Unlike love and death, silence does not receive separate and substantive coverage, nor does it occupy a clearly defined place within Rahner's dogmatics. In the absence of such treatment, I suspect many readers pass over Rahner's repeated invocations of "silence" as merely a favored metaphor or perhaps a verbal tic. Indeed, Rahner's use of silence has received very little scholarly attention.[1] Yet close scrutiny reveals that while Rahner deploys images of silence broadly, he does so with an underlying consistency.[2]

Rahner infuses his grammar with silence, using it in several parts of speech—as noun, verb, adverb, and adjective. In doing so he indicates a kind of occurrence (experiences of silence), depicts a characteristic (describes an act, disposition, or way of being), and employs a discursive strategy to identifiable ends (invokes silence to locate his subject

---

1 One exception to this is Stefan Raueiser (1996, 166-174). Raueiser briefly argues that silence can be seen as a positive mode of communication in Rahner's theology, highlighting the image of silence as the earthly expression of the eternal Word.

2 While I argue that Rahner employs the image of silence with considerable consistency and identifiable meaning, I do not claim he uses it the same way every time, or that my analysis is exhaustive. There are times when he uses silence differently. For example, in Rahner (1966c, 47), "silent" means merely "unspoken."

both without and within language). He portrays the act of being silent as clearing away distractions and offering space, time, and attention to the mysterious other. He describes persons and acts as silent insofar as they embody such openness to the other and acknowledgement of mystery. Finally, given Rahner's conviction that silence and speech are not opposites, but rather mutually conditioning elements of discourse, using images of silence to depict occurrences and describe characteristics simultaneously marks these as both beyond what can be adequately articulated in speech and yet inescapably related to the realm of language.

Within Rahner's various incantations of silence, there is a strong coherence. Silence marks the reality and acknowledgement of distance, difference, and otherness between persons, a reality that is both painful and necessary for freedom, love, faith, and community. Openness to otherness between persons is ultimately grounded in humanity's connection to the radical other, the one mystery, the Silent One, God. Rahner uses silence in his portrayal of the relationship of God and humanity to emphasize the reality of otherness, its acceptance in openness, and the centrality of mystery.

## IMAGES OF SILENCE

Rahner employs images of silence—stillness, listening, quiet, silence—often in describing the relationship between God and humanity. He invokes the image of silence to capture the character of the infinite horizon that is the term and source of human transcendence, the horizon of our knowledge and love, calling it "the silent immensity" (1967e, 33). Rahner writes:

> The term of transcendence admits of no control over itself because then we would be reaching beyond it and incorporating it within another, higher and broader horizon. This contradicts the very nature of this transcendence and of the real term of this transcendence. This infinite and silent term is what disposes of us. It presents itself to us in the mode of withdrawal, of silence, of distance, of being always inexpressible, so that speaking of it, if it is to make sense, always requires listening to its silence [*Dieses Woraufhin ist die unendliche, stumme Verfügung über uns. Es gibt sich uns im Modus des Sichversagens, des Schweigens, der Ferne, des dauernden Sichhaltens in einer Unausdrücklichkeit, so dass alles Reden von ihm immer—damit*

*es vernehmlich sei—des Hörens auf sein Schweigen bedarf]* (Rahner 1982, 64; 1976a, 73)

He calls the term of our transcendence "the ontologically silent horizon of every intellectual and spiritual encounter with realities" and "the ineffable and silent source and term of everything, which in fear and trembling and before the final silence could be called 'God'" (1982, 77, 85).

Since Rahner equates the mystery of this transcendental horizon with God, silence becomes a descriptor for the Divine. Rahner states that transcendental experience is "an experience in which he whom we call 'God' encounters man in silence [*schweigend dem Menschen zusagt*], encounters him as the absolute and the incomprehensible, as the term of his transcendence which cannot really be incorporated into any system of coordinates" (21; 1976a, 32). He characterizes the transcendental experience of mystery as "silently present and silencing its presence" (1983c, 196). Making the point that our transcendental experience of God is an aspect of knowing our concrete, historical reality, Rahner states "Everyday reality then becomes itself a pointer to this transcendental experience of the Spirit, which is always present silently and apparently facelessly" (199). He calls God "the silent and all-sheltering mystery" and refers to "that mysterious, silent, impalpable reality that we call God and his will" (203, 201).

Rahner invokes images of silence in describing both God and our experience of God, sometimes without clear differentiation between the two. He depicts our transcendental experience as "beyond words" and writes of "God's silent incomprehensibility" (1982, 126; 1983c, 201). This reflects the content of Rahner's theology, in which our experience of God is given as grace, and this gracious experience is fitting to our created nature. In transcendence, humanity does not grasp and comprehend God in accordance with our ways of knowing, but rather our spiritual nature opens up to the infinity that disposes of us, to that which creates, sustains, and ultimately shatters all of our knowing. Our transcendence

> appears as what it is only in the self-disclosure of that towards which the movement of transcendence tends. It exists by means of that which gives itself in this transcendence as the other, the other which distinguishes this transcendence from itself and enables it to

be experienced as mystery by the subject who is constituted as such by this transcendence. By its very nature subjectivity is always a transcendence which listens, which does not control, which is overwhelmed by mystery and opened up by mystery. (1982, 58)

Rahner also uses silence to refer to faithful responses to God, to saying "yes." Rahner's theology emphasizes that spiritual encounter with God happens always and everywhere. At the same time, he holds an important place for human freedom, when a choice is made to accept the relation between God and humanity and to open oneself to the otherness of God. In this way he can also write about particular times in which God is known in a more intense or vivid way through spiritual discipline, through attempts to focus on transcendental experience, and through the conceptualization and thematization of grace. He can therefore both assert that God is present to everyone and write: "What are the facts? God is present to the one who is silent, who lets everything recede into his finite limitation and who looks towards its horizon in order to look beyond it despite the fact that there is not 'anything' to be seen there" (1967e, 30). Rahner can also coherently claim that grace is the innermost element of humanity and that "[i]t takes place within you when you are silent, when you wait and when in faith, hope and charity, you interpret correctly (i.e. in the light of Christmas) what you experience" (29).

## DIVINE/HUMAN DIALOGUE

These images of silence take place within a portrayal of the divine-human relation modeled on a dialogue between unequal partners. He writes: "The unity between transcendence and its term cannot be understood as a unity between two elements related equally to each other, but only as the unity between that which grounds and disposes freely and that which is grounded. It is a unity in the sense of a unity between an original word and the response to it which is made possible by the word" (1982, 58).

This divine/human dialogue begins with creation, in which the world is created as the addressee of the Word. Humanity exists as the hearers of the Word, the one whom God created in order possibly to self-communicate with something other than God. This points to a

deep connection between the creation of humanity and its assumption
in hypostatic union. Rahner writes of God:

> Therefore his capacity to be creator, that is, the capacity merely to
> establish the other without giving himself, is only a derived, delim-
> ited and secondary possibility which ultimately is grounded in this
> real and primordial possibility of God, namely, to be able to give
> himself to what is not God, and thereby really to have his own his-
> tory in the other, but as his own history. In their innermost essen-
> tial ground creatures must be understood as the possibility of being
> able to be assumed, of being the material for a possible history of
> God. God establishes creatures by his creative power insofar as he
> establishes them from out of nothing in their own non-divine real-
> ity as the *grammar of God's possible self-expression*. (222, 223)

The possibility of human nature is grounded in the possibility of Jesus Christ. It could have been the case that human beings existed and
there were no incarnation, yet even then, the possibility of hypostatic
union would have been the ground of the existence of humanity (223).
Humanity is "the utterance in which God could empty himself, could
express himself" (224). "From this perspective we could define man,
driving him all the way back to his deepest and most obscure mystery,
as that which comes to be when God's self-expression, his Word, is
uttered into the emptiness of the Godless void in love" (224). Thus, in
Rahner's thought, human nature is deeply and intrinsically connected
to the nature of God even in its difference and distinction: "When
God wants to be what is not God, man comes to be" (225).

In other writings, Rahner takes the idea of human nature as the
grammar of God's self-expression still further. Discussing the possibility of legitimately envisioning prayer as a dialogue with God, Rahner questions: "How would it be, however, if we said and were permit-
ted to say that in prayer we experience ourselves as the ones spoken by
God…If we said that what God primarily says to us is ourselves …?"
(1975a, 66). If we are hearers of the Word, and are also words of God,
then, "we are ourselves . . . the utterance and address of God which
listens to itself" (66).

This means prayer is not merely occasional, verbal conversation, but
rather is the structure of human life (67). Rahner writes:

> When a person, in the Spirit and by grace, experiences himself as
> the one spoken by God to himself and understands this as his true

essence to the concreteness of which the gratuitous grace of God's self-communication also belongs, and when he admits this existence and freely accepts it in prayer as the word of God in which God promises himself to man with his Word, his prayer is already... dialogic, an exchange with God. The person then hears himself as God's address, heavy with God's self-promise, in the grace-filled self-communication of God by faith, hope and love. He does not hear "something" in addition to himself as one already presupposed in his dead facticity, but hears himself as the self-promised word in which God sets up a listener and to which he speaks himself as an answer. (67)

How does understanding all persons as spoken by God relate to Christological claims that Jesus is *the* Word of God? Rahner states that the humanity of Jesus Christ is the expression of God, and

This is not contradicted by the fact that there are also other men, namely, we ourselves, who are not this self-expression of God becoming other. For "what" he is as the self-expression of the Logos and "what" we are is the same. We call it "human nature." But the unbridgeable difference is constituted by the fact that this "what" in him is spoken as his self-expression, and this is not the case with us. (1982, 224)

At this point, one can see the Christological center of Rahner's theological anthropology. God creates humanity as the hearers of a possible word and the grammar of such a possible word. That Word, Jesus Christ, is the logic, structure, and climax of God's gracious self-communication. Both human nature and the self-offering of God in the supernatural existential can be understood as lesser possibilities that are grounded in the greater possibility of the incarnation. The possibility of the Word is the logic behind human nature and the supernatural existential.[3]

---

3 We see this clearly when Rahner describes human self-transcendence as the obediential potency for the supernatural existential and the supernatural existential as the obediential potency for hypostatic union. Again, the relationship is emphasized when Rahner takes pains to avoid extrinsicism in describing the supernatural existential, and identifies the supernatural existential in the mode of acceptance with the Holy Spirit, that is, with the Spirit of Jesus Christ (1961a, 308, 309, 315; 1982, 218, 124, 125). See also Endean (1996, 286-287) and Coffey (2001).

As the possibility of the incarnation is the ground of human nature—the creation of partners in the dialogue—the resurrection is the
final content of God's address. In the resurrection, Jesus' claim of the
new and unsurpassable closeness of God which demands a decision
is experienced as permanently valid and accepted by God—he is vin-
dicated as absolute saviour (279). Rahner describes this in dialogical
metaphor, saying that before the Christ event, "the dialogue between
God and humanity was an open thing—no one knew which way it
would go or how it would be terminated" (1993b, 288). The hypostatic union closes God's side of the conversation (288, 289).

Thus Rahner's use of images of silence in describing the relationship
between God and humanity is found within a larger pattern of depicting this relationship as a dialogue, in which God says "yes" to humanity
and enables us to respond. The depiction of this dialogue is given further dimension in Rahner's spiritual writings, where he wrestles with
the painful silence of God.

Rahner's spiritual texts, like his more theological writings, describe
the human person as a finite creature who sees beyond herself into
the silent infinity of God. Knowing ourselves in the context of and
in distinction from this silent horizon of God, we are presented with
the question of ourselves in our totality. Portraying the experience of
God as the distant horizon of our lives, Rahner speaks in a Lenten
sermon:

> he is mute and silent in refusal, as if he embraces our existence only
> as an empty, distant horizon would embrace it; our thoughts and
> the demands of our heart go astray in this pathless infinity and
> wander around, never to find their way out...God seems to us to be
> only that unreal, inaccessible infinity which, to our torment, makes
> our tiny bit of reality seem still more finite and questionable. This
> infinity makes us seem homeless even in *our* world, because it leads
> us to the extravagance of a yearning that we can never fulfill, and
> that even he does not seem to fulfill. (Rahner 1993a, 115)

The distance from this silent God is frightening, and it creates in
us a longing for the infinite that is deeply painful. This horizon is a
mystery that we can never understand, and even knowing it is there
threatens and disrupts our conceptions of an ordered and comprehensible reality. Rahner states, "There is a distance of God that permeates

the pious and the impious, that perplexes the mind and unspeakably terrifies the heart" (115, 116). He prays:

> Why do You torment me with Your Infinity, if I can never really measure it? Why do You constrain me to walk along Your paths, if they lead only to the awful darkness of Your night, where only You can see?... Why have You kindled in me the flame of faith, this dark light which lures us out of the bright security of our little huts into Your night? (Rahner 1999, 4, 5)

To assuage this pain, we can attempt to evade the silent horizon that surrounds us by focusing on the finite cares of our daily lives. We can try to retreat into our huts and stay there. However, our transcendence will render the attempt useless, because we cannot know the mundane realities of our lives without also knowing the horizon that encompasses them. It is precisely in knowing our finitude that we transcend it and touch upon infinity. Rahner contemplates fleeing from God and prays:

> And yet, where shall I go? If the narrow hut of this earthly life with its dear, familiar trivialities, its joys and sorrows both great and small—if this were my real home, wouldn't it still be surrounded by Your distant Endlessness?...Suppose I tried to be satisfied with what so many today profess to be the purpose of their lives. Suppose I defiantly determined to admit my finiteness, and glory in it alone. I could only begin to recognize this finiteness and accept it as my sole destiny, because I had previously so often stared out into the vast reaches of limitless space, to those hazy horizons where Your Endless Life is just beginning...I could never feel the pain of longing, not even deliberately resign myself to being content with this world, had not my mind again and again soared out over its own limitations into the hushed reaches which are filled by You alone, the Silent Infinite. (6)

In discussing how one can go about being present to this distant God, Rahner begins to describe a kind of silent prayer in which one can become aware that this horizon has drawn near to us in love and become the center of our being. In two different writings, one for Lent and one for Christmastime, Rahner describes the activity of this silence. Both sermons depict the difficulty of facing this silence and portray it as quite dreadful. Yet, within it, there is the possibility of awareness of experience of God. Rahner preaches:

Make *yourself* block up every exit; only the exits to the finite, the paths that lead to what is really trackless, will be dammed up. Do not be frightened over the loneliness and abandonment of your interior dungeon, which seems to be so dead—like a grave. For if you stand firm, if you do not run from despair, if in despair over the idols which up to now you called God you do not despair in the true God, if you thus stand firm—this is already a wonder of grace—then you will suddenly perceive that your grave-dungeon only blocks the futile finiteness; you will become aware that your deadly void is only the breadth of God's intimacy, that the silence is filled up by a word without words, by the one who is above every name and is all in all. That silence is God's silence. It tells you that he is there. (Rahner 1993a, 116, 117)

Rahner indicates that God's eloquent silence will communicate God's presence to us if we have the courage and steadfastness to wait in silence. He understands the pain and frustration of experiencing God's silence, but also says that the silence of God "can also be a grace-given experience" (Rahner 1975a, 71). Silence here is clearly not the mere absence nor opposite of words, as the silence of God contains a word without words and is "a mode of speech" (Rahner 1979a, 154).

Rahner describes the same silence in a different context when he offers instruction on how to prepare for Christmas:

First of all, then, persevere for a while on your own. Perhaps you can find a room where you can be on your own. Or you may know a quiet path or a lonely church.

Then do not talk to yourself the way you do with others, the people we argue and quarrel with even when they are not there. Wait, listen, without expecting any unusual experience. Do not pour yourself out in accusation, do not indulge yourself. Allow yourself to meet yourself in silence. Perhaps then you will have a terrible feeling. Perhaps you will realize how remote all the people are whom you are dealing with every day and to whom you are supposed to be bound by ties of love. Perhaps you will perceive nothing but a sinister feeling of emptiness and deadness.

Bear with yourself. You will discover how everything that emerges in such silence is surrounded by an indefinable distance, permeated as it were by something that resembles a void. Do not yet call it God! It is only what points to God and, by its namelessness and limitlessness, intimates to us that God is something other than one more thing added to those we usually have to deal with. It makes

us aware of God's presence, if we are still and do not flee in terror
from the mystery which is present and prevails in the silence—do
not flee even to the Christmas-tree or to the more tangible religious
concepts which can kill religion.

...If you persevere in this way and, by keeping silence, allow God
to speak, this silence which cries out is strangely ambiguous. It is
both fear of death and the promise of the infinity which is close to
you in benediction. And these are too close together and too similar for us to be able of ourselves to interpret this infinity which is
remote and yet close. But precisely in this strangeness and mystery
we learn to understand ourselves rightly and to accept the dear fa-
miliarity of this strange mystery. And that is precisely the message
of Christmas: that in reality God is close to you, just where you are,
if you are open to this infinity. For then God's remoteness is at the
same time his unfathomable presence, pervading all things. (Rahner 1968, 24, 25)[4]

Note the way that Rahner piles up apparently contradictory descriptions. Certainly any "silence which cries out is strangely ambiguous,"
and the silence Rahner speaks of is particularly so, for it cries about a
familiar mystery. Recognizing silence as a mode of speech, Rahner also
uses of the theme of silence to indicate communication that is less concrete and more difficult to comprehend than ordinary propositional
language. This can be useful, for the experience of remaining in silence
can help us to be aware of the term of transcendence and can thereby
unsettle comfortable notions of God as "one more thing." Mystery prevails in silence, communicating the presence of God without reducing
God to something that can be comprehended and circumscribed.

The communication between God and humanity that Rahner is
describing hinges on each party offering silence to the other—giving
space and attention for the other to speak their own word. Rahner
repeatedly agonizes over the difficulty of this process, both of offering
silence to God and of bearing God's silence as response.

Rahner demands of God in prayer, "What can I say to You, my God?
Shall I reproach You with being so far from me or with Your silence
which is so terrible and lasts a life-time?" (Rahner 1997a, 4). He prays
to God about being "deaf to the eloquent sounds of Your silence" and
says that in the "blessed and terrible hour" of his death, "You will still

---

4 See also Rahner (1967e, 24-28), which is quite similar.

be silent. You will still let me do all the talking, speaking out my own self to You" (Rahner 1999, 23-25). Rahner says that God's silence at such times is called "the dark night of the soul" (25). He writes about the decisive moment in his life when he will be able to pour out his own self to God, a moment which will last until his death. He prays:

> And after this moment shall have come for me, after the hour of *my* love, which is shrouded in Your silence, then will come the endless day of *Your* love, the eternity of the beatific vision. But for now...I must just wait in the courtyard before Your sanctuary and mine. I must empty it of all the noise of the world, and quietly endure the bitter silence and desolation thus produced—the terrible "night of the senses"—in Your grace and in pure faith. This, then, is the ultimate meaning of my daily prayers, this awful waiting. (25. )

Along with a sense of how bitter and painful this silence can be there also emerges a picture of a relationship with God wherein God is silent in order that we might speak. The most appropriate response is if we then offer silence to God and await God's word to us. Silence is not the opposite of speech; God's silence can tell us God is there and our silence can say "yes" to God. Offering silence is a way of saying "yes," of being open to God as God has been open to us. Rahner murmurs:

> Why are You so silent? Why do You enjoin me to speak with You, when You don't pay any attention to me? Isn't Your silence a sure sign that You're not listening?
>
> Or do You really listen quite attentively, do You perhaps listen my whole life long, until I have told You everything, until I have spoken out my entire self to You? Do You remain so silent precisely because You are waiting until I am really finished, so that You can then speak Your word to me, the word of Your eternity? Are You so silent so that You can one day bring to a close the life-long monologue of a poor human being, burdened by the darkness of this world, by speaking the luminous word of eternal life, in which You will express Your very Self in the depths of my heart? . . . Is Your silence when I pray really a discourse filled with infinite promise, unimaginably more meaningful than any audible word You could speak to the limited understanding of my narrow heart, a word that would itself have to become as small and poor as I am? (20, 21)

Here God's silence is described as a meaningful discourse, one that can communicate to a human being more than any human words and concepts. Silence becomes a medium for communication of content that cannot be categorized. It is capable of communicating mystery as mystery, without reduction.

In this passage, Rahner is describing human life as a dialogue with God, in which we speak ourselves to a God whose silence makes room for our voices, and then, after the close of our lives and the completion of our response to God in rejection or acceptance, God speaks to us the word of God's eternity. Rahner writes, "Then at last, everything will be quiet in death; then I shall have finished with all my learning and suffering. Then will begin the great silence, in which no other sound will be heard but You, O Word resounding from eternity to eternity" (32, 33). Again, note that God's Word is not opposed to silence. The great silence is not empty, or filled with our words, but resounds with God's Word.

In an angry and frustrated prayer demanding answers from God about the painful silence of his loved ones who have died, Rahner says:

> But why am I asking this of You? You are as silent to me as my dead. I love You too, as I love my dead, the quiet and distant ones who have entered into night. And yet not even You give me answer, when my loving heart calls upon You for a sign that You and Your Love are present to me. So how can I complain about my dead, when their silence is only the echo of Yours? Or can it be that Your silence is Your answer to my complaint about theirs?
>
> That must be the way it is, since You are the last answer, even though incomprehensible, to all the questions of my heart. I know why You are silent: Your silence is the framework of my faith, the boundless space where my love finds the strength to believe in Your Love.
>
> If it were all perfectly evident to me here on earth, if Your Love of me were so manifest that I could ask no more anxious questions about it, if You had made absolutely crystal clear the most important thing about me, namely, that I am someone loved by You, how then could I prove the daring courage and fidelity of my love? How could I even have such love? How could I lift myself up in the ecstasy of faith and charity, and transport myself out of this world into Your world, into Your heart?
>
> Your Love has hidden itself in silence, so that my love can reveal itself in faith. You have left me, so that I can discover You. If You were with me, then in my search for You I should always discover

only myself. But I must go out of myself, if I am to find You—and find You there, where You can be Yourself.

Since Your Love is infinite, it can abide only in Your Infinity; and since You will to manifest Your infinite Love to me, You have hidden it in my finiteness, where You issue Your call to me. My faith in You is nothing but the dark path in the night between the abandoned shack of my poor, dim earthly life and the brilliance of Your Eternity. And Your silence in this time of my pilgrimage is nothing but the earthly manifestation of the eternal word of Your Love. (56, 57)

This passage contains and illumines much of what Rahner is doing with the theme of silence. First, it is part of a prayer in which Rahner is grieving for loved ones and missing them terribly. He rails at God about their silence, because their silence is his loss and loneliness. Silence marks the distance between him and his loved ones. The prayer also accuses God of not answering, attacks God for God's silence in response to the earnest prayers of the faithful. God is just as distant as the dead. Silence here also indicates the pain of not knowing, especially of not knowing about the beloved. At the same time, there is a description of a relationship in which silence is a necessary and enabling element. God's silence is the space in which Rahner can come to believe freely. If the creator of the universe spoke clearly all that is true, there would be no way for a mere human not to accept such truth entirely. If another human being were to speak incessantly, this would not preclude the possibility of our speech, although it might make it more difficult. But it is quite a difference case with God. The darkness of God's silence makes room for our freedom and subjectivity.[5] It marks the difference and distinction between God and human persons that allows a real relationship. It is distance, but that distance between persons is necessary for community. It is constitutive of otherness. It is the necessary space in which faith, love, and grace can be given.[6]

---

5 It might be possible to perceive resonances here with John Hick's "epistemic distance" necessary for soul-making. While there may be some similarities, Rahner does not offer this dialogue image as a theodicy. Much of Rahner's theology, especially regarding the importance of the incomprehensibility of God, leads Rahner away from the project of theodicy. See Rahner (1983b, 95).

6 In another text, Rahner (1969c) describes the concealment and secrecy of

Again we see the divine-human relationship in the metaphor of a dialogue. After speaking us that we might hear God's Word, God is silent that we might also speak. Yet God's silence continues to communicate to us in a way that does not destroy our freedom and subjectivity, because it remains hidden, uncategorized, and ineffable. It communicates God's presence while still making room for us. God's silence gives us the opportunity to accept God as something other than a function of our own understanding, a character in our own script. It communicates without dissolving mystery. In response to God's offered silence, we pray, a prayer that is, ultimately and at best, a silent waiting for God, a listening to the eloquence of God's silence. After our death, we cease to speak out our lives to God and instead, God speaks God's Word of beatific vision and eternal life.

The imagery of dialogue between God and man appears in many places in Rahner's work. Humanity is the hearer of a possible word, the grammar of a possible word. We are all—in some sense—words

---

God as a necessary condition of grace. This passage, while directly addressing the relationship between philosophy and theology, explicates Rahner's view of the importance of a distinction between human nature and grace. It is necessary both to prevent viewing the natural as meaningless and simply sinful, while also securing the gratuity of grace and underlining the distinction between Jesus and humanity. He writes:

> grace, understood as the absolute self-communication of God himself, must always presuppose as a condition of its own possibility (in order to be itself) someone to whom it can address itself and someone to whom it is not owed; which therefore means also someone who can be thought of without contradiction even apart from this communication…God has created the servant only in order to make him his child; but he was able to create the child of grace, in distinction to his only-begotten Son, only by creating the addressee without claim to sonship, i.e. the servant. In the same way, God has willed the truth of philosophy only because he willed the truth of his own self-revelation, ie. the absolute, beatifying truth which he is himself and which for us is the vision which is the nearness and not the distance of the absolutely Incomprehensible…For this reason he had to create the one from whom he could keep this truth a secret, ie. the philosopher who, because he himself experienced God as the one who conceals himself, could accept revelation from him *as a grace.* (1969c, 75)

spoken by God. We are those to whom the one, unique, absolute Word of God is spoken, and a word to God in response is demanded of us. Through both the *Foundations* and Rahner's more spiritual writings, a picture emerges in which God speaks us in order that we might listen to God's Word, and God hears us in order that we might speak a word to God. Speech and silence are both elements of this dialogue, for both parties. The "ontologically silent horizon" is the God who speaks the Word (Rahner 1982, 77); the words spoken by God to be hearers are required to speak a word of response; we can speak a "yes" by offering silence to hear the Word of God.

In the context of this dialogical understanding of the relationship between God and humanity, Rahner describes Jesus Christ, the Word of God, with images of silence. He names Jesus as "the hidden, silent, sacrificed God" (Rahner 1997g, 128). He imagines Jesus as following him "down the wandering path of [his] life constantly and silently, leaving bloody footprints behind" (Rahner 1997d, 59). In a similar passage, Rahner prays to Jesus, "You speak Yourself through Your Spirit into my heart, and as You silently meet me in the events of my life, as the experience of Your indwelling grace" (Rahner 1997e, 82). Again, Rahner prays, "We kneel, O Lord, before Your Sacrament, as Your people. Before the Sacrament of Your death, which gives us life; before the Sacrament of Your silence, which speaks out more clearly than all the chatter of our own hearts" (Rahner 1997f, 97). As Jesus' death is life-giving for us, so the Word speaks to us in silence. The Sacrament of the Word is silence; the Word meets us silently in the world; Jesus is the silent, hidden God. In Jesus, God communicates Godself to us in radical intimacy through the hypostatic union. At the same time, Jesus is a human being, marked by the same difference and otherness that unavoidably separate persons. This Word both reveals Godself to us in incredible nearness and maintains and respects our otherness and freedom in relation to God.

In Rahner's works, silence marks distance and difference between persons, both the blunt realities of otherness (the pain of loss, loneliness, and isolation) and the possibility that freely offered silence (space, respect, attention offered to the other) is part of how God affirms humanity and how humanity says "yes" to God. Speech and silence are not opposites, but rather silence is a mode of speech that risks the reconfiguration of the self in acknowledging the unmanipulable other. Within the dialogical relationship between God and humanity, both parties must speak themselves and can do so by offering silence, thus speaking themselves as openness to the mysterious other. In this context, Jesus is a Word of a piece with silence, who speaks Godself to us in a way that still allows for our freedom of response.

## GOD IN LANGUAGE

It is tempting to imagine that Rahner's descriptions of God as silent are intended to indicate that God remains securely outside the confines of human discourse. Yet this is not what Rahner says. Rahner does not see silence as the opposite or absence of speech, but rather as an element of discourse. Silence and speech are different but connected, mutually implicated. Every mention of silence also invokes speech. Thus when Rahner describes God as silent, he both indicates that God cannot be comprehended in language, and that human knowledge of God takes place within the sphere of language. Note that, in *Foundations*, Rahner does not offer a strong philosophical argument for why the term of transcendence can be equated with God. What he offers, instead, is a linguistic analysis.

Rahner's move to label the term of our transcendence "God" involves two different but related patterns of reasoning. First, Rahner states that the only way we can really know what the term "God" means is from and through our orientation to mystery. We know what this word means when we accept and reflectively objectify our transcendental experience, as it is elevated in the supernatural existential (Rahner 1982, 44). The second pattern, which indicates *why* we would let our transcendental experience shape our understanding of the word "God," moves through an exploration of the term to argue that this word marks where the human person is confronted with the question of herself. This is the word that humanity uses to acknowledge that our finitude touches infinity and that we are face to face with mystery. Thus Rahner first asserts that we should let our transcendental experience shape our understanding of what the word "God" means, and second, we should do this because the word "God" marks the place where we transcend our finitude. Rahner's explication of the word "God" is

particularly interesting to the investigation of how silence functions in
his theology. I will outline it using much of Rahner's own prose.

"It is natural to begin with a brief reflection on the word 'God,'" Rahner writes. "This is so not merely because, in contrast to a thousand
other experiences which can get a hearing even without words, it could
be that in this case the *word* alone is capable of giving us access to what
it means" (44). The word "God" does not function like other words
that refer to categorical objects within our experience. Unlike "tree" or
"table," "God" does not refer to anything that appears within our system of coordinates, but rather to the ever-present horizon on which
our matrix of understanding is located. Thus, the word "God" cannot
point to the reality it names, nor does it carry directly any information
about its referent. In this way, "God" functions as a proper name (46).
Nevertheless, Rahner finds the fact that this word is "so very much
without contour" appropriate. He writes:

> the present form of the word reflects what the word refers to: the
> "ineffable one," the "nameless one" who does not enter into the
> world we can name as a part of it. It means the "silent one" [*das*
> *"Schweigende"*]who is always there, and yet can always be over-
> looked, unheard, and, because it expresses the whole in its unity
> and totality, can be passed over as meaningless. It means that which
> really is wordless, because every word receives its limits, its own
> sound and hence its intelligible sense only within a field of words.
> Hence what has become faceless, that is, the word "God" which no
> longer refers by itself to a definite, individual experience, has as-
> sumed the right form to be able to speak to us of God. For it is the
> final word before we become silent [*vor dem Verstummen*], the word
> which allows all the individual things we can name to disappear
> into the background, the word in which we are dealing with the
> totality which grounds them all. (46, 47; 1976a, 56)

At this point one could make connections between Rahner's "God"
and Derrida's "transcendental signified"—that illusory, singular truth
that stabilizes and anchors the entire system of language by being
signified without, in turn, functioning to signify something else. The
transcendental signified is the point of pure presence that governs the
structure and limits of language without itself being bound by language (Derrida 1978, 279). Derrida critiques this notion as arising
from a human desire for certainty. He declares that the center is in

exile, the point of pure presence is absent, and language is better understood through function and play than reference and stability. Rahner's work here can be read as a shining example of the modern view Derrida attacks wherein God is the ground of language that cannot yet be contained within it. However, I believe there is more going on here. Rahner is not building a modern structure of linguistic and ontological stability. While postmodern criticisms of Rahner's work will be taken up more fully in Chapter Five, for now it is important to note that Rahner, in the midst of his complex images of silence as a form of speech, is using the concepts of absence and presence in non-binary patterns. As God's silence tells us God is there, God's absence communicates God's presence. This linguistic pattern should be noted in conjunction with the fact that Rahner is most decidedly not seeking certainty. The power of the word "God" is not that it indicates the stable point and anchor, but rather that it confronts the human person with the question of herself in her totality. Its power is that of the radical question; it asks us who we are. Human beings, who are the grammar and words of God, face the question of themselves in the word "God."

"God," as a name for the "silent one," brings the human person "face to face with the single whole of reality" and "with the single whole of his own existence" (Rahner 1982, 46-47). Thus the word "God" is essential to our humanity, for without it

> [m]an would forget all about himself in his preoccupation with all the individual details of his world and his existence. *Ex supposito* he would never face the totality of the world and of himself helplessly, silently and anxiously. He would not notice any more that he was only an individual existent, and not being as such. He would not notice that he only considered questions, and not the question about questioning, itself (48).

The idea of questioning ourselves in our totality is so important to Rahner's theological anthropology that without this question, which is exactly what the word "God" confronts us with, we would cease to be human. If this word did not exist, humanity would have forgotten the "silent mystery," "the totality and its ground" (48; 1976a, 58). Even more, Rahner states, "man...would have forgotten that he had forgotten" (Rahner 1982, 48). He writes, "We can only say that man exists when this living being in reflection, in words and in freedom places the totality of the world and of existence before himself in question, even if he might become helplessly silent [*ratlos verstummen*] before *this* one and total question" (48; 1976a, 58.).

Furthermore, it is not merely the case that the word "God" indicates the kind of questioning that happens when a person is confronted with the term of transcendence. The word itself provokes such questioning. This word presents us with the question of ourselves in our totality in relation to reality as a single whole. It does this precisely by indicating the empowering ground of language. Rahner writes:

> For the word "God" places in question the whole world of language in which reality is present for us. For it asks about reality as a whole and in its original ground. Moreover, the question about the totality of the world of language exists in that peculiar paradox which is proper precisely to language because language itself is a part of the world, and at the same time it is the whole of it as known. When language speaks of anything it also expresses itself, itself as a whole and in relation to its ground, which is distant but present in its distance. It is precisely this that is pointed to when we say "God," although we do not mean thereby identically the same thing as language itself as a whole, but rather its empowering ground. (Rahner 1982, 49, 50)

Rahner is neither imagining a way to know God outside of language, nor is he describing the reality of God as a function or production of human discourse. God, as the empowering ground of language and the horizon of human transcendence, is always present, even when distant or absent. In Rahner's theology and spirituality, God is present even in the absence that creates the possibility of our own presence to ourselves and to each other. God is present as the infinite that reveals all of our finite attempts at fullness to be empty. We can know God, for Rahner, in the void of human meaninglessness as well as in God's absence.

"God," as the term that confronts us with the question of the whole of ourselves and the whole of the world, is a word that we "*hear and receive*" (50). It comes to us from the history of language that shapes us, a history that presents us with the question of this word. Yet the history of language is not sufficient to answer the question with which it presents us. Rahner writes of the word "God:"

It is always open to Wittgenstein's protest, which bids us to be silent [*schweigen*] about things which we cannot speak about clearly.
Notice, however, that he violates this rule in formulating it. The
word itself agrees with this maxim if correctly understood. For it
is itself the final word before wordless and worshipful silence [*vor
dem anbetend verstummenden Schweigen*] in the face of the ineffable
mystery. It is the word which must be spoken at the conclusion of all
speaking if, instead of silence in worship [*Schweigen in Anbetung*],
there is not to follow that death in which man becomes a resource-
ful animal or a sinner lost forever. (51; 1976a, 60, 61)

Rahner approaches the linguistic analysis of why we can call the
term of transcendence "God" from two directions. On the one hand,
we should allow our experience of transcendence to shape what "God"
means. On the other hand, the word itself plays a role in prompting
the experience itself. The word hearkens back to the experience, even
as the experience is called forth by the word.[7]

In trying to describe the meaning of this word which has been
uttered, which points to an experience that could not get a hearing
without words, Rahner relies heavily on images of silence. God is the
Silent One and the word "God," which points to this silence, is the
only necessary word. At least in part, this serves to indicate that the
meaning of the word "God" is outside of our categorical matrix and
therefore cannot be objectified in words. It is the empowering ground
of language and therefore cannot be adequately contained within it. It
is incomprehensible mystery, the experience of which is transcendental and unthematic. In part, Rahner's use of "silence" marks the place
where words fail. Yet this failure is not a truly negative inadequacy;
it is not the case that words should be able to capture the content of
the word "God" and somehow fall down on the job. Indeed, it seems
as if silence might be the appropriate response to the recognition that
the meaning of the word "God" is mystery. Worshipful silence is the
desired conclusion to all speaking. Even being "helplessly silent" is part
of what makes us human and not clever animals (Rahner 1982, 48). It
is only if we were to try and force the word "God" out of existence—to
somehow negate the ground of language—that we would keep "dead
silence" or "absolutely silent" (Rahner 1982, 45, 49; 1976a, 55, 59).

---

7 This pattern resonates with a nonfoundationalist approach to Rahner as a
whole.

Having argued that it is appropriate to name the infinite horizon "God," Rahner tends to use other terms, such as holy mystery, instead. He wants to examine the "experience and the term of the experience together before what is experienced can be called 'God'" (Rahner 1982, 61). No matter what name we use, Rahner states, "[w]e have really understood this process of naming only if we understand it as simply pointing to the silence [*Schweigen*] of transcendental experience" (62; 1976a, 71).

It is clear that Rahner is not using silence as the opposite or absence of speech, nor is he invoking silence as a way to leap out of language and generate a theology unbounded by discursive constraints.[8] Rahner famously wrote four thousand things—he was not invested in avoiding words.[9] Furthermore, we only know about the place of silence in his life in so far as he wrote about it, inscribed it on the page and thereby entrenched it in language. The repeated use of images of silence in Rahner's theological and spiritual texts can best be understood as a discursive strategy. Frequently he employs images of silence to indicate the inadequacy of speech. At the very same time, however, he is performatively asserting the inescapability of language.

## LANGUAGE AND EXPERIENCE

Yet could Rahner still be understood as trying to escape language in a more subtle sense by placing a pre-linguistic experience of God at the center of his theology and spirituality? Even if we accept a reading of Rahner that is not philosophically foundationalist, must we concede that he secures the heart of Christianity in an inner, silent core that cannot be assailed by language?[10] To answer this question, we need to explore how Rahner understands language. Then we can return to his use of images of silence in order to better understand just what experience Rahner has in view and what role it plays in his theology.

---

8 Derrida discusses these problems in relation to negative theology. Derrida (1992).

9 See also his defense of speaking about God (1988, 111).

10  This question is connected to a concern raised by Endean: "The claim that Rahner's theology proceeds from his experience of God is in danger of collapsing into the claim that his theological achievement depends on some form of private revelation" (Endean 2001, 142).

Rahner emphasizes the importance and universality of experience of God. Harvey Egan states that "God's experiential self-communication" is "one of the main pillars" of Rahner's thought (Egan 1998, 32).[11] This experience is vital to Rahner's thought both in terms of content, with transcendence and the supernatural existential, and in terms of method, with his mystagogical, apologetic style and his anthropological starting point. Many scholars view this experience of God as a pre-linguistic foundation to Rahner's theology. For example, Geffrey Kelly writes, "In this experience, according to Rahner, one is immersed in the silence of being and orientated to the holy mystery even before theological reflection can infuse verbal meaning into the reality or proclaim the spiritual dimension of human existence...It is an *original* knowledge of God and thus a vital *a priori* of theological affirmation" (Kelly 1992, 41).[12]

Rahner's theology invokes and evokes experience throughout. This is perhaps clearest when he speaks in an apologetic voice. Writing within the context of Christianity struggling to come to terms with modern secularism, atheism, and pluralism, Rahner recognizes that Christians no longer grow up in a society in which Christianity itself is unquestioned. We can no longer rely on external indoctrination to make us Christians. Such external formation will only be effective if it resonates and answers our own internal experience of Mystery. Rahner says:

> even the "normal" self-critical and well-disposed person of today (in contrast to somebody of fifty, sixty, or a hundred years ago) is far less ready to accept as self-evident any indoctrination from outside about the meaning of life....Today things are not quite that simple. There exists that well-known, much heralded pluralism of world

11  Egan continues:

> Ignatius was convinced that during the Exercises the exercitant experiences the *immediacy* of God's self-communication and that the Creator and the creature work directly with each other. This Ignatian insight is almost a short formula for the entire Rahnerian enterprise. (32)

12  While I offer another option for understanding Rahner's view on experience of God and language, I also note that Kelly's introduction is excellent and that he notices Rahner's use of silence (or at least quotes and invokes it) more than most scholars.

views. The result is that if Christians really want to be Christians, they have to assume direct personal responsibility for building Christianity anew from within, more independently than used to be the case. Fundamentally included in that is what other people and I call the "experience of God." (Rahner 1991a, 179)

And elsewhere,

> Today a lively Christianity can exist even in an atheistic society only when the exterior message of Christianity knows that it is not powerful in itself alone, but is willing to encounter the innermost experience of the person, which is the mystical component of Christianity, and actualize it, making it come alive, digging it out from under the rubbish of everyday awareness. (Rahner 1986b, 183)

Rahner summarizes his vision of the future of Christianity by stating, "the devout Christian of the future will either be a 'mystic,' one who has 'experienced' something, or he will cease to be anything at all" (Rahner 1971a, 15).

Rahner believes that we experience God in the depths of our being and, therefore, the hum-drum banality of our daily lives is not exempt from grace. God offers Godself to us everywhere and always and, more often than not, our acceptance or rejection of this offer does not take place in dramatic moments of grand decision, but in how we handle the day to day routine of life, with its small commitments, miniscule duties, friendships, and obligations. Thus Rahner speaks of a "mysticism of everyday life" (Rahner 1992a, 84). If the essence of mysticism is immediate experience of God and, as Rahner argues, God's gift of self is the core of our being, then every one of us is implicitly a mystic. When asked what he meant by writing that the church of tomorrow would be a church of mystics, Rahner replied,

> With this expression I wanted to take a position opposed to an opinion which used to be dominant, according to which knowing about God was thought to be only something indoctrinated from outside a person . . . [in contrast] I think that people must understand that they have an implicit but true knowledge of God perhaps not reflected upon and not verbalized—or better expressed: a genuine experience of God, which is ultimately rooted in their spiritual existence, in their transcendentality, in their personality, or whatever you want to name it. (Rahner 1991a, 115)

Since this experience of God is so important for Rahner's theology and spirituality, and given that he repeatedly invokes images of silence in describing the experience of transcendence and of God, is he preserving a non-linguistic center to Christianity? Does Rahner present a picture of Christian faith in which the central moment is exempt from language? These are important questions in assessing Rahner's continuing relevance for contemporary theology.

As the ripples from the linguistic turn in philosophy continue to move outward, any picture of the human person that relies upon a non-linguistic core becomes less persuasive. Philip Endean discusses two problems inherent in Rahner's work understood as grounded on pre-linguistic experience of God. First, it fails to acknowledge the ways in which language is formative of experience and we, as those who experience, are formed in language. He writes, "It is not that we have experience and then clothe it, so to speak, in words: language is a necessary condition of our being able, at least in one sense of the word 'experience,' to have an experience at all" (Endean 2001, 140). Second, the notion that such an experience provides warrant for theological claims prevents, rather than encourages, rigorous thought, criticism, and further communicability (141, 42).

At times Rahner does appear to embrace a sense of pre-linguistic experience instead of acknowledging the ways in which our experience itself is always shaped by discourse, even before it is subject to reflection and attempted communication. For example, he writes, "we should show again and again that all these theological concepts do not make the reality itself present to man from outside of him, but they are rather the expression of what has already been experienced and lived through more originally in the depths of existence" (Rahner 1982, 17). This seems to follow a pattern of identifying experience and knowledge, common to all individuals, to which words then refer. Fergus Kerr criticizes Rahner on this point:

> Rahner's natural assumption—that communication comes after language, and language comes after having concepts—is precisely what the Cartesian tradition has reinforced. His example suggests that, when I am in pain, I first have the thought that I am in pain, I then put it into words and finally I find someone to whom to communicate it. ...The picture would thus be that I enjoy immediate

non-linguistic knowledge of my own inner experiences..." (Kerr 1997a, 11)

George Lindbeck characterizes Rahner's theology as utilizing a combination of two types of approaches: a "cognitivist" approach that sees doctrines as "truth claims about objective realities" and an "experiential-expressive" approach that "interprets doctrines as noninformative and nondiscursive symbols of inner feelings, attitudes, or existential orientations" (Lindbeck 1984, 16, 17). Lindbeck sees this as generating many problems, including relying on a universal experience that, due to its pre-conceptual nature, cannot be meaningfully articulated. In contrast, Lindbeck offers a "cultural-linguistic approach" in which

> [A] religion can be viewed as a kind of cultural and/or linguistic framework or medium that shapes the entirety of life and thought. It functions somewhat like a Kantian *a priori*, although in this case the *a priori* is a set of acquired skills that could be different. It is not primarily an array of beliefs about the true and the good (though it may involve these), or a symbolism expressive of basic attitudes, feelings, or sentiments (though these will be generated). Rather, it is similar to an idiom that makes possible the description of realities, the formulation of beliefs, and the experiencing of inner attitudes, feelings, and sentiments. Like a culture or language, it is a communal phenomenon that shapes the subjectivities of individuals rather than being primarily a manifestation of those subjectivities. (33)

Nicholas Adams summarizes the contrast succinctly by stating that "Rahner's argumentation *starts* with experience" while Lindbeck "*starts* with languages" and "moves subsequently to identify particular experiences which such languages make possible" (Adams 2005, 218). Adams also places Rahner's theology within a context in which "[d]ominant voices in his tradition advocated a strong identification of church teaching with truth," even implying that official church teaching was "the *only* access to such truth" (219).[13]

However, both Kerr's statement and Lindbeck's analysis neglect aspects of Rahner's theology that suggest a much more nuanced interplay between experience and language. Francis Caponi argues that Rahner's theology includes two conflicting views of religious language: "an 'incarnational' approach in which language is a necessary and con-

13  For other current discussions of Lindbeck and Rahner, see Marmion (2003, 201-207) and Kerr (2007, 92-93).

stitutive dimension of revelation, and an 'optional' approach in which language is the subsequent and ultimately unnecessary embodiment of an *a priori*, 'transcendental revelation.'"(Caponi 202)[14] Having argued above against reading Rahner's work as a seamless, systematic unity, I will not here demand that his many remarks on language form a univocal statement. Instead, I suggest simply that without offering an extended linguistic theory, Rahner's writings acknowledge many functions of language. Furthermore, many of his texts move towards a complex perspective on the mutually forming relation of language and experience.

In *Foundations*, Rahner is concerned with portraying a unity in distinction between experience and reflection, such that each requires the other (Rahner 1982, 15). He distinguishes this view from both "rationalism" and "modernism." He writes:

> For basically every rationalism is based upon the conviction that a reality is present for man in spiritual and free self-possession only through the objectifying concept, and this becomes genuinely and fully real in scientific knowledge. Conversely, what is called "modernism" in the classical understanding lives by the conviction that the concept or reflection is something *absolutely* secondary in relation to the original self-possession of existence in self-consciousness and freedom, so that reflection could also be dispensed with.
>
> But there is not just the purely objective "in itself" of a reality on the one hand, and the "clear and distinct idea" of it on the other, but there is also a more original unity, not indeed for everything and anything, but certainly for the actualization of human existence, and this is a unity of reality and its "self-presence" which is more, and is more original, than the unity of this reality and the concept which objectifies it. When I love, when I am tormented by questions, when I am sad, when I am faithful, when I feel longing, this

14  Caponi (2007) sees this contradiction as evidence that Rahner's idea of "transcendental revelation" should be exised (218). This would have immense repercussions in Rahner's theology, as well as mitigating its usefulness for liberation and political theologies. While Caponi does not address this directly, he does call for "clearer development" of "the normative nature of liturgical and Magisterial language within Roman Catholic systematics, and the real necessity of dogma and an authoritative teaching office for the vital proclamation of the gospel" (220). I find Caponi's charge that Rahner's work presents two contradictory views on language to be predicated upon a foundationalist reading of Rahner that presumes systematic unity.

> human and existentiell reality is a unity, an original unity of reality
> and its own self-presence which is not *totally* mediated by the con-
> cept which objectifies it in scientific knowledge. (15, 16)[15]

Rahner claims that we know things about ourselves at a level more
original than words and concepts, such that what we know and our
knowing of it is in a unity prior to the conceptualization of our knowledge. At the same time, this original knowledge also includes reflection and cannot be separated from language. Even when we cannot put
our experiences and emotions into words, our knowing of them is still
bound up in the language that forms and shapes our knowledge. We
are not creatures who have emotions without reflecting upon them;
we question our sorrows, celebrate our triumphs, dwell on our loves,
and plan the fulfillment of our desires. And even if words cannot capture our knowledge of ourselves, we attempt to communicate in words
our experiences to others. Rahner states, "This original unity which we
are driving at between reality and its knowledge of itself always exists
in man only with and in and through what we can call language, and
thus also reflection and communicability. At that moment when this
element of reflection would no longer be present, this original self-
possession would also cease to exist" (16). If we experienced our self-
knowledge entirely without concepts and did not reflect upon it, we
would cease to be spiritual beings and be merely animals.[16]

While original knowledge always moves "towards greater conceptualization, towards language, towards communication, and also towards theoretical knowledge of itself," there is also a way in which our
language and concepts and theoretical knowledge are always turning
towards this original knowledge (Rahner 1982, 16). The tension between original knowledge and its conceptualization is fluid and dynamic, as original knowledge moves toward conceptualization and
"conceptualization and language have a necessary orientation to that

---

15  Translator William V. Dych offers the note that "existentiell" "refers to
the free, personal and subjective appropriation and actualization of something which can also be spoken of in abstract theory or objective concepts
without such a subjective and personal realization" (16 n.).

16  Rahner is clearly assuming a person, without significant disabilities, who
has reached the age of reason. Issues regarding such assumptions will be addressed in Chapter Five.

original knowledge, to that original experience in which what is meant and the experience of what is meant are still one" (17).

This kind of relationship between language and experience was seen above in the discussion of the word "God." What the word "God" means can only be known through experience, yet that experience is prompted by the word "God" itself. Rahner says something similar in *The Love of Jesus and the Love of Neighbor*. Here he explains that the words of this book "signify a challenge—a challenge to allow what the words say to summon up the content of one's own life experience, and so afford them entry into one's mind and heart" (Rahner 1983f, 11). Rahner both assumes that the reader has relevant life experience and that words can "summon" them. This can, and I think should, be understood as saying something more than that words are reminders of prior, pre-verbal experiences.

Within his theology, Rahner presents a view of language functioning symbolically, as he describes in "The Theology of the Symbol." Here Rahner states

> [A] symbol is not something separate from the symbolized (or different, but really or mentally united with the symbolized by a mere process of addition), which indicates the object but does not contain it. On the contrary, the symbol is the reality, constituted by the thing symbolized as an inner moment of itself, which reveals and proclaims the thing symbolized, and is itself full of the thing symbolized, being its concrete form of existence. (Rahner 1966f, 251)

Some scholars emphasize that the movement in Rahner's symbolic view of language is unidirectional. For example, Robert Kress states that the symbol always receives "its being and identity" from that which is symbolized (Kress 1982, 44). Yet Rahner gives two examples of a symbol that each point to something more complex. The first is that Jesus Christ is the symbol of the Father, in whom the Father is present, and through whom the Father comes to be Himself (Rahner 1966f, 236). The second, what Rahner calls "a profane example," is that of a marriage, when two people say "yes" in a wedding ceremony. Rahner explains:

> this external, freely spoken word, which is to be uttered with certain formalities, is the symbolic reality. It is not a subsequent and extrinsic sign, which merely refers from outside to the "thing" (the

inward consent). The consent is given in the audible expression, so much so, that the intended effect (the permanent marriage bond) cannot be realized without this audible expression. The expression and the thing expressed really are related here like body and soul. (240, n. 13)

This is the classic illustration of a performative utterance, given by J. L. Austin in *How to Do Things with Words* (Austin 1975).[17] While Rahner does not describe the statement "I do" as one that performs, or makes happen, what it states, he uses this famous example to claim that words have a more than expressive function.

In the case of both Jesus and wedding vows, the symbol does more than express or fulfill what is symbolized. Furthermore, it is not simply the case that the being and identity of the symbol is "received" from that which is symbolized, without any movement in the other direction. The process of symbolization is integral to the identity, reality, and actualization of that which is symbolized.[18]

Rahner's presentation of language as functioning symbolically is also developed when he compares the relationship of body and soul to the relationship of thought and word. He writes:

> Our word is more than a thought: it is thought become incarnate. If it is true that body and soul exist in substantial unity, as Scholasticism teaches, then the word is more than a mere externalization in sound, a signalling of a thought which could equally well exist without the accompaniment of this animal noise. As if the thought were a mere conventional signal in the brute spiritlessness of the animal and material world which we—spirits—are constrained to frequent! No, the word is rather the corporeal state in which what we now experience and think first begins to exist by fashioning itself into this its word-body. To be more precise: the word is the embodied thought, not the embodiment of the thought. It is more than the thought and more original than the thought, just as the

---

17  Describing a performative utterance, Austin writes, "the issuing of the utterance is the performing of an action" (6).

18  Stephen Fields, S.J. (2000) explores Rahner's use of symbol in a very different way. This text places the issue in the context of philosophy, metaphysics, and—to a lesser degree—art. Fields traces sources of Rahner's thought on symbol in order to create a "philosophy of the Realsymbol's history" (17). As the contexts, assumptions, and issues of Field's text are quite different from my own, he offers a different take on Rahner's symbolic language.

> entire man is more than, and more original than, his body and his
> soul considered separately. (Rahner 1967b, 295)

Rahner is clearly envisioning a more complex relationship than one
of mere expression. He states: "men always think in conceptual words
and not in wordless concepts" (Rahner 1967a, 321). Thought is not
simply antecedent to language.

In "Priest and Poet," Rahner views language as symbolic, transcendent, and redemptive. Recognizing that words have different meanings according to context and usage such that his typology is necessarily inadequate, Rahner sketches two categories: utility words and
primordial words. He writes:

> Some words are clear because they are shallow and without mys-
> tery; they suffice for the mind; by means of them one acquires mas-
> tery over things. Other words are perhaps obscure because they
> evoke the blinding mystery of things. They pour out of the heart
> and sound forth in hymns. They open the doors to great works and
> they decide over eternities. Such words, which spring up out of the
> heart, which hold us in their power, which enchant us, the glorify-
> ing, heaven-sent words, I should like to call primordial words (*Ur-
> worte*). The remainder could be named fabricated, technical, utility
> words. (Rahner 1967b, 296)

This typology provides both a criticism of the inadequacy of refer-
ential views of language, and the claim that some words function differently. Primordial words can, "by a kind of enchantment produce in
the person who listens to them what they are expressing" (295). They
are "gifts of God, not creations of men, even though perhaps they came
to us through men" (296). Primordial words cannot be defined, but
rather "evoke the mystery" as "children of God, who possess something
of the luminous darkness of their Father"(297). Rahner writes poeti-
cally of primordial words, explaining that in them "spirit and flesh, the
signified and its symbol, concept and word, things and image, are still
freshly and originally one—which does not mean, simply the same"
(297, 298). A primordial word is something quite different than a reference to an object or concept. It is "in the proper sense the presentation of the thing itself" (299). Rahner states, "whenever a primordial
word of this kind is pronounced, something happens: the advent of
the thing itself to the listener" (299).

Rahner goes on to relate that, since every individual thing has its being with the whole, the fulfillment of each entity is related to the fulfillment of all. For persons, this means that they find their completion in knowledge and love—knowing, loving, being known, and being loved. And, Rahner claims, non-persons reach completion by being spoken by persons. He states "All realities sigh for their own unveiling. They want themselves to enter, if not as knowers at least as objects of knowledge, into the light of knowledge and of love." (300). Words spoken bring realities into the presence of hearers and more fully into themselves. Thus Rahner writes, "Everything is redeemed by the word. It is the perfection of things" (300).

Primordial words signify finite realities in such a way that windows are opened into infinity. In this movement from the finite to the infinite, these words participate in transcendence (298). Rahner writes:

> But among all the modes of expressing himself that man uses in all the arts, the word alone possesses something which is not shared by any other creation of man: it lives in transcendence. Were it not to sound *exclusively* negative, and therefore destructive, one could say that negation alone lives in it. The word alone is the gesture which transcends everything that can be represented and imagined, to refer us to infinity. It alone can redeem that which constitutes the ultimate imprisonment of all realities which are not expressed in word: the dumbness of their reference to God. (302)

In *Foundations*, Rahner suggests that perhaps the experience of God cannot get a hearing without words. In this essay he goes much further, stating that God comes to humanity in word, and indeed cannot come otherwise without taking humanity out of the world (304). It is through the word that God can come to humankind without robbing us of our freedom and humanity and without diminishing Godself. The word "alone lives in a conscious way that transcendence which both negates and liberates. It alone is capable of making God present as the God of mysteries to the man who does not yet see him, in such a way that this presence not only *is* in us by grace, but is *there* for us to perceive" (303, 304). Thus Rahner, who continually reiterates that God is the innermost center of the human person, can also coherently state that the word makes God present in the world, as "God's grace itself only reaches its own fulfillment when it is spoken. Then it is really *present*. It is present in virtue of being proclaimed" (305).

Rahner's symbolic view of language reaches its own conclusion and climax with the recognition that the experience of God, the gift of grace in transcendence and the supernatural existential, becomes fully present in the proclamation of the word of God. The experience of God, which Rahner so often describes using images of silence, becomes fully itself only when it is spoken in language. Rahner presents a world in which humans both access and actualize reality in and through language. The objects around us sigh for the deeper existence of articulation. Even the grace of God—the innermost constitutive element of humanity—is only fully present when the word of God is proclaimed.

Rahner does not articulate a single, fully-developed view of language. Indeed, his remarks on language differ from text to text. However, it seems clear he does not have a post-structuralist view of language, in which meaning is generated by the process of signification, by the interplay between signs within discourse. At the same time, neither does he have an expressivist view in which language is purely posterior to knowledge and thought. While he does not depict truth and meaning as produced entirely within human discourse, neither does he imagine that the human processes of knowing can bypass language.

Unlike many authors, both modern and postmodern, Rahner does not detail the connection between experience and language as one in which specifics of language deeply shape the content and character of our spiritual experiences. He does say language can summon, invoke, or even enchantingly produce certain experiences, which in turn move towards conceptualization and articulation. Every articulation of experience moves back, trying to approach the experience while also fulfilling it. Furthermore, Rahner appreciates ways in which the human subject always exists in language. He writes,

> Every individual in his intellectual and spiritual existence lives by the language of all. He has his ever so individual and unique experience of existence only in and with the language in which he lives, from which he does not escape, and whose verbal associations, perspectives and selective a prioris he appropriates, even when he protests against them and when he is himself involved in the ever-ongoing history of language. (Rahner 1982, 49)

These kinds of remarks lead Kevin Hogan to conclude that for Rahner, "Words are not only communicative, but redemptive and formative of being" (Hogan 1998, 197).

What does this mean regarding the experience of God that is given always and everywhere in the supernatural existential? Does Rahner ground Christian faith on a pre-linguistic experience and understand all of Christianity as the expression of this experience? Such a view would be unconvincing to many people today who grant a larger and more formative role to language and culture, in Derridian, Lindbeckian, or other ways. It would likewise be unpersuasive to many if it is seen as a form of positivism, in which a particular "pure" experience forms the content and basis of faith.

I believe Rahner's theology presents a significantly subtler picture. For Rahner, there is a transcendental element to all human experience. Mystical experience is distinct from, and yet intimately bound up with, ordinary experience. We cannot know God outside of our worldly existence. There is not a touchstone or foundation that resides outside of life and language that we can build upon. Rahner's affirmation of humanity's experience of God does not provide a path to sidestep the linguistic and worldly texture of human life. In contrast, he proclaims that God is experienced, known, and loved precisely in our mundane reality—that the commonplace utterances and daily tasks of life are steeped in the grace of God, symbolically realizing the presence of God among us.[19]

---

19   Philip Endean (2001) grapples with the possibility that Rahner understands the experience of grace as non-linguistic. Endean clearly rejects such a reading, insists "that all human experience involves language," and interprets Rahner's use of descriptors such as "ineffable," "nameless," and "non-conceptual" as indicating that knowledge of God "can never be a discourse of control, of grasping"(171). Endean writes, "The climax of the Christian life may indeed be silence and abandonment before the mystery of God, but that mystery is given us in word and symbol"(169). While I do not disagree with Endean's conclusions on this matter, I find parts of his discussion problematic. While stating that Rahner sometimes laboured under "an excessively crude theory of language" (169) and asserting that language and reality can relate in many ways, Endean assumes that all speech about reality that is beyond language, "unsayable," or "nameless," must be incoherent and self-contradictory (166-167). The possibility that speech about silence might be an intentional discursive strategy to communicate certain things about the reality so de-

While Kilby does not investigate Rahner's view of language, her non-foundationalist reading of his work relates to this subject. When Rahner takes up an apologetic style, he calls on the reader to look to her own experiences, which he interprets in accordance with his view of Christianity. Kilby interprets this not as relying on an experience that is accessed and understood independently of Christianity and only subsequently interpreting it in a Christian frame, but rather as presenting a Christian interpretation of experience that "initiates" the hearer into a certain kind of experience and into Christianity (Kilby 2004, 113). She writes, "We do not adopt faith because a prior experience leads us to do so, but we adopt an understanding of experience because our faith points us to it" (105). The experience of God that is so vital to Rahner's theology is not, in Kilby's view, the starting point of Rahner's theology, but rather "one of its conclusions" (98). Endean also claims that Rahner's apologetics do not rely on a neutrally-verifiable experience that is only subsequently interpreted by Christianity. He states, "the grounding of Rahner's 'I encountered God' turns…on the validity of the tradition enabling such a claim to be made in the first place" (Endean 2001, 182)[20]

Putting Kilby's reading into the context of Rahner's view of language, we can see how it is possible to talk about an experience that goes beyond language, and yet is only accessed within it. This experience gets its hearing in words, is produced by the enchantment of primordial words, provoked by the challenge of the word "God" that calls all things into question. Rahner affirms experience that is not generated simply or entirely within discourse, that cannot be captured and

---

scribed does not seem to be recognized. Endean concludes that such language from Rahner is informed by three concerns, apparently without imagining that Rahner deploys language to highlight these concerns. In short, Endean's commitment to the linguistic nature of human experience prevents him from fully exploring Rahner's references to silence, which might have been quite profitable within an exceptional book on Rahner and Ignatian spirituality. Framing the book with a story of a notebook of blank pages, ending with an image of theology as clearing space for the disclosure of God's grace, discussing the importance of verbal negation, Endean unaccountably misses the opportunity to explore this rich topic.

20  See also 224, 225, 230-233. For another view on the relationship between interpretation and experience in Rahner, see Lash (1988, 247-249).

contained in language, and that reaches towards an infinite horizon. But even this experience is summoned and fulfilled by the word. Rahner is doing something different here from simple expressivism, from poststructuralism, and from a cultural-linguistic view of religion. He offers—in his multiple, occasional texts—a view of language as humanly created and historical, and yet also God-given and redemptive. He does this through an understanding of symbol that dovetails with his description of the transcendental and categorical, in which what is symbolized comes to be fully itself in and through the symbol.

Such a symbolic view of language does not fit neatly into the categories of contemporary discussions about language. It does, however, bear out patterns familiar in certain traditions of Christian thought. Recall Rahner's use of opposition in describing the "silence which cries out," the familiar mystery, the luminous darkness of God, and the presence of God in absence. Note that, for Rahner, words have the power to gesture towards the infinite precisely in signifying the finite, living the transcendence that "negates and liberates" (Rahner 1967b, 304). The word is redemptive because, through the negation that lives in it, it can become the sacrament of the "conscious presence in the world of the God who is superior to the world" (304, See also 302). These patterns resonate with the traditions of negative theology, deploying language in unexpected ways in order to speak of mystery. Rahner's discursive patterns and discussions of language, as well as his related emphasis on mystery, indicate the apophatic leanings of his theology.

These tendencies in his theology are important to note within a theological discussion of silence. They point to the question: what is the relationship of silence and theology for Rahner? The definition of "theology" in the *Theological Dictionary* written by Rahner and Herbert Vorgrimler states:

> In the strict sense (as distinct from philosophy, metaphysics, mythology, and natural knowledge of God) it is essentially the conscious effort of the Christian to hearken to the actual verbal revelation which God has promulgated in history, to acquire a knowledge of it by the methods of scholarship and to reflect upon its implications. Thus it does not produce verbal revelation but presupposes it, and yet theology cannot be sharply distinguished against revelation, because the latter is promulgated in human terms and thus already

contains an element of human reflexion of which God has made use.

...In no other science is there such a gulf between the statement and what is stated, between what is expressed and what is implied, between what we lay hold on and the mystery which lays hold on us; and therefore it is not only the right but the duty of theology to allow this gulf to be sensed ever more keenly, to refer men from the apparent clarity of its conceptions to the blinding brilliance of mystery which seems to us to be darkness. (Rahner and Vorgrimler 1965, 456-457)

This is a brief quote from a lengthy definition, in which theology is noticeably not presented primarily as an activity of talking about God. Rather, it is about listening to and hearing God's revelation. Theology is essentially the effort to "hearken" to revelation; theology is based on "an undistorted hearing of God's word;" "revelation is meant to be heard;" theology "listens" to the word of God; "theology is always an effort to hear and understand;" the secular historical experience of a person "must embody itself in the act of theology if he is to hear God's word" (456-457). There is a remarkable contrasting lack of active verbs describing speech. Elsewhere Rahner states, "theology is nothing but the exact listening to God's revelation with every means of grace and nature available to a person" (Rahner 1993a, 312). Theology is about listening, and what is listened to is the revelation of God.

Yet silence is a part of discourse, and cannot be viewed apart from speech. Both silence and speech are integral to Rahner's understanding of theology. Rahner uses the image of silence while saying the experience of God, above all others, requires, involves, questions, and demands language. He writes, in considerable continuity with negative theology, that the "distinctive relativity in theological statements"

is one that cannot be replaced by an attitude of silent adoration, by a *theologia meditativa* which effectively reduces itself to silence. Nor can we express these statements in a form which suggests that the actual formulation of them in human words is the ultimate goal at which we are aiming. Rather it is the attitude of trembling and silent adoration which is intended to beget these statements, and this belongs to that deathly silence in which man's lips are sealed with Christ's in death. It is, therefore, a very difficult task with which theology has to cope in these statements. They must be expressed in words in order that we can arrive at the authentic silence which we need. They must be borne with in patience and hope in respect both of their necessity and of their incommensurability, in which they attempt to utter the ineffable. I believe that theology today has still very much to learn before it speaks in such a manner that men can achieve a direct, effective, and clear recognition of the special quality of this language. (Rahner 1974b, 112)

## RAHNER'S USE OF SILENCE

Thus far I have noted Rahner's repeated, consistent use of silence in describing God, experience of God, and appropriate response to God. This has been seen in the context of divine/human relationship understood as a dialogue between two parties, each offering both speech and silence to the other, communicating in love and freedom. This dialogue is further contextualized within a view of language that falls neatly neither into a modern or postmodern framework, but rather relies on a notion of symbol that, for Rahner, is tied to the unity of body and soul and to the corporate nature of creation. I have noted that, in Rahner's texts, silence is neither the opposite of speech nor the absence of communication.

What, then, are we to make of Rahner's use of silence? A consistent pattern emerges. First, silence is, for Rahner, interpersonal. He does not write about silence of uninhabited deserts or about the quiet of a mind engaged only with itself.[21] He even states that even if God were to remain silent, "God's silence would always once again presuppose ears to hear the silence of God" (Rahner 1982, 223). Rahner writes about silence within the larger dialogue between humanity and God—silence as perceived and performed by persons both human and divine. Second, within this dialogue, silence is an important and enabling part of discourse. It is the silence of God that makes room for our speaking; our silence allows us to hear the communication of God. Third, silence is thus both a condition of this dialogue and its pinnacle. God's eloquent silence tells us God is there and our earthly, worshipful silence is the prayer God desires, the summit of our speech. Even Jesus Christ, the Word of God, accompanies us in silence. Fourth, following the above, silence also marks the limits of language. It gestures towards all that cannot be thematized, conceptualized, and circumscribed. Si-

---

21   Rachel Muers (2004) makes a similar point about Bonhoeffer.

lence moves towards mystery, which, in Rahner's work, is both the ocean that supports human knowing and the rock upon which human knowing shatters.

These comments all indicate the space within language that silence occupies for Rahner. But what does it mean? Does it really only signify that something goes beyond the grasp of language? When Rahner repeatedly uses images of silence to characterize God, our experiences of God, and saying "yes" to God, surely there is some content to this description.

In the above passages tracing Rahner's use of silence, we see that images of silence are used to mark the pain and isolation of the human person. There is an enormous gulf of difference between ourselves and all others, both human and divine, that brings with it confusion, loneliness, and loss. In our transcendence to the Silent Infinite, we know ourselves as finite and God as distant, withdrawn, and unknowable. In grieving, when we mourn the silence of our loved ones, we feel the brutal realities of human life that mean we can be separated from our closest companions. Rahner uses images of silence to indicate the distance between persons that is the very substance of otherness.[22]

This otherness and difference is undeniably painful, but it is also the precondition for real relation, instead of mere self-extension. We become ourselves when we reach beyond ourselves to the other in love. Rahner portrays loving relations as those that acknowledge difference, recognize otherness, and avoid self-serving manipulation. This means that while he affirms that humanity is an intercommunion and that God is present in the center of the human self, he also honors human individuality and the distinction between God and humanity (Rahner 1982, 193). In Rahner's view, this is not paradoxical. Rather, it is the nature of loving relation that difference is required.

---

22  The importance of otherness in Rahner's thought has been explored by Michael Purcell (1998). This text brings Levinas and Rahner together as complementary thinkers, operating within the disciplines of philosophy and ethics. Andrew Tallon (1982) discusses two forms of otherness, embodiment and interpersonal, in Rahner's thought. Tallon likewise engages Rahner in a fairly philosophical context while addressing ethical concerns, particularly regarding the individual and the community. The importance of the other will be touched upon frequently in the next two chapters and most fully addressed in Chapter Five.

Therefore, without shedding any of the negative connotations mentioned above, images of silence in Rahner's work also indicate a communicative openness that makes room for the voice of the other. Silence indicates attention, space, and time granted to the other in order
to hear her word, her silence. At times, silence is used to evoke an
intimate communion that goes beyond words.

Silence between persons indicates both otherness and openness.
God, as the term of our transcendence, is the radical other to which
we are intrinsically open in our very humanity. Openness to this other
is the core of human spirituality. God cannot be known apart from
this experience of openness to otherness, and God relates to humanity as one who is profoundly other and yet offers Godself to us and
is open to our response. Finally, we say "yes" to God by acknowledging this structured dialogue, by recognizing and accepting ourselves as
self-possessing openness, as individuals who come to be in intercommunion, as sinful humans sanctified by the gift of God's own future.

Indeed, otherness and openness are so central to Rahner's depiction
of the human condition that one could ask how merely being open to
otherness could constitute a "yes" at all. Is it not merely being human?
Yes. That is, it is becoming fully human. He writes, "The real and total
and comprehensive task of a Christian as a Christian is to be a human
being, a human being of course whose depths are divine" (1982, 403).
Rahner's spirituality is structured as the acknowledgement—in disposition and deed—and awareness of the reality of the relationship between God and humanity. Saying "yes" for Rahner, in whatever form,
is a process of accepting who we are and, in so doing, fully becoming
ourselves.[23]

In his theological anthropology, Rahner describes the human person as self-possessing openness to the other. In his use of silence, these
same characteristics mark saying "yes" to God, accepting God's grace
and our God-given identity. This can be seen in Rahner's conclusion
to his exploration of the word "God," where he states : "We are familiar with the Latin expression *amor fati*, the love of one's destiny.
This resolve in the face of one's destiny means literally 'love for the
word that has been uttered,' that is, for that *fatum* which is our destiny.

---

23  For a different gloss on self-acceptance in Rahner, see Lash (1988,
245).

Only this love for what is necessary liberates our freedom. This *fatum* is ultimately the word 'God.'" (Rahner 1982, 51). For Rahner, silence marks a posture of openness to the unknown, unmanipulable other, such that silence is one form of *amor fati*, one characteristic of saying "yes" to God.

# CHAPTER 3

## LOVE

*Only one who loves his or her neighbor can know who God actually is. And only one who ultimately loves God (whether he or she is reflexively aware of this or not is another matter) can manage unconditionally to abandon himself or herself to another person, and not make that person the means of his or her own self-assertion.* (Rahner 1983f, 71)

### INTRODUCTION

In Chapter One, I explained Rahner's claim that human beings have a fundamental freedom to say "yes" or "no" to God's offer of Godself. Three events in which this "yes" can be affirmed are silence, love, and death. Each one of these events, if it is to be a "yes," involves a posture of openness to the unknown other. In silence, the difference and distance from the other is affirmed as part of freedom and love; in love, the fundamental orientation to the other is accepted.

Rahner has two basic insights about love that are pivotal in his theology. First, any act of love is an implicit affirmation of faith in God. Second, it is in the act of loving that we know God most fully. These two insights open the way for Rahner's proposal concerning "anonymous Christians," form the basis of his reinterpretation of mysticism, and become resources for the liberation and political theologians whom Rahner influences.

When Rahner writes about love he is not focusing on affection or sentiment, or even on great acts of sacrifice. What he is concerned with are any acts, large or small, whose positive meaning cannot be derived solely from the worldly consequences. Whenever someone is loyal when loyalty goes unrewarded, whenever someone is honest when dishonesty would be approved, whenever someone offers kindness that is not required, such a person is affirming a meaning and value that cannot be accounted for in purely human terms. They are, according to Rahner, enacting an implicit faith that this world is contained within a much larger meaning-making structure, in which things like honesty, loyalty, and kindness have enormous value. People who love are choosing to shape their lives around an affirmation of meaning. Rahner understands this enacted affirmation to be faith, faith that, despite overwhelming evidence to the contrary, the chaos and pain of this world are held within the horizon of a loving God.

Rahner's second insight concerning love is that it is in the act of loving that our ever-present knowledge of God is actualized. We possess certain kinds of knowledge that are most accessible to us in the "doing." We know how to tie shoelaces, but if asked to explain the procedure, many of us would need to reach down and actually tie them in order to observe our own knowledge in action. Although of course far more complex, our knowledge of God is similar to this. Rahner asserts that God offers Godself to each of us, gracing us with a vocation to be in communion with God. The knowledge of God that we gain from this revelation, however, is transcendental. We cannot access this knowledge directly; we can only be aware of this knowledge in and through our interactions in the world. One might expect a theologian to claim that we are aware of our own sense of God when someone offers us kindness that, by analogy, reassures us of a loving creator. However, Rahner argues that we can most fully access our own God-given knowledge of God when we love other people.[1]

This is related to Rahner's understanding of knowledge itself. In an essay titled "The Concept of Mystery in Catholic Theology," Rahner criticizes modern understandings of reason and mystery, wherein mystery is seen as merely something that the rational has yet to grasp. Mystery is provisional and negatively defined. In contrast, Rahner wants to understand mystery not as a "defective mode of knowledge" but rather as "the primordial and fundamental [that] is the ultimate transcendental condition of possibility of knowledge" (Rahner 1966c, 42). Describing his familiar view of humanity, Rahner states that the mystery, which makes knowledge possible, also demands that the subject take up a stance in relation to it, commit a basic and comprehensive act of either love or despair. For Rahner, knowledge is grounded in mystery and realized in love. Reason itself is "a potentiality only to

---

1 See also Rahner (2005) where he states that "knowledge ultimately terminates in bodily action" (93) and that "truth is first the truth which we *do*, the deed in which we firmly posit ourself for ourself and for others" (96).

be actualized in love." From this perspective, "mystery is not merely a way of saying that reason has not yet completed its victory. It is the goal where reason arrives when it attains its perfection by becoming love" (43).

From an anthropological starting point that begins with the knowing subject and transcendence understood primarily in epistemologically terms, as discussed in the last chapter, Rahner moves towards love as the actualization of knowledge within a transcendence that is understood primarily in interpersonal terms. Of the three interrelated moments addressed in this book—silence, love, and death—love is the one that Rahner writes about most directly. He repeatedly states that persons say "yes" to God by loving. For example, Rahner writes:

> Somewhere, even in the most normal course of a middle-class life (to which the whole of our cultural process belongs), there are moments in which that process calls a relative halt. It contains gaps and cracks—which look like empty fissures, but which, once we look hard, permit glimpses into the infinite. What seems to be the only reality then becomes just the starting point and framework for a gaze of awareness and freedom that loses itself in the infinite and no longer remains what one busies oneself with "soberly and realistically." More importantly: From time to time there seem to occur, in every human life no matter whose, moments in which the sober everyday love that can scarcely be distinguished from reasonable selfishness suddenly finds itself confronted by the invitation to love without hope of requital, to trust without looking back, to dare to love where only a foolish adventure can reasonably be expected, one that "would never be worth it."
>
> At such moments, human beings' freedom finds itself standing before the choice either of being cautiously cowardly—denying itself, and not daring to risk itself—or, in a foolhardy trustfulness, seemingly absurd (and yet—wonder of wonders—there it is), of taking the risk, of risking our freedom and our free subject without looking back, of risking really loving in the proper sense of the word. There is no longer any ground to tap in advance to see if it is solid or not; then freedom dares more than is granted it by a calculating rationality, risks itself and its own subject, and plunges into the unfathomable, unbounded dwelling place of God, who can ultimately be experienced only in this bottomless, headlong plunge.
>
> …The launching pad, if we may so call it, may be flimsy and narrow, and rise so scarcely above the flat plain of the everyday as to be

hardly noticed at all. But these trivialities—the biblical glass of wa-
ter to someone thirsty, a kind word at someone's sickbed, the refusal
to take some small, mean advantage even of someone whose selfishness has infuriated us, or a thousand other everyday trifles—can
be the unassuming accomplishment by which the actual attitude of
unselfish brotherly and sisterly communion is consummated, And
this communion is life's proper deed. (Rahner 1983f, 102, 103)[2]

## THE LOVE OF GOD AND
## THE LOVE OF NEIGHBOR

For Rahner, the love of God is not one achievement among others but
is the radical and definitive act of human freedom in which a person
says "yes" to God's offer of self-communication. The God who is loved
in this radical act remains incomprehensible mystery, even to the lover,
such that we cannot fully grasp and measure God and then make a
rational decision that it is in our best interests to love this intelligible
deity. Rather, the love of God calls us out of ourselves, away from our
calculations for our own self-promotion and into the self-forgetful
position of casting our lot with an elusive and uncontrollable other.
Thus Rahner describes our loving, affirmative answer to God in terms
of self-abandonment and self-surrender (Rahner 1983f, 70, 45). He
writes:

> The love of God is the totality of the free fulfillment of human ex-
> istence. It is not, in the last analysis, the content of an individual
> commandment, but is at once the basis and the goal of all individual
> commandments. And it is what it must be only when God is loved
> for his own sake—when love for him is produced and experienced
> not with a view to human self-assertion and interior self-fulfillment,
> in the accomplishment of certain individual exploits which people
> require of themselves, but when human beings, ultimately without
> self-seeking, go out of themselves, forget themselves because of
> God, and really lose themselves in the ineffable mystery to which
> they willingly surrender. (70)

At different points in his writings, Rahner discusses both the love
of God and the love of Jesus. Given Rahner's Christology, which af-

---

2 I find interesting resonances here with the work of Luce Irigaray. See Irigaray (1985).

firms traditional Christian claims that Jesus Christ is the incarnation of God, the love of God and the love of Jesus are both the same and distinct. I begin this discussion assuming their unity. Rahner asserts, "Unconditional love for Jesus…and the unconditional self-surrender of the human being to God…are, at bottom, one" (45). The distinction between love of God and love of Jesus, in that Jesus Christ is eternally the mediator and form of God to us, becomes clearer in the section focused on Christology below.

When writing about the love of neighbor, Rahner uses words and phrases that resonate with his descriptions of the love of God even before he begins to explicate the relationship between the two. Like the love of God, the love of neighbor is not a discrete action to be completed, but rather refers to "the fundamental act of human moral reality, of man himself" (Rahner 1968, 110). Rahner states, "Love of neighbour…is not to begin with just any of the many co-existing morally right reactions of man towards his own reality and that of his surroundings, but is the basis and sum total of the moral as such" (Rahner 1969d, 239, 240). Likewise, he writes, "The act of personal love for another human being is therefore the all-embracing basic act of man which gives meaning, direction and measure to everything else (241). Love of neighbor is described, like love of God, as the self-defining act of human freedom, our "free self-disposal" (241).

The similarity of these descriptions makes clear that the relationship between love of God and love of neighbor that Rahner envisions is a particularly intimate one. He is grappling with the Biblical witness to their unity, which is attested to in several different texts. Matthew 22:36-40 reads:

> 'Teacher, which commandment in the law is the greatest?' He said to him, 'You shall love the Lord your God with all your heart, and with all your soul, and with all your mind. This is the greatest and first commandment. And a second is like it: 'You shall love your neighbor as yourself.' On these two commandments hang all the law and the prophets.

Mark 12:28-31 is quite similar and Luke 10:25-28 combines love of God and love of neighbor into one commandment upon which the inheritance of eternal life rests. Matthew 25:40 makes love of neighbor the standard of eternal judgment, recounting Jesus saying "as you did it to one of the least of these who are members of my family, you did it to me." The theme of love of neighbor and its relationship with love of God is also addressed in the Fourth Gospel and taken up in the Pauline corpus.

Rahner rejects several ways of understanding the connection between love of God and love of neighbor. It is not the case, as some have thought, that love of neighbor is a proof of love of God, or even a kind of test case (Rahner 1969d, 235). Neither is it a "juridical fiction," such that loving neighbor somehow counts as loving God (Rahner 1968, 114).[3] The connection is deeper than that.

At the same time, it is not the case that the two can be understood as simply identical such that after love for neighbor, love for God is unnecessary. Rahner aims carefully to avoid elevating or endorsing secular humanism by simplistically collapsing love of God into love of neighbor. The relationship between the two, he says, "must not of course be understood in the sense of secular humanism, as if love for God were only an old-fashioned, mythological expression for love of neighbor—so that, when all is said and done, one could simply skip over it today if one could still maintain an inexorable, unselfish love for human beings without it" (Rahner 1983f, 71).

Nor should the relationship be collapsed too simplistically in the other direction, such that love of neighbor is only love for God played out in interactions with one's neighbor. Rahner writes that "'love for God's sake'…does not mean love of God alone in the 'material' of our neighbour merely seen as an opportunity for pure love of God, but really means the love of our neighbour himself, a love empowered by God to attain its ultimate radicality and a love which really terminates and rests in our neighbour" (Rahner 1969d, 244).

Rahner describes the relationship of love of God and love of neighbor as one of "mutual conditioning" and "mutual inclusion" (Rahner 1983g, 71).[4] There are two implications of this description that Rahner draws out. First, in this understanding, the love of God is included in the love of neighbor such that every act of loving one's neighbor is an act of loving God. This claim is not particularly radical; it is in

---

3  See also Rahner (1969d, 234).

4  See also Rahner (1968, 107, 108).

keeping with Rahner's understanding of Catholic tradition and scholastic theology (Rahner 1969d, 236).

The second implication of Rahner's description is that the love of
neighbor is included in the love of God, such that every act of loving
God is an act of loving one's neighbor. This is a more radical claim and
Rahner acknowledges that this goes a good bit further than scholastic
theology (237).

Drawing on his theological anthropology and the Biblical witness
(most specifically the gospel of John and the Pauline letters), Rahner
defines the relationship between love of God and love of neighbor as a
reciprocal one. He writes:

> Love of neighbor is not only a love that is demanded by the love of
> God, an achievement flowing from it; it is also in a certain sense
> its antecedent condition. ...There is no love for God that is not, in
> itself, already a love for neighbor; and love for God only comes to its
> own identity through its fulfillment in a love for neighbor. (Rahner
> 1983f, 71)

The reasoning behind Rahner's understanding of the relationship
between love of God and love of neighbor builds on his theological anthropology, discussed in the previous chapters. Love of God and love
of neighbor are mutually inclusive and mutually conditioning because
of who we are as human beings: God is both the horizon and inmost
center of our humanity. The love of neighbor is both an achievement
of and antecedent condition for love of God because, in Jesus Christ,
God has come to abide in humanity and humanity has been accepted
by God.

Rahner understands the unity of love of God and love of neighbor
as existing entirely due to God's grace. Drawing on scholastic theology, Rahner writes of love of neighbor within traditional discussions
of charity and emphasizes that both kinds of love he is considering
are enabled by the prevenient grace of God (Rahner 1968, 108, 109).
If love of neighbor were not a gift of grace, Rahner's claim that every
act of love of neighbor is an act of love of God would be theologically
dangerous, implying that we could muster the means of our own salvation.[5] This danger is seen more directly in light of Rahner's descrip-

---

5 In Rahner's view, "damnation is ultimately only the despairing incapacity to
love God" (1968, 102).

tion of love of neighbor as the eternity-making disposal of ourselves in freedom, his assertion of its radicality. Because of its relationship to love of God, love of neighbor is of ultimate importance.

Thus in this context, as in all of Rahner's theology, the necessity and abundance of grace is underlined. We cannot love God without God first loving us. "Theologically speaking," Rahner writes, "the radical character of love for Jesus Christ is made possible only by the anticipating force of Love itself, which Love is always available to our freedom and is ultimately God himself" (Rahner 1983f, 39). Likewise, loving our neighbor is supported and made possible by grace. In Rahner's words, "if we have turned in love from self to our neighbour, we have come to God, not by our strength but by God's grace" (Rahner 1968, 114). Finally, the organic, intimate relationship between loving God and loving neighbor is also established by grace, by "the universal saving will of God" (110).

This sense of grace permeates Rahner's theological anthropology, which then leads to his understanding of love. Rahner's theological anthropology describes the human person as dynamically transcendent unto the mysterious horizon, oriented towards God. In our knowing of categorical objects, we have unthematic knowledge of God as the horizon that makes our knowing possible. As with knowledge, so too with love. Rahner argues that all love of neighbor is also love of God because "it is orientated towards God, not indeed by an explicitly categorised motive but…by its inescapably given transcendental horizon, which is given gratuitously by God's always prevenient saving grace" (Rahner 1969d, 238). Rahner understands the orientation of the spirit to God to include "an element of (transcendental) revelation and possibility of faith" which gives moral acts (preeminently neighbor love) "that sufficient character of 'faith' necessary for a moral act being a salvific act" (239). Our transcendental orientation to God is a gift of grace, a gift that, within the present economy of salvation, divinizes our love of neighbor (239).

Rahner emphasizes that God is not one categorical object among others that we can know or love. Rather, God is the horizon of our knowing and loving, which we encounter in "mediated immediacy" in and through our encounters with categorical objects. This indicates both why love of neighbor is also love of God and why love of God cannot take place without love of neighbor. Rahner writes:

> God is not an object towards which the intentionality of man can be directed in the same fragmentary and particular way as it is towards the multiplicity of objects and persons encountered within the categories of intramundane experience.... In the original act which precedes all reflex systematisations, God is always given as the subjectively and objectively all-bearing *ground* of experience, a ground which is beyond this world; he is therefore given indirectly in a kind of boundary experience as the origin and destination of an act which is objectively directed towards the world. (244)

If we wanted to love God directly, apart from the world we live in, how would we go about it? In a Rahnerian framework, such an unworldly love of God is impossible and any attempt at such love is wrongheaded. It misses the ways in which God enables, empowers, and encompasses our relationships with the world around us. From Rahner's perspective, if we think we can aim our love solely at God, we have chosen to restrict our view such that the creator of the universe appears target-sized. If we imagine we can love God alone, we falsely envision God as one object among many. Rahner's theological anthropology claims that we know and love God in and through our interactions with the world, most specifically, in and through our relationships with other persons (245, 246). Thus he writes, "It is radically true, i.e. by an ontological and not merely 'moral' or psychological necessity, that whoever does not love the brother whom he 'sees,' also cannot love God whom he does not see, and that one can love God whom one does not see only *by* loving one's visible brother lovingly" (247).

Rahner's understanding of the unity of love of God and love of neighbor is clearly influenced by 1 John chapter four. Verse 12 states, "if we love one another, God lives in us and his love is perfected in us"; verse 16 reads, "God is love, and those who abide in love abide in God, and God abides in them." Rahner draws on the statement that "God abides in us" to help explain how it is that when we love our neighbor, we love God. As the permanent beginning and guarantor of God's offer of Godself to humanity, Jesus Christ is the reason that God abides in us. In and through Jesus Christ, God becomes human and humanity is accepted into God. The incarnation means that, for all eternity, God abides in human flesh and humanity is divinized. Rahner writes:

> It is truly the case that we meet the incarnate Word of God in the other human being, because God himself really is in this other. If we love him, if we do not as it were culpably impede the dynamism of this love and fundamentally turn it back towards ourselves, then there occurs precisely the divine descent into the flesh of man, so that God is in the place where we are and gazes at us in a human being. This divine descent continues through us and it then happens that we, because God loves us, love our neighbour and have already loved God by the very fact of loving our neighbour. For, of course, we cannot achieve this love at all except on the basis of that divine love for us which in fact made itself our brother. The Christological side, if I may so call it, of our brotherly love would have to be taken really seriously and really realized in life. Where the other human being confronts me, there Christ really is, asking me whether I will love him, the incarnate Word of God, and if I say Yes, he replies that he is in the least of his brethren. (Rahner 1968, 114, 115)

Throughout his discussions of God and neighbor love, Rahner reminds us that he is pointing to something ultimate and decisive, to a self-surrender, self-abandonment, and self-commitment. He is thinking neither of romantic gestures and great acts nor of moments of affection and mutual goodwill. He is thinking, rather, of those instances when we put another's interests before our own, when we stand by someone when it would be easier and pleasanter to leave, when we trust another person with our own selves, and when we, in turn, are truly open to the unknown and uncontrollable reality of another person's identity. These instances occur most frequently in the minor decisions of mundane existence. At the same time, they have a character of radicality and absoluteness.

This kind of love is risky. It requires putting oneself on the line and opening oneself up to the possibilities of pain and disappointment. It would only make sense for a person to love in this manner if she had enough knowledge of the beloved and the surrounding circumstances to be certain she would be safe. Yet that kind of certainty is unavailable. Other people are too *other* for us to know them so thoroughly and far too flawed to warrant such trust. Even if one were to attempt or pretend to love another human being unconditionally, the falsehood of this unfounded love would distort it into perversity. "It would be inauthentic. It would be ascribing to the lover, and even more to the beloved, an unconditionality and absolute validity which is simply not attributable to them. It would be feigning a certainty and security which it simply does not possess in reality, and it would end by anxiously overstraining its limits through this self-deception" (Rahner 1983f, 40). Rahner gives the example of someone who claims to be willing to go hell with their beloved (42). This kind of unwarranted unconditionality is clearly a distorted and destructive love. Rahner thus concludes that earthly, human love both reaches for unconditionality and yet contains a measure of "secret reservation" (40).

Rahner contrasts this love with love for Jesus. "The last reservations and insecurities of all human love are transcended in the case of love for Jesus, and love can be really unconditional, unconditional in the last extreme and in all dimensions" (41). Love for Jesus has "the right of extravagance" (41). The unconditionality of God is behind this love, both in that Jesus can be loved absolutely without perversity because he is the incarnation of the God of faithfulness, and in that the power for a human being to love Jesus is a gift from God's own love (41).[6] In love for Jesus, God can grant love the right of extravagance by standing surety for both parties, enabling the lover and making the beloved worthy of unconditional love by association with God's own unconditionality (42).

Rahner reasons that the secret reservations of love for a human being can be removed without falsehood if the beloved "enjoys an absolute and definitive union with God" or if God has unconditionally accepted the beloved (42). Each of these ways—union with God and unconditional acceptance by God—apply properly only to Jesus. In this regard, the right of extravagance rests only upon love of Jesus. It is only in Jesus Christ that God has irrevocably offered God's love to the

---

6 Note again that love for God and love for Jesus cannot be separated for Rahner: "…this salvific love for Jesus occurs by the power and as the consummation of the infused supernatural virtue of divine faith, in which God, through his prevenient grace, is himself principle, guarantor, and vessel of this love of a human being for God. Love for Jesus Christ has an unconditionality that is precisely the unconditionality of the love of a human being for God…" (41).

world in the hypostatic union and only in Jesus Christ that God has unconditionally and absolutely accepted a human being.

Yet in Jesus the love of God has been offered to the *whole* world, and in Jesus God has accepted *all* of humanity. The hypostatic union functions as the ground of the love and acceptance that God offers to all people (43). Rahner reasons further that as one can love Jesus with extravagance, one can also love with extravagance someone who belongs to Jesus, who is "included in his affirmation" (42). We can love human beings unconditionally in the belief that God has loved them unconditionally in and through God's absolute affirmation of Jesus Christ (43). Thus Jesus Christ provides both the foundation and irrevocable commitment of God's love for humanity and the enabling ground of neighbor love.[7]

There is a strand of Christian tradition that warns against loving any human being too much. Only God should be loved absolutely. To love anything or anyone else that much is a sign of sinfulness, disordered priorities, and idolatry. Without advocating disordered love, Rahner reinterprets the relation between loving God and loving neighbors, such that this warning loses its purchase. Loving another human being extravagantly and genuinely is only possible for someone who loves God. True, only God is worthy of absolute love. But it would also be right to unconditionally love anyone in union with God, or anyone whom God has accepted. Most properly, that means Jesus. However, in Jesus God has accepted all of humanity. Therefore it is not sinful to love another human being with abandon; it is salvific.

Rahner mitigates the radicality of this claim in a number of ways that embed the loving relationship within the grace of God. He states that real love is beyond our power to generate on our own. We can only manage it when God empowers us. When real love happens, God is present—abiding in the beloved, descending into the lover, grounding the love itself. While this surely raises human love to new heights, it does so within the love of God. Any merely human attempts to offer unconditional love to another human being directly—apart from the grace and presence of God—will fail, becoming relative and possibly idolatrous (Rahner 1967d, 269).

---

7 See also Rahner (1979c, 222-223).

In keeping with his understanding of silence discussed in the previous chapter, Rahner describes both the love of neighbor and the love of God as acts of being radically open to the mysterious other. In his discussions concerning our relationship with God, Rahner speaks of self-abandonment and surrender to the mysterious abyss. He repeatedly warns against reducing God to something comprehensible and manipulable, against imagining God to be another object within our matrix of coordinates. He continually emphasizes the ineffability of God, identifying faith with loving God precisely as mystery. In his discussions of love of neighbor, Rahner uses the same terms of self-abandonment and self-surrender and warns against the same errors, against reducing our neighbor to someone we can completely understand, use to our advantage, or see only as a support for our own self-understandings. In contrast, love is a "free self-disposal, [that] when morally right and perfect, is precisely the loving communication with the human *Thou* as such (not as mere negation of nor as something different from the 'ego' which wants merely to find *itself*, even though in the other)" (Rahner 1969d, 241). And elsewhere: "the lover loves and affirms the other precisely *as* other, certainly not seeking simply to absorb the beloved into his or her own peculiar way of being" (Rahner 1983f, 21).[8]

With both God and neighbor, we are tempted to accept and "love" only insofar as God and neighbor are comprehensible and useful to our own identities, only insofar as they serve as stable markers within our organized view of ourselves and the world around us. We are tempted to understand them by placing them neatly within our conceptual framework and not, as Rahner hopes for us, by opening ourselves to them and accepting the possibility that knowing them freely might wreck total havoc upon our tidy visions of reality, might disturb and transform our knowledge entirely.

In Rahner's view, mystery is the foundation of true knowledge. Knowledge, which is only truly realized in becoming love, necessarily contains an element of unknowing, of mystery (Rahner 1966c, 41, 43). This is very important in Rahner's understanding of how humans know God—if we think we fully comprehend God, we are no longer discussing the God of Jesus Christ but merely an idol of our own cre-

---

8 See also, in regard to love and mystery, Rahner (1966c, 41).

ation. It is also key to his view of how humans love God and one another. Love, as the perfection of knowledge, acknowledges the mystery
of the beloved.

The unity between love of neighbor and love of God is such that
each love has a character of openness to the other, precisely the posture of openness indicated by Rahner's use of "silence" in discussions
of human persons in relationship with God. One who loves assumes
a posture of self-giving openness to the mysterious Divine Other and
to the mysterious human other. The task of loving mystery *as mystery*
encompasses both love of God and love of neighbor. In both cases,
love requires the self-surrender of openness to the other as other, not
merely as a function of ourselves. Rahner writes:

> But the human being is ultimately a—no, *the* mystery. We are only
> ourselves when and where we trustingly and lovingly surrender, in
> freedom, in unbounded openness as the infinite question, to the
> incomprehensible mystery we call God. Thus the mystery of the
> human being is conditioned by and grounded in the mystery of
> God, but not ultimately via a thirst for a controlling knowledge and
> perception—rather only in the experience of the wonder of love.
>
> One human being will be dealing with another in a love of neigh-
> bor. This love of neighbor will make the loving person over to the
> other, surrender him or her to the other, not simply in this or that
> serveillable and manipulable particularity (of utility, objective ad-
> vantage, comfort in one's vital needs, esthetic infatuation, and so
> on), but as a whole—as "subject," as a person with an unsurveillable,
> limitless breadth of unbounded consciousness and concrete free-
> dom, as a person who surrenders and loses himself or herself in
> abandonment to God. And vice versa: The beloved accepts the
> other in this love of neighbor, accepts the other as this incalcula-
> bly mysterious subject. Love of neighbor is the compenetration of
> two such mysteries, in which Mystery *simpliciter*—God—is present
> and thereby ultimately renders all boundaries of these two subjects
> unrecognizable, inasmuch as at least what we Christians call grace
> makes God himself, as such, the inward determination of the finite
> subject, and thus God himself becomes an inward determination in
> both subjects' exchange through love of neighbor, or brotherly and
> sisterly communion. (Rahner 1983f, 99, 100)[9]

---

9  Rahner (1966c) states clearly that there is only one mystery, God. Humans
are mystery through reference to God. See especially (1966c, 44, 47).

By this point, it becomes clear that Rahner is describing love between persons as a mystical experience of God.[10] This seems rather radical, but it is merely a logical consequence of other aspects of Rahner's theology. It follows from his vision of everyday mysticism. It follows from his theological anthropology, in which Rahner asserts that we know God in and through knowing the world around us, understood primarily as the world of persons. It follows from his conception of the supernatural existential, which claims that God is at the core of every human person. It follows from his Christology, which states that God has come to abide eternally in humanity and has accepted humanity in Jesus Christ. It follows quite directly from his discussion of the unity of love of God and love of neighbor.

In addressing the unity of love of God and love of neighbor, Rahner begins with an affirmation supported by traditional scholastic theology, that in this economy of grace, every act of love of neighbor is an act of love of God. He takes this further, to say that every act of love of God is an act of love of neighbor. He moves further still, to describe love between human beings as a mystical experience of the presence of God. This is both a bold claim and a completely mundane, predictable outgrowth of his fundamental theological commitments.

What Rahner offers in this depiction of neighbor love as a mystical encounter with God is a vision of what Christian relationships ought to be as they are enabled by, and interpreted in light of, Jesus Christ. Rahner focuses on the challenges of managing to love someone, of assuming a posture of openness to the other. Speaking on a fairly abstract level, Rahner exhorts Christians to open themselves up to the mysterious other. This abstract depiction of openness is made concrete in statements about honesty, loyalty, and forgiveness that could be misapplied so as to encourage someone to submit to abuse or mistreatment. He does not offer, in this context, concrete norms and guidelines for limiting openness to the other or determining with whom one can safely be open. Given the drastic harms human beings inflict upon one another, such boundaries are terribly important. As the momentum of Rahner's theology moves toward openness to the

---

10   For a discussion of problematic elements related to this view, see Susan Abraham (2004, 48-50).

mystery of God, he does not articulate such boundaries nearly as well as he paints the vision of what openness can be.

However, there are some resources within Rahner's theology that can be marshaled on this point. These include his insistence that love must always respect the otherness and mystery of the beloved. He contends that true love begins only where the beloved is loved precisely in his "incalculable individuality." "Otherwise one is loving only one's own ideal, and the other person only as object of, or means to, its realization; in other words one is loving only oneself" (Rahner 1967d, 268, 269). This normative statement about love excludes abusive or domineering relationships. Love is the best way to understand the act of faith, of saying "yes" to God, because in love there is "an acceptance of what is not comprehended, an acceptance of what we have not ourselves perceived and consequently not mastered in the other person, the person who is loved" (Rahner 1983b, 101). Rahner contrasts love with knowledge on this point. He writes that knowledge in our ordinary lives "bears in itself the character of appropriation and domination of what is known, while this is not the case in genuine interpersonal love" (101). While Rahner does not offer clear instructions on when not to be open to the other, he does provide a standard by which to judge whether or not a relationship is loving. This standard includes the mutual recognition and respect of otherness and mystery.

Furthermore, Rahner is not exhorting Christians into self-abnegating submission. Rahner is too adamant that the other is not to be used for one's own self-assertion to imagine that he would somehow condone this in an inverted sense of defining oneself in terms of the other. Rahner's elevation of self-abandonment, self-surrender, and overcoming selfishness is not about denying or disparaging self-assertion. It is about having the courage to fully encounter the uncontrollable mystery that is the center of the self, the center of the neighbor, and the radically other mystery of God. Rahner views individuality and freedom as necessary for the inter-communion of radical interpersonal love. He states that love is

> …not a natural flowing out of the self, but is the free self-bestowal of a person who possesses himself, who therefore can refuse himself, whose giving away of self, therefore, is always an event of wonder and grace. And love, in the full, personal sense, is not merely any

sort of relation between two persons who meet one another in some third thing, whether this third thing is a work, a truth or anything else. Rather, love is the abandoning and opening of one's innermost self to and for the other, who is loved. (Rahner 1960, 141)[11]

The disposition of openness to the other is not about sacrificing one's identity, although it is about risking its reconfiguration. Rahner believes that the identity of the self is not lost in this encounter, but rather the true identity of the self is found. He states that we find ourselves by abandoning ourselves and lovingly sinking into the other (Rahner 1983f, 17).[12] He remarks, "one can and must quite soberly take oneself seriously, in really loving the other person by service to him. But that does not alter the fact that it is only by loving other people that one enters into a right relationship with oneself" (Rahner, 1972b, 201).

---

11   This is quoted in and translated by Mark Lloyd Taylor (1986, 69).

12   While I argue that Rahner does not intend a destructive self-abandonment in which the lover's own identity is built upon, or lost within, the identity of the beloved, it is important to place these considerations briefly within a larger discussion. In a groundbreaking article, Valerie Saiving Goldstein (1960) argues that the views of love and sin proposed by Protestant theologians Reinhold Neibuhr and Anders Nygren, which focus on sin as primarily or fundamentally prideful self-assertion, are inadequate to the experience of women. Many feminists have continued this discussion, most notably Judith Plaskow (1980). In this text, Plaskow describes women's experience of sin as "self-abnegation," or "the failure to take responsibility for self-actualization."(3) Several feminist theologians thus argue against Christian exhortations to selfless love as making a vice into a virtue and as further socializing women into subservient roles (for example, see Plaskow 87). While a full comparison of Rahner's call to self-abandonment in relation to this conversation would be out of place in this context, it is important to note that, as a Roman Catholic, Rahner is operating with very different theological assumptions concerning sin, the self, and love. In contrast to the Protestant theologians addressed by Saiving Goldstein and Plaskow, Rahner does not focus on sin, does not build a view of love in opposition to sin, and does not view the center of the self as a focal point in opposition to God. For further discussion of these issues, see Jacquelyn Grant (1993), Daphne Hampson (1990), Susan Nelson Dunfee (1982; 1989), and Delores Williams (1993). For further consideration of Rahner's thought in this context, see Rahner (1983g, 211-217) and Rahner (1961c, 205). See also Malcolm (2005, 126-127).

In the context of Rahner's theology, wherein the center of the neighbor is the mystery of God, this self-possessing openness is part of a relationship between the self and God. Human subjectivity and freedom are gifts from God and increased intensity of relationship with God does not limit or dilute them, but rather radicalizes them. He writes, "the nearer one is to God, the more one is a human being, in all human freedom" (Rahner 1983f, 33). In loving both God and neighbor we are encountering life-changing mystery.

## ANONYMOUS CHRISTIANS

Rahner furthers his view of love by asserting that Jesus functions as the enabling ground of human love even where Jesus is not known to the human lovers. Having said love that risks itself for the other is how we say "yes" to God's offer of self-communication, and having explained that such love is only possible because of God's grace in Jesus and in graced human nature, Rahner claims that wherever human love attains this radical character of self-risk, it does so on the ground and basis of Jesus. This means that it is possible for people to say "yes" to God and be saved by Jesus even if they do not explicitly believe in Jesus at all. Over the course of his career, Rahner described this in different ways, using different terms. He writes that "[i]mplicit Christianity—it could also be termed 'anonymous Christianity'—is what we call the condition of a man who lives on the one hand in a state of grace and justification, and yet on the other hand has not come into contact with the explicit preaching of the Gospel and is consequently not in a position to call himself a 'Christian'" (Rahner 1972a, 145). The term "anonymous Christianity" was sharply criticized and Rahner conceded that at times "anonymous Christian" was more appropriate (Rahner 1976b, 281).[13] However, the substance of his view did not

---

13  This was done primarily in response to criticism by de Lubac. See also Rahner (1974a, 162-165) for earlier discussion of de Lubac's criticism. Also note Rahner (1969a, 398), where Rahner writes, "the name itself is unimportant." For a fine discussion of the controversy over language, Rahner's own inconsistency on this point, and an evaluation of how little the change in terminology reflected a change in Rahner's thought, see Conway (1993, 28-33).

change, and indeed was nothing more than an explication of the logical implications of his understanding of love.

Eamonn Conway notes that Rahner began writing about anonymous Christians in 1960 in the context of an increasingly secular Europe, where significant numbers of people were beginning to understand themselves as atheists (Conway 1993, 10, 19). Rahner's theory of anonymous Christians was intended to help the church understand itself in relation to growing "secularism, pluralism, and atheism" (25). In this setting, Rahner's theory allowed Christians to understand those non-Christians around them as not destined for damnation, but rather called into a future with God. Rahner writes,

> [C]an the Christian believe even for a moment that the overwhelming mass of his brothers, not only those before the appearance of Christ right back to the most distant past (whose horizons are being constantly extended by palaeontology) but also those of the present and of the future before us, are unquestionably and in principle excluded from the fulfillment of their lives and condemned to eternal meaninglessness? He must reject any such suggestion, and his faith is itself in agreement with his doing so. (Rahner 1969a, 391)

Rahner finds the idea of persons having no chance of salvation antithetical to Christianity as the proclamation of the nearness and grace of God. Rahner writes of the Christian, "He does not seek any heaven from which some other man is excluded from the outset" (Rahner 1976b, 294). Contemporary awareness of the sheer numbers of non-Christians throughout history requires, Rahner thinks, asserting that salvation is possible outside explicit Christianity (Rahner 1974a, 175). Rahner's theory thus portrays non-Christians as graced and possibly saved while continuing to hold fast to the conviction that salvation comes through Jesus Christ (Rahner 1969a, 396)[14]. This does not diminish the importance of salvation through Jesus, but rather expands it exponentially. Rahner writes: "Today we can recognize the full length and breadth of non-Christian human history, and evaluate the power of the Cross of Christ at its true worth, and in view of this we can no longer assume that a majority of mankind is destined to perdition" (Rahner 1974a, 175).

---

14  See also Rahner (1979c, 218).

Thus the theory of anonymous Christians is shaped to give "comfort" and "strength" to Christians whose faith and hope are "sorely tried" by concern for unbelievers (Rahner 1969a, 396). People who love are saying "yes" to God and are saved by Jesus, even if they do not know it. Rahner writes,

> Where love can really abandon all reservations, definitely and with absolute assurance, where love can really live out to the last its most proper, most original nature as unconditional self-giving and surrender to the other, there Jesus as such is "co-loved" as the Ground of this love—even where that blessed Name is as yet altogether unknown to the one who loves. But we Christians can name this primordially and radically loved person. We call him Jesus of Nazareth. (Rahner 1983f, 44)

While Rahner's description of anonymous Christians is intended to help Christians in their understanding of God, the church, and themselves, questions concerning people of other faiths inevitably follows. Rahner's mature view of non-Christian religions is presented straightforwardly in *Foundations*, where he claims that Jesus Christ is present in non-Christian religions. He is clear that he is staging an *a priori* argument for this claim, not one that would draw upon the concrete history of religions. Rahner then makes two assertions. "First of all," he writes, "we shall presuppose a universal and supernatural salvific will of God which is really operative in the world" (Rahner 1982, 313. His emphasis removed.). God loves and wills to save every human being. This universal salvific will of God has already been asserted and explicated in Rahner's theological anthropology, specifically in his description of the supernatural existential. This supernatural elevation of human transcendentality, present always and everywhere, is the offer of God's own self to humanity, the gift of a vocation to eternal communion with God. His second assertion is this: "when a non-Christian attains salvation through faith, hope and love, non-Christian religions cannot be understood in such a way that they do not play a role, or play only a negative role in the attainment of justification and salvation" (314). For Rahner, this second statement follows from the historical and social nature of salvation, as attested to in the ecclesial nature of Christianity. Note that here Rahner uses the importance of the church in Christianity to argue for salvation outside the explicit,

confessing church.[15] This is not as awkward as it sounds—Rahner is
noting that Christianity claims that divine revelation takes place historically and communally, which is in accordance with the nature of
humanity. Therefore, it would contradict a Christian understanding
of the human person and of divine revelation to imagine that salvation
could take place in a radically individual or ahistorical way. Rahner
writes, "For even in his most personal history man is still a social being whose innermost decisions are mediated by the concreteness of
his social and historical life, and are not acted out in a special realm
which is separate" (Rahner 1982, 314). Therefore, Rahner argues, a
non-Christian could not say "yes" to God's offer of salvation outside of,
or apart from, her lived, historical, and social reality. She can only say
"yes" within this reality, and so we must understand any non-Christian
religion she is involved in to play, at the very least potentially, a positive
role in her salvation.[16]

There is another assertion, an important presupposition, operative
in Rahner's argument that is not explicitly identified as such in this
discussion, although it is clearly present. Rahner presupposes that salvation comes through Jesus.[17] This is why the possibility of salvation
in non-Christian religions must entail a presence of Jesus in such religions. In Rahner's words:

> Such a "presence" of Jesus Christ throughout the whole history of
> salvation and in relation to all people cannot be denied or over-
> looked by Christians if they believe in Jesus Christ as the salvation
> of *all* people, and do not think that the salvation of non-Christians
> is brought about by God and his mercy independently of Jesus
> Christ. (Rahner 1982, 312)

Elsewhere Rahner takes care to exclude interpretations of God's
universal salvific will wherein non-Christians may be saved through
"natural morality" or even through some "primitive" revelation that has

---

15   Rahner (1969a) argues for "degrees of membership" within the church,
such that anonymous Christians are within the church, instead of advocating
salvation outside the church (391). This is connected to his conversation with
de Lubac over terminology, discussed above.

16   See also Rahner (1983d). Rahner argues that "non-Christian religions
can be categorical mediations of genuine salvific acts" (294).

17   This assumption is stated clearly in Rahner (1979c, 216).

been handed down through the ages (Rahner 1976b, 291, 286). As we have seen above, Rahner strives in his description of the supernatural existential to emphasize that the offer of God's self is not natural, but supernatural. Any "attempt to account for the grace of redemption and nearness to God" as "given already by the mere fact of being human" would "negate it *as* grace" (Rahner 1969a, 392).

These three claims form the structure of Rahner's argument for the presence of Jesus in non-Christian religions: God wills salvation for everyone; non-Christian religions play a positive role in salvation; salvation comes through Jesus; therefore, Jesus is present in non-Christian religions.

How is Jesus present in non-Christian religions? Rahner says that Jesus is present in his Spirit. This claim rests on two related theological moves that Rahner makes. The first is to identify the supernatural existential, in the mode of acceptance, as experience of the Holy Spirit. The second is to explicate the Trinitarian relations such that the Holy Spirit is perceived as the Spirit of Jesus, even while acknowledging these separate persons within the Trinity.

In regards to the first claim, the relationship between the supernatural existential and the Holy Spirit is not articulated specifically and consistently throughout Rahner's writings. David Coffey examines the various descriptions of the supernatural existential in Rahner's work and notes that formulating "the theology of the supernatural existential in trinitarian terms…was never a concern of Rahner's, at least not in a systematic way" (Coffey 2004, 117). However, this minimal assertion is clear: the supernatural existential, in the mode of acceptance, is the indwelling of the Holy Spirit. In *Foundations*, after writing about the event of God's absolute self-communication to humanity (the supernatural existential) as a vocation to beatific vision, Rahner says "This is what is expressed in the Christian doctrine which says that in grace, that is, in the communication of God's Holy Spirit, the event of immediacy to God as man's fulfillment is prepared for in such a way that we must say of man here and now that he participates in God's being." (Rahner 1982, 120; See also 118). Rahner ends this chapter on the supernatural existential with a section on the Trinity. In this section, Rahner writes, "Insofar as he has come as the salvation which divinizes us in the innermost center of the existence of the individual person, we call him really and truly 'Holy Spirit' or 'Holy Ghost.'" (136).[18]

It is likewise apparent in Rahner's more spiritual writings. Rahner describes the activity of the Holy Spirit in a sermon for Pentecost. While the terms he uses are different from those he employs in his more academic writings, the connection to the supernatural existential is clear. Rahner describes the Holy Spirit as the innermost principle of humanity, which makes God our absolute future as long as we do not cut ourselves off from God. Further, his description of the work of the Holy Spirit in the world echoes his accounts of how human beings say "yes" to God's offer of Godself in the supernatural existential. He writes:

> If we look out for inner freedom in which a person, regardless of herself, remains faithful to the dictate of her conscience; if someone succeeds, without knowing how, in really breaking out of the prison of her egoism; if someone not only gets his pleasures and delights, but possesses that joy which knows no limit; if someone with mute resignation allows death to take her and at the same time entrusts herself to an ultimate mystery in which she believes as unity, meaning, and love: when these things happen, what we Christians call the Holy Spirit is at work, precisely because in these and similar experiences what is involved is not a controllable and definable factor of the world of our experience. The Spirit is at work precisely because this world of experience is delivered up to its incomprehensible ground, to its innermost center which is no longer its very own.
>
> We Christians least of all need to think of this nameless Holy Spirit, "poured out upon all flesh," as locked up within the walls of the church. Rather do we form the church as the community of those who confess explicitly in historical and social forms that God loved the world (not merely us Christians) and made his Spirit the innermost dynamic principle of the world, through whom everyone finds God as his absolute future, as long as he does not cut himself off from God through the deep-rooted sin of a whole life. If we see the gift of the Spirit to the world in this way, then it is perhaps not

---

18   See also Rahner (1983c), where he states, "The experience of transcendence permitting God to be present (because of God's salvific will in regard to all human beings, by which man is oriented to God's immediacy) is in fact always experience of the Holy Spirit" (198). Full consideration of the relation between Rahner's view of the supernatural existential, his pneumatology, and his Trinitarian theology, is beyond the scope of this inquiry.

so difficult to find in this world the Holy Spirit in whom we profess
our faith at Pentecost as our innermost mystery and even more as
God's mystery. (Rahner 1993a, 216)

In his exposition of the supernatural existential, Rahner already has
operating, as a vital element of his theology, an understanding of the
Holy Spirit as offered always and everywhere within the structures of
a graced humanity. Thus the significant point he must make to argue
that Jesus is present in non-Christian religions is that this Holy Spirit
is the Spirit of Jesus. This point would be easily accepted by many
Christians as a fairly common understanding of Spirit promised by Jesus and given at Pentecost, and, according to Rahner, it would be supported by Catholic scholastic theology (Rahner 1982, 316). It is also
apparent in the way that Rahner asserts that the grace given always
and everywhere is, in itself, deeply connected to the historical event of
the cross of Jesus. He affirms that "God's free salvific will" is "the *a priori* cause of the Incarnation and of the cross of Christ, a cause which
is not conditional upon anything outside of God" (317). At the same
time, "the Incarnation and the cross are, in scholastic terminology, the
'final cause' of the universal self-communication of God to the world
which we call the Holy Spirit" (317).[19] The Incarnation and cross of
Jesus are the final cause of the giving of the Holy Spirit and the giving
of the Holy Spirit is the efficient cause of the Incarnation and cross of
Jesus. While the Holy Spirit and Jesus are two persons of the Trinity
that cannot be collapsed into one, they are also inextricably bound in
a relationship of mutual causality. Rahner can thus describe the Holy
Spirit and Jesus as intrinsically related in "unity and difference," and in
"a relationship of mutual conditioning" (318). He states, "it can truly
be said that this Spirit is everywhere and from the outset the Spirit of
*Jesus* Christ, the Logos of God who became man (318).[20]

---

19   Rahner (1979c, 213-215), where he describes this dynamic in terms of
symbol and sacramental causality. In this essay, Rahner articulates the presence of Christ to anonymous Christians not by speaking of the Holy Spirit,
but by describing "a Christology of quest" (220-222).

20   See also Rahner (1974a, 173-175). Rahner describes grace has having
an inherent incarnational dynamism, such that "everywhere and in all cases"
grace is "a grace of Christ" (174). David Coffey explores the relationship between Jesus and the Holy Spirit in Rahner's theology in (Coffey 2001).

The logical structure of Rahner's position on anonymous Christians is laid out clearly in an essay entitled "Experience of the Holy Spirit." This essay serves as a well-ordered summary of some of the central aspects of Rahner's theology, concisely moving step-by-step through the plotline of his thought. He begins by asserting that Christians have an experience of the Spirit "as an offer to [their] freedom" (Rahner 1983c, 195). In order to "draw attention to" that experience, Rahner describes human knowledge and freedom in terms of transcendence (195). His account of transcendence is as discussed in Chapter One: in encountering individual objects, we also reach beyond them, grasping them within a wider horizon of knowledge and freedom (196). Rahner then asserts that this movement towards the infinite horizon is an orientation toward God (197). Therefore, in our ordinary encounters with the world around us, we have a kind of transcendental experience in which we encounter God (197). Given that God has offered Godself to each of us, this experience of transcendence is radicalized, such that it is an offer of the Holy Spirit. This is the elevation of human transcendence into the supernatural existential. Rahner writes:

> [I]n the actual order of reality, experience of transcendence (which is experience of God) is always also experience of grace, since the radicalness of the experience of transcendence and its dynamism are sustained in the innermost core of our existence by God's self-communication making all this possible, by the self-communication of God as goal and as strength of the movement toward him that we describe as grace, as the Holy Spirit. (198)

This means every human being—in her mundane, everyday interactions with the world—experiences the offer of the Holy Spirit, and experiences the indwelling of the Holy Spirit if she manages to say "yes" to God's offer in love (200). We drink "the pure wine of the Spirit, filled with the Holy Spirit, at least to the extent that we do not thrust back the chalice when it is offered to us" (205).

Having thus summarized his view of the human person, Rahner plots out the implications in his view of anonymous Christianity. He says that this experience is shared both inside and outside the bounds of explicit Christianity, leading Christians to affirm that God "wills the salvation of *all* human beings…that the grace of Christ is effective in a mysterious way beyond the limits of verbalized and institutionalized Christianity" (205). Finally, Rahner underscores the deep connection between the Holy Spirit and Jesus Christ, such that "[i]n this life the chalice of the Holy Spirit is identical with the chalice of Christ" (206).

In his description of anonymous Christians, Rahner has the courage to think through systematically what it means to say that Jesus is the savior of the world. He does this in a way that not only allows him to affirm salvation beyond the explicit membership of the church, but also to respect that non-Christian religions play a positive role in the attainment of salvation. Without ever questioning the primacy of Christianity, Rahner conceptualizes a way in which non-Christian religions can have value and even have much to teach a Christian (Rahner 1986b, 134). Faced with a diverse and pluralistic world on the one hand, and a conviction regarding salvation through Jesus on the other, Rahner generates a logical framework in which to hold the two together. He explains this in an interview:

> "Anonymous Christianity" means that a person lives in the grace of God and attains salvation outside explicitly constituted Christianity. A Protestant Christian is, of course, "no anonymous Christian"; that is perfectly clear. But, let us say, a Buddhist monk (or anyone else I might suppose) who, because he follows his conscience, attains salvation and lives in the grace of God; of him I must say that he is an anonymous Christian; if not, I would have to presuppose that there is a genuine path to salvation that really attains that goal, but that simply has nothing to do with Jesus Christ. But I cannot do that. And so if I hold that everyone depends upon Jesus Christ for salvation, and if at the same time I hold that many live in the world who have not expressly recognized Jesus Christ, then there remains in my opinion nothing else but to take up this postulate of anonymous Christianity. (Rahner 1986b, 207)[21]

Note that logically, there is another option open to Rahner. He could deny salvation outside the explicit church. However, Rahner repeatedly asserts that belief in salvation outside the church is a longstanding part of Roman Catholic teaching. He states bluntly: "In the tradition of the Church since about the time of Ambrose right up to Vatican II, there is an irreformable teaching which says the following: if persons are true to their conscience, they are living in God's

---

21   See, in relation, Rahner (1979c, 219).

grace and can reach eternal salvation even if they are neither baptized nor members of the Roman Catholic Church. In other words, such persons are justified, made holy, and are temples of the Holy Spirit" (Rahner 1991a, 102).[22]

In his discussions of love and its implications, Rahner rejects the modern separation of the world into distinct realms of secular and sacred. All of human life is permeated and surrounded by the grace of God, the Spirit of Jesus Christ. This is implied by many aspects of Rahner's theology, but becomes most explicit in his discussions of anonymous Christianity as he refuses to see the church as the site at which the grace of God is dispensed to confessing Christians.

Rahner's understanding of anonymous Christians has been controversial in a number of ways. Most prominently, it has been understood as challenging the Roman Catholic Church's understanding of mission. Rahner's rejection of the secular/sacred divide takes away the role of the church as carrying the sacred into the secular world: the sacred is already there.[23] Traditional views of missionary activity as saving souls that would otherwise be damned do not apply in Rahner's schema. However, he argues that missionary work actually presupposes an understanding similar to his view of anonymous Christianity, in that it assumes that grace is already at work before evangelization. He writes: "Only in the light of grace can we recognize and accept the light of the gospel. The grace of faith is the necessary prior condition for the teaching of the faith" (Rahner 1974a, 170). It would not make sense, in Rahner's view, to imagine that such grace was given in the instant before preaching began. While, indeed, the grace of faith becomes "actual, effective, and demanding" upon the hearing of the gospel, it has been present beforehand as an offer at the center of the human person (170).

At the same time, Rahner characterizes grace in general as having an incarnational quality. This means that while the effectiveness of preaching requires grace already offered to the hearer, it is also the case that the grace offered always and everywhere by its very nature "seeks its historical embodiment in the word and above all in the sacrament"

---

22   See also Kerr (2007, 96-97) for a discussion of Rahner's theory in relation to Roman Catholic tradition.

23   This issue will be taken up again in Chapter Five.

(173, 174). Thus Rahner states, "[p]recisely because it is prior to the preaching the grace itself demands that it shall be preached" (174). This means that from Rahner's perspective, the theory of anonymous Christians does not endanger mission but rather enables it, or, in his words, "anonymous Christianity does not render explicit Christianity superfluous, but rather itself demands it" (174).

How can Rahner's view of anonymous Christianity, especially when seen as an element presumed in missionary activity, be understood in a non-foundationalist framework? It seems that Rahner claims an external, independent universal experience as the sure foundation upon which Christianity is built. In response to such questions, Kilby reiterates her argument that Rahner is not grounding theological claims on ideas or experiences outside of Christian faith. Rather, he speaks squarely from within Christianity, offering an interpretation of human experience that also initiates the hearer into such experience. Such a view effectively dismisses many criticisms of the theory of anonymous Christianity that are rooted in methodological concerns.[24] This reading also undermines claims that Rahner's theory erodes the distinctiveness of Christianity and the significance of the church. It is not the case that explicit Christianity is irrelevant since what happens there happens everywhere else, as well. Instead, explicit Christianity and the traditions of the church offer a theological interpretation of what happens everywhere, an interpretation which shapes the experiences of those who participate in it.

Rahner himself repeatedly emphasizes the importance of the church, both as a community and in terms of the obligation for explicit Christians to seek their salvation in and through the church. Rahner understands the church as a whole in primarily theological terms, as sacrament and symbol. The church is the continuing historical presence of God's grace in the world. The public and communal profession of faith in Jesus, dependent upon the Holy Spirit, is "the continuation of God's offer of himself in Jesus" that is "an intrinsic and constitutive element in God's offer" (Rahner 1982, 330). Indeed, explicit, communal Christian faith is "an intrinsic element" of the resurrection of Jesus Christ (267). While it is possible, in Rahner's theology, for people to be saved beyond the explicit bound of the concrete Christian

---

24   See Kilby (2004, 115-126).

church, the existence of the church is an integral element of the history of grace that creates this possibility. People can be saved beyond the church, but not without it.

As Rahner emphasizes the importance of the church as a whole, so too he defends the necessity of ecclesial Christianity for individual Christians. Following out the implications of his view of the incarnational dynamism inherent in grace, Rahner claims that grace presses towards its own historical embodiment and conceptual objectification. This means both that the anonymous Christian really has faith and that the person who is introduced, in a meaningful way, to explicit Christianity should not imagine that it is just as well to be indifferent to the church. He writes,

> [F]aith as it exists in the pagan is properly speaking designed to follow its own inherent dynamism in such a way as to develop into that faith which is objectified and articulated through the gospel, that faith which we simply call the Christian faith. The seed has no right to seek not to grow into a plant. But the fact that it is not yet developed into a plant is no reason for refusing to give the name which we give to the plant destined to grow from it to the seed as well. (Rahner 1976b, 291)

Rahner states this view over and over again: "the moment it becomes clear to you, in a binding way, that the concreteness of the confession of Jesus Christ is precisely the concreteness of the ultimate relationship to God, then you can no longer say: Christianity does not concern me, I am going to seek my salvation in another way" (Rahner 1991a, 102). And again:

> [W]hen, and to the extent that, the ultimate self-expression of God in Jesus Christ has encountered you explicitly, you may not say: "That does not interest me!"...You as a Christian can't pretend that you didn't know more explicitly, in a more developed and more radical way than a non-Christian, about the ultimate meaning of life. You have this knowledge precisely because of your encounter with Jesus Christ through the message of the gospel and through the Church. (118)[25]

---

25 See also Rahner (1986b, 207).

Once a person encounters Jesus in a binding way, they cannot be absolved of the responsibility of seeking their salvation through Christianity.

Rahner's view of anonymous Christianity also has caused controversy among people who find it denigrating to non-Christian religions. Rahner's view of "anonymous Christianity" affirms that there is value in non-Christian religions. However, that value is not intrinsic to those religions but rather is based in Christianity, in the Spirit of Jesus.[26] Such religions may be respected, to a degree, but can only be seen as provisional and as less than Christianity (Rahner 1982, 314). Rahner's view of other religions, then, can be seen as condescending. The Buddhist monk may attain salvation, but he is deceived about the means and manner of that salvation, whereas, the Christian truly understands what has happened to the Buddhist monk.

Rahner clearly assumes that Christianity interprets the relationship between God and humanity better than other religions by affirming Jesus Christ as the one savior. He acknowledges that non-Christians may think it is "presumption" for Christians to assert that all that is holy, sound, or sanctified is rooted in the grace of Jesus Christ. However, Rahner states "the Christian cannot renounce this 'presumption' which is really the source of the greatest humility both for himself and for the Church" (Rahner 1966a, 134). Rahner sees clearly the paradox that this theory holds. On one hand, it is a view that strips Christianity of any claims to be the sole site or recipient of God's grace and revelation. On the other hand, it awards Christianity the status of being the religion that best understands the grace given always and everywhere. Thus Rahner writes that the understanding of anonymous Christians provides a basis on which "one can be tolerant, humble and yet firm towards all non-Christian religions" (134).

From a standpoint critical of Rahner's modernist tendencies, the difficulty of Rahner's condescension can be given a more precise diagnosis. In claiming that all religions are, in some sense, the same, Rahner creates a situation in which they can be compared and hierarchically ranked from best to worse. All religions attempt "to mediate the origi-

---

26 Other religions, as interpretations of transcendental experience, may well contain religious truth that does not thematically reference Jesus. However, that truth is ultimately dependent on Jesus Christ.

nal, unreflexive and non-objective revelation historically, to make it reflexive and to interpret it in propositions" (Rahner 1982, 173). Rahner
claims that Christianity is the most successful attempt. In addition
to being condescending or disrespectful, this can be seen as ignoring
the differences of concrete religions. Jeannine Hill Fletcher characterizes Rahner's view as "a self-referential construction of the 'other'"
that "erases the differences among religions" (Fletcher 2005, 246). On
a theoretical and theological level, when it comes to other religions,
Rahner does not advocate openness to the unknown other. Given
the emphasis on such openness in his use of images of silence and his
discussions of love, this appears to be a significant incoherence in his
thought. Also, postmodern scholars point out the many drawbacks of
modern movements towards equality and justice, as such movements
rest on accounts of humanity as fundamentally the same and therefore
obscure the differences among people. This erasure of difference, they
argue, ultimately moves towards inequality and injustice by declaring
those who differ from the central norm to be inferior.

To evaluate such criticism of Rahner's notion of anonymous Christians, it is important to place the idea in historical context. Rahner is
speaking both out of, and into, Christian community. He offers a theological claim about grace and a specifically Christian interpretation of
human experience. His theory is intended first and foremost to assure
confessing Christians of the goodness and mercy of God. Rahner does
not set out to provide a framework for inter-religious dialogue, but
rather to find a coherent and faithful way for Christians to hope for
those around them in a secular and pluralist society.

Furthermore, his articulation of a coherent Christian account of
salvation outside the institutional church had significant influence on
attitudes and practices among Christians, in ways that concretely respected and acknowledged difference. For example, while Rahner defends his theory as not undermining Christian mission, it certainly
does take the salvific urgency out of proselytizing. Non-Christian
communities are seen as loved and graced by God; non-Christian religions are acknowledged as carrying truth and aiding salvation. Quite
concretely, a shift took place in Roman Catholic practice, such that
before Vatican II, churches prayed for the conversion of the Jews, then
after Vatican II, Catholic congregations began to pray that the Jews

would remain true to their own faith. Rahner's affirmation of the universal salvific will of God had some part in this change in the views of Catholics. While it may well be that new contexts require new articulations of God's love, it should be acknowledged that in the particular situation in which he wrote, Rahner's theory of anonymous Christians contributed to a larger Christian sensibility in which the otherness of non-Christian religions was granted greater respect.

## LONELY DECISION IN COMMUNITY

Rahner often begins his theology by addressing the topic of theological anthropology, explicating a vision of the human person as an individual. In this text I am offering a non-foundationalist reading of Rahner that does not assume he grounds his theology on neutral reflection on the individual knowing subject, but rather that he addresses the individual human person from a Christian standpoint and offers a theological interpretation of human experience. While such a reading shifts the tenor and importance of Rahner's anthropological starting point, there remains a movement from the individual to the interpersonal in Rahner's work in two different ways. First, Rahner's depiction of the human person moves from a focus on the individual to a more interpersonal model of humanity over the course of his career.[27] His earliest writings, particularly philosophical texts such as *Spirit in the World*, have the most strictly anthropological, philosophical, and individualistic bent. In his subsequent theological writings, Rahner explains some of the key points of his thought in more relational and communal terms and spends more time discussing the interpersonal. For example, while his earliest works describe transcendence primarily in terms of knowing, often focusing on knowing objects in the world, in later publications Rahner describes human transcendence as transcendence to the other. Thus he writes of "the essential *a priori* openness to the other human being which must be undertaken freely" (Rahner 1969d, 241). This does not necessarily mean that his view of relationality is a late development in his theology. Rather, the importance of the interpersonal is articulated more fully and emphasized

---

27  Many scholars note this, including Marmion (2003), Purcell (1998), and Tallon (1982).

more after his initial publications.[28] In an essay about the love commandment, written in 1961, Rahner states

> One may speak of a commandment of love as long as one does not forget that this law does not command man to do something or other but simply commands him to fulfil himself, and charges man with himself, i.e. himself as the possibility of love in the acceptance of the love in which God does not give something but gives Himself. (Rahner 1966b, 456)

Clearly there is already a strong sense of the human person as being actualized in love and, therefore, as fundamentally interpersonal. Titus F. Guenther argues persuasively that this idea is present in Rahner's work as early as 1946 (Guenther 1994, 220).[29]

The second form of movement from the individual to the interpersonal in Rahner's work takes place in his pattern of narration. When he tells the story of who we are, he begins with the individual as a knower and moves towards the person who actualizes her fulfillment in community. This pattern of narration remains in place throughout the major writings of his career. In *Foundations*, a later work first published in German in 1976, Rahner's initial presentation of the human person in the earlier chapters of the book lists the "social nature" of humanity as an existential of humanity with almost no justification or discussion of implications (Rahner 1982, 26). Yet Rahner's brevity on this point in his description of the human person does not mean the social nature of humanity is unimportant or marginal in his theology. On the contrary, throughout the text of *Foundations* the social, interpersonal, and communal nature of humanity becomes increasingly apparent. By the end of the book, it is clear that love of neighbor is a central element of Rahner's theology, so much so that even the initial explication of the human person can only be fully understood in light of this. At the very end of *Foundations*, Rahner offers a few brief creedal statements. His "Brief Anthropological Creed" reads as follows:

---

28  See Taylor (1986, 64-70) for a brief and useful index of the argument concerning the importance of the interpersonal and its development in Rahner's thought.

29  Note also that interpreting Rahner's work as philosophically foundationalist renders his discussions of intersubjectivity problematic and possibly incoherent.

A person really discovers his true self in a genuine act of self-realization only if he risks himself radically for another. If he does this, he grasps unthematically or explicitly what we mean by God as the horizon, the guarantor and the radical depths of this love, the God who in his existentiell and historical self-communication made himself the realm within which such love is possible. This love is meant in both an interpersonal and a social sense, and in the radical unity of both of these elements it is the ground and the essence of the church. (456 Emphasis removed.)

While Rahner's work begins with the individual, it moves inexorably towards love, and therefore towards the social, interpersonal, and communal.

Rahner puts forth a view of the human person in which a strong sense of individual freedom is held in tension with the idea that a person becomes most fully herself only in the act of loving an other. Indeed, for Rahner, the strong sense of freedom—and the individuality it supports—is necessary in order to have a real community. Difference and distinction are necessary for love. If there is no clear demarcation between you and me, when I love you, I may only love some part of my own self, my own worldview, my own interests, or my own picture of who you ought to be. Individuality is critical for the posture of openness to the unknown other. It is this posture, marked by silence and characterized by love, which Rahner understands to be a critical element of faith, of saying "yes" to God. Holding together individuality and relationality, Rahner describes the free decision to say "yes" to God as a lonely decision that is worked out in community. He writes:

Of course, there is one last, lonely responsibility and deed to be done, in a freedom which ultimately cannot be shared or transferred, and it is one of the essentials of Christian spirituality. When all is said and done, it is each of us individually—all communion and love of neighbor aside for the moment (though concretely it will have been precisely in virtue of this communion and love of neighbor)—who must become this particular person, of whom there is only one, and who only as this unique individual can manage an ultimate contribution to the actualization of the communion of saints. (Rahner 1983f, 81)

Here Rahner categorizes unique individuality as a prerequisite for the actualization of the communion of the saints. This eschatological context, which will be discussed further in the next chapter, is important for understanding the dynamic between individual and community in Rahner's work. He is not envisioning this dynamism primarily within the political context of the nation state in which communal relations are aimed at maximizing individual freedom. Rather, he is considering this in a sacramental and eschatological context of eternal communion, in which individual freedom and dependence on the divine are not in conflict, in which difference and unity are not opposed.

Since Rahner's view of love is not a sentimental one, but is rather a mystical concept of risking one's own stable identity in openness to the other, his statements about saying "yes" to God in love have implications beyond loving relationships among individuals. Rahner says in an interview:

> Only when we love each other can we love God. Love of neighbor is not just one among various commandments of God; it is the actual way in which human beings can encounter God. That too sounds pretty abstract, I grant, but what I am getting at is this: As soon as anyone realizes that what we call Christian love of neighbor as the way God saves us is not only the norm of the family circle or of private life, but today has a social and political dimension, this old commandment speaks to us also of political responsibility. (Rahner 1986b, 268-269)

Some of the implications of Rahner's account of love, with its tension between the individual and the communal, can be seen in the complex relationship between Rahner's theology and the political and liberation theologies that emerged in the latter half of the 20th century.[30] Rahner

---

30 For a more detailed explication and analysis of the relationship between Rahner's theology and liberation theology, see Martinez (2001). Martinez examines Rahner's work and its influence on the theologies of Johann Baptist Metz, Gustavo Gutierrez, and David Tracy. He argues that the forms of theology represented by these three scholars move from Rahner's focus on transcendence towards more historically and socially grounded theology, yet ultimately reaffirm the mystery of God that Rahner so emphasized. The intensification of their own historical approaches, Martinez argues, leads each of these theologians to highlight this mystery, in methodological difference and theological resonance with Rahner.

defends, encourages,[31] argues with, and learns from the political and liberation theologies that were being developed in the later decades of his life (Rahner 1991a, 64; 1986b, 168-169, 202). These different responses reflect some changes in Rahner's view, the complexity of the relationship between his thought and these theologies, and the variety of expressions of liberation theologies.

One of Rahner's most prominent students is J.B. Metz, who developed his own political theology in conversation and contention with Rahner's work. Metz' primary criticism of Rahner's work is that the focus on transcendence generates an ahistorical theology that cannot do justice either to the historical specificity of Christianity or to the concrete struggles of Christians today.[32] Rahner clearly learns from Metz, often disagrees with him, and makes seemingly contradictory statements about the relationship of his own work to political theology.[33] While Rahner does not work out fully the political and communal implications of his theology, he does, following Metz' example, begin to do so in *Politische Dimensionen des Christentums: Ausgewahlte Texte zu Fragen der Zeit* (Rahner 1986a). Rahner says both: "*Theology must always be 'political' theology*" (Rahner 1972b, 189) and "I never developed any political theology" (Rahner 1986b, 269). Rahner appreciates some of the insights of political theology, while also being wary of the possible loss of the mystical elements of spirituality and the theological affirmation of the mystery of God.

The middle years of Rahner's career coincide with the emergence, in the 1960s, of a new development in Christian theology. Liberation theology is theological action and reflection done within the ongoing struggle for liberation of the poor and oppressed. Phillip Berryman

31  See also the letter Rahner wrote two weeks before his death in which he defends the orthodoxy of Gustavo Gutierrez' work (Rahner 1990, 351-352).

32  See Metz (1980) This brief essay summarizes this criticism in regards to both the theory of anonymous Christians and political theology. Further discussion of Metz' criticisms will be taken up in Chapter Five.

33  Guenther (1994) analyzes the relationship between the theologies of Rahner and Metz and argues that Rahner's work is itself political. In addition to this interpretation, the book offers valuable historical framing for Rahner's work and an account of the links between love of neighbor and political theology.

describes liberation theology as "an interpretation of Christian faith out of the experience of the poor...[and] an attempt to help the poor interpret their own faith in a new way" (Berryman 1987, 4, 5).[34] The distinguishing features of liberation theology include a methodological commitment to doing theology within and for a given historical and social location and an emphasis on Christian affirmations that God cares for the poor and oppressed.

Rahner is acknowledged as having helped to create a space within Roman Catholic theology in which liberation theology could exist. His understanding of how human beings attain salvation through neighbor love is part of this, as well as his depiction of Christian experience of God in everyday life (Endean 2001, 226). Additionally, Rahner's stance on several specific issues contributes to making an environment in which liberation theology could grow. For example, his hope that Vatican II marked the beginning of a real world Christianity that would no longer be an European export (Rahner 1983f, 77-79), his recognition that some traditional forms ought to change in different cultural settings (Rahner 1986b, 271), and his hope that the Roman Catholic Church teaching could be structured from the bottom up (269).[35]

Rahner agrees with many of the basic principles of liberation theology, including the preferential option for the poor, writing, "According to the example of Jesus the Church may not and must not regard all classes as equal to one another. She must take the part of the poor" (Rahner 1991a, 63). He knew that he himself was not a liberation theologian, reflecting theologically on lived experience of ongo-

---

34 This book is a helpful historical and theological introduction to liberation theology.

35 Also, there are some methodological similarities. The occasional and unsystematic, pastoral nature of Rahner's indicates ways in which his theology acknowledges its location in concrete situations and aims to address them. Furthermore, his understanding of the relationship between knowledge and love indicates that we can know most fully in actively loving the other. Rahner attempts to make "clear that love (praxis)—perhaps today we would also say freedom—can be and must be also the condition of knowledge of the true (theory), so that this very relationship of a perichoresis of the two transcendentals [good and true] reaches its most radical essential realization in the presence of the incomprehensibility of God" (Rahner 1983b, 102).

ing struggle for liberation. At the same time, he quite clearly saw the need for liberation theology and the possibility of its legitimacy for the church. While being interviewed about liberation theology emerging in Latin America, Rahner says:

> I am convinced that a true Catholic theology of liberation can and must exist. (I gladly confess to having been a theologian of late European individualism.) I can only rejoice when a theology develops in Latin America which is built up on the experience of community, on the grassroots experience of the Church, on the sociopolitical task of the Church. (Rahner 1986b, 201, 202)

At the same time, Rahner is skeptical about certain tendencies with liberation theologies. Most of the time, this skepticism emerges from his resistance to reducing the mystery of God and of humanity in any way. This leads him to be suspicious of any "theological turn to the world" that might diminish God into "a stopgap for human beings, their happiness and their so-called self-realization" (Rahner 1991a, 50). He has deep theological reservations about quickly and easily identifying social movements or accomplishments with the coming of God's new creation (51). To do so would be to diminish God, in part by claiming such full comprehension of God, in part by imagining that the grace of God can be measured in human terms, and in part by identifying grace and salvation with political and social liberation. While the concrete issues of human necessities and human rights are vitally important, the spiritual reality of a human person ought not be reduced to their material, social, and political well-being. He asserts:

> It's obvious that all of Christianity has a social, not to say political dimension, whereby the social dimension of humanity refers not to a particular aspect of men and women but to the whole of their humanity...On the other side, Christianity cannot of course let itself be reduced to a movement of social emancipation. Christianity rightly objects to that sort of thing, because individual persons cannot be reduced to their social roles and because human beings and their history are always transcending themselves into the absolute mystery that we call God, to God who has been revealed in Jesus Christ as the power over all in history and has been promised to us as our absolute future. Because of all this we have to view the theology of liberation with some reservation. If we conceive liberation in the New Testament sense of *eleutheria* we can subsume under this

key word everything that Christianity has to say to humanity about itself and its God. But then this freedom, for which God's grace in Jesus Christ has freed us, is not to be simply identified with a social emancipation of humankind, for even if this fully occurred, people would not yet be fully free. (Rahner 1986b, 135)

Rahner is eager to assert that Christian love of neighbor has political aspects, but is also unwilling to confine the activity of grace to that sphere. He consistently claims that the grace of God is present always and everywhere in human life, and that human beings may say "yes" to God in many ways, on various levels of thematic conceptualization. In response to certain forms of liberation and political theologies that can appear to emphasize the political to such an extent that other forums for relation with God fade from view, Rahner states, "[a]ll well and good, but my mother was an authentic Christian and she never took a political stand in her life" (273). This is in keeping with his general stance of writing within and for the society that Rahner appears to take as the normal or average—that of the middle-class. It is also in keeping with his existentialist tendencies, for Rahner recognizes that the most ordinary and mundane life—and even the most privileged—has moments of great anguish and requires fateful choices. Also, having rejected a modern division of the secular and sacred, Rahner is clear that Christian faith involves the whole person, including her political life. For the same reason, he is unwilling to view the political realm as the only, or even primary, arena for faith.

Because it is grounded in a mystical understanding of the indwelling of the Holy Spirit, Rahner's articulation of the freedom of the individual and of the individual's self-actualization in love for the other both contributes to the space in which liberation theology could develop and means that Rahner himself cannot accept all the tropes of liberation theology wholeheartedly. It would be inaccurate to say that the emphasis on social and political liberation pulls liberation theologies too far away from the individual and towards the communal for Rahner, since he offers a picture of the human person in which the individual and the communal are not in an oppositional, dualistic relationship. For Rahner, individuality is a necessary condition for the possibility of love—of friendship, kindness, self-giving, and even political action—and cannot be discounted in concern for the social.[36] At the same time, the most intensely individualistic spiritual experience of grace is mediated within a social location and always moves towards being actualized in love for another person. We do, indeed, in Rahner's eyes, each have our own offer of grace in the depths of our being, our own experience of God that demands a response from us that no one else can give. But we can only know this offer, experience this grace, and make our response to it when we love other people. We know God as individuals, but we cannot know God alone.

Metz' criticism of Rahner's ahistorical transcendentalism is echoed in contemporary terms by John Milbank. For both Rahner and liberation theologies, Milbank asserts, the relationship between the individual and the social remains oppositional, only traversed by the non-theological and ahistorical means of Kantian ethics. So while a Rahnerian-liberationist view of the human person can provide a general motivation for an anonymous, unspecified love of neighbor, the particularly "religious" aspect of salvation can only be understood in terms of the individual person (Milbank 1990, 206-240).[37] While issues of historicity will be addressed in Chapter Five, at this point it is important to note that Rahner unfolds the implications of the supernatural existential not merely in ethical terms, such that it provides a motivation for love, but in mystical terms, such that love is the means of encounter with the divine. Neighbor love is not primarily action towards the goal of expanded freedom for individuals in community. It is the foretaste of beatific vision.

Thus while Rahner's theology had significant influence on the political and liberation theologies that developed in the latter half of the twentieth century, his basic theological perspective is of a different

---

36  Note that Rahner writes that the Spiritual Exercises of Ignatius "demand only that their user take and accept himself in his ultimate permanent solitude before God, and they must therefore expose flight into the masses (even ecclesial), not encourage it" (1975a, 70).

37  Like Metz, Milbank appears to find the theory of anonymous Christians to be troubling in ecclesiological terms not primarily because it undermines mission or relativizes the status of the church, but rather because it arises from a fundamentally ahistorical and individualistic methodology that, in its inadequacy to the concrete, performative, and historical reality of humanity, can then never account for what the church, at its best, can be.

sort. He struggles to articulate the political implications of his thought without abandoning his Christocentric spirituality and his affirmation of the mystery of God. When an interviewer asks Rahner what he would emphasize if he were to "start over again as a theologian," Rahner replies:

> I would, on the one hand, say that the unity of love of God and love of neighbor needs to be worked out in a more radical way, that Christianity, the Church has a task toward society that is political in the strictest sense of the word. On the other hand, I would perhaps emphasize more that when humans are truly open to the absolute mystery of God, and entrust themselves to God in a worshiping, loving, forward-looking, hopeful way, that Christianity is only present when it looks at the crucified and risen Jesus Christ. This Christianity which stresses the adoration of the living God can not be replaced by a sociopolitical humanism, however respectable that humanism might be. (Rahner 1986b, 202-203)

## SPIRITUALITY AND THEOLOGY OF LOVE

For Rahner, love of the human other is inextricably bound up with love of the divine Other and both of these loves are the actualization of a transcendent nature radicalized by grace. God has come near to us. In our divinely-empowered freedom, we must say "yes" or "no" to the offer of eternal intimacy with the Divine. Saying "yes" requires an openness to the other, a self-abandonment and self-risk. This necessitates a sturdy assessment of the individual and culminates in a view of humanity as actualized in mystical union. Thus Rahner attempts to describe what it is to be a human being in such a way that individuality and community are mutual requirements. We cannot have community without individuality, and no one can be a fully realized individual without opening themselves to others in community. Both of these terms—individual and community—are defined by the gift of Godself, offered to each person and present in loving encounter.

In this chapter and the one before it, I have argued that Rahner uses both silence and love to indicate the disposition of openness to the mysterious other which is an acceptance of God's offer of grace. In Rahner's theological anthropology, we are transcendent into a silent term and this can also be described as a "transcendentality towards the

other who is to be loved" (Rahner 1969d, 243). The term of our transcendence is the silent mystery and radical otherness of God, which,
through the gracious elevation of our transcendentality into the supernatural existential, is present to us in mediated immediacy in our relationships with other human beings. Our transcendental nature means
that we exist in both otherness and openness to God. This ontological
claim cannot be separated, for Rahner, from the claim that our transcendental nature means that we exist in both otherness and openness
to our neighbors.

Rahner's Christian interpretation of the human person thus depicts
us as self-possessing and open to the other, as granted this identity by
God and as stepping into this identity in our free acceptance. Freely
loving is how we accept our openness and orientation to the other, say
"yes" to God's offer, and become our true selves. "The one moral (or im-
moral) basic act in which man comes to himself and decides basically
about himself is also the (loving or hating) communication with the
concrete Thou in which man experiences, accepts or denies his basic
*a priori* reference to the Thou as such" (241). This means that love of
neighbor is not a nicety, nor a secondary implication of Christianity.
It is of eternal significance and it is the very substance of faith. The
demand for love is written into the structures of spiritual existence.

In Rahner's description of love, he maintains a mutual relationship
of requirement between individuality and community. He describes
humanity such that the distance and difference between persons is inescapable, as is the orientation to the other. Part of what it is to have
faith, for Rahner, is to freely accept this condition—to acknowledge
and respect otherness and difference, while also giving ourselves to
others and recognizing humanity as "intercommunicative existence"
(Rahner 1972c, 176, 177). In both silence and love we accept this
condition, accept who we are as individuals deeply bound to others
and grounded in God, and accept the mystery of the other as mystery
without reduction. Silence, understood as self-given openness to the
other, is the character of the act that is love.

# CHAPTER 4

## DEATH

*Judgment when refused, blissful future when accepted, this grace perme-*
*ates history, and in the cross of Jesus it has already reached the point*
*where it can no longer be defeated.* (Rahner 1981b, 75)

### INTRODUCTION

In the previous chapters, I examined two ways in which Rahner describes saying "yes" to God's offer of salvation: silence and love. Each of these involves a paradox that is central to Rahner's understanding of the relationship between God and humanity. As free persons burdened with self-crafting freedom, we accomplish our fullest act of self-creation when we accept who we are as created by God. Saying "yes" to God is both a free, creative act and an acceptance of God-conferred identity. Explained somewhat differently, we step into greater self-possession by abandoning self into the mystery of God.

Silence is invoked by Rahner to emphasize the mystery of God that can be comprehended neither within, nor apart from, language. It signals the acknowledgement and acceptance of otherness, the individual's chosen posture of openness to the other in the dialogue between God and humanity.

Love is Rahner's explicit answer to the question of how we say "yes" to God's offer of self-communication. Love is the disposition and deed of openness to the unknown and unmanipulable other, both human and divine. Rahner depicts love of neighbor as an interpersonal relation in which persons risk the stability of their own identities through such openness. He offers a vision of love as held within the larger framework of divine love in Jesus Christ, such that the self is realized precisely when it is risked in loving relation.

There are differences between how Rahner uses silence and how he describes love. Silence functions primarily to describe individual experiences and actions within the divine/human dialogue. Love is pro-

foundly interpersonal, as Rahner claims that human and divine relationship is necessarily bound up with inter-human love. Yet in both of
these, we see the dialectic between self-possession and openness to the
other that is vital to Rahner's theological anthropology. I have argued
that saying "yes" in Rahner's theology is an act of love, characterized by
silence.

In this chapter, I explore another way that Rahner portrays saying
"yes" to God: death. He identifies death, like love, as an explicit form
of "yes" or "no" to God's offer of self. In words echoing his description
of love, Rahner states: "death is also not only an act, but 'the act,' the
act of freedom" (Rahner 1964, 92). Likewise, he calls death "the highest moral act, whereby man freely consummates his whole existence"
(103).

Rahner addresses the subject of death in several scattered texts, including the book, *On the Theology of Death*. His view of death is not
stagnant, and those who chart the development of Rahner's theology
over the course of his career perceive a familiar pattern moving from a
more individual to a more communal focus. Peter C. Phan describes
Rahner's view of death as moving through three overlapping phases:
"individualist-existentialist," "existentialist-interpersonal," and "socio-
political" (Phan 2005, 176, 177). While there are grounds for noting
such dynamism in Rahner's thought, it should also not be overstated.
Phan notes that the development and evolution of Rahner's eschatology is "without any radical reversal" (189).

In explicating his view of death Rahner often begins, as he does with
love, by stating what it is not. He flatly rejects the idea that death is a
passage to an afterlife that is some sort of further extension in time,
"that 'things go on' after death, as though we only changed horses, as
Feuerbach put it, and rode on" (Rahner 1966e, 347). While Rahner
accepts the Catholic, doctrinal description of death as the separation of body and soul, he finds this definition on its own to be inadequate (Rahner 1964, 24, 25). It contains no information about what
is unique to human death and it can be seen as a domestication of
death, based on a falsely overstated dichotomy between body and soul
within the human person (Rahner 1975b, 179; 1964, 92). Rahner
therefore emphasizes that "death is something that affects the whole
man" (Rahner 1975b, 179). He likewise insists that descriptions of

death as a natural event must be significantly nuanced. It does have a "natural essence," or neutral element, that allows us to say both that all persons die the same death and that death can either be an event of salvation or damnation (Rahner 1964, 44). However, attempts to take away death's sting by viewing it as a merely natural biological process are efforts to evade the eternity-making decision of "yes" or "no" and, as such, they are the beginnings of damnation (63).

For Rahner, death is a profoundly theological event and should be recognized as such. Even statements about the universality of death are, in Rahner's view, only justifiable on theological grounds. Without revelation, we could imagine that someday doctors will find a way to keep death at bay indefinitely. Our certainty that everyone must die is a Christian truth, based on theological anthropology. "There is a factor in man, in his very nature and in the way in which he was originally fashioned, which makes it impossible for him ever to escape from or do away with the necessity of dying, that makes it absolutely certain that he will always die" (Rahner 1971b, 286). This factor is human freedom, the burden of saying "yes" or "no" to God in meaningful and definitive way.

This choice to be made, grounded and enabled by God's offer of salvation, is precisely why palliative accounts of death (the immortality of the soul alone, the afterlife as an extension of time, and death as merely natural) are unacceptable to Christians. It is because we have been offered eternal life that death's apparent negation of human life threatens us. Rahner writes, "It is only because we have become immortal in our life that death with its menacing and impenetrable mask of destructivity is for us so deadly" (Rahner 1966e, 349). And elsewhere: "In his tending towards grace and the supernatural end of the sharing the life of God, there is given to man a real-ontological element of life which contradicts death" (Rahner 1964, 45). A Christian should not attempt to conceal from herself "the comfortless absurdity of death," but rather should recognize death as the "arch-contradiction of existence" (Rahner 1975b, 179, 180). It is as such a threat to our immortality and hoped-for beatitude that death demands a decision, either to despair of God's promises or to fall trustingly into the unknown future.

The fact that death demands such a decision is not, for Rahner, inconsistent with the brutal reality that death comes to us from without, "unmastering" us (Rahner 1964, 55). Death is "a destruction, an accident, which strikes man from without, unforeseeably, with no assurance that it will strike him at the moment in which he has prepared himself for it interiorly. Death is for man a dark fate, the thief in the night; it is an emptying, an ending" (48). Death is truly an event in which the human person is passive, overtaken and unmastered by forces external to herself.

## DEATH AS ACT

While Rahner recognizes the passivity of death, he focuses on death as an act of the human person. Robert Ochs identifies two approaches to death as an act in Rahner's thought (Ochs 1973, 121). The first is that human freedom requires a final culmination. Rahner repeatedly asserts that time stretching endlessly into the future would be worse than hell. Since every decision taken could be changed in future moments, all decisions would be meaningless (Rahner 1971b, 288; 1974c, 320). "Time becomes madness if it cannot reach fulfillment" (Rahner 1982, 271). Therefore human beings, as free creatures, inherently "crave," "seek," and "hunger for" a final consummation of their free decision (Rahner 1971b, 288; 1974c, 319).[1] Death is an act since human beings will their own deaths as culminations of their freedom.

Clearly Rahner is speaking at a high level of abstraction here. Death, as it comes to the individual, is still the thief in the night, the external destruction of a life. In saying that persons seek their own deaths he is not talking about suicidal tendencies, but rather acknowledging that people want to craft their characters as coherent in some sense. Consider the way some people talk about how they want to be remembered—as a good mother, an honest man, a loyal friend, someone who loved the land, etc. Such language conveys a desire for a permanent personal identity. Rahner points out that such identity cannot

---

1 Note the implication that Adam and Eve would also have had some sort of consummation even if they had not sinned. Rahner states that they would have experienced an end to temporal life in another manner, one which maintained "the integrity of [their] bodily constitution" (1964, 42). See also Rahner (1971b, 288).

be created in unending time. One is only "remembered" in this sense after death, after the choice has been made and the character cannot be re-crafted. Rahner writes, "Death brings man, as a moral-spiritual person, a kind of finality and consummation which renders his decision for or against God, reached during the time of his bodily life, final and unalterable" (Rahner 1964, 35).

This view of death as an act is based on Rahner's understanding of the relationship between time and eternity. Eternity is not something that comes after time. Rather, it is what comes to be "*in* time, as its own mature fruit" (Rahner 1966e, 348). The purpose of time is the coming to be of that which is eternal, the final validity of a "personal history of freedom" (Rahner 1982, 271; 1975b, 175). Death is the completion and consummation of this history, its "birth" into full realization, and the moment at which it can never be lost through further decision (Rahner 1975b, 175). Thus Rahner asserts, "through death—not after it—*there is* (not: begins to take place) the achieved definitiveness of the freely matured existence of man. What has come to be is there as the hard-won and untrammeled validity of what was once temporal; it progressed as spirit and freedom, in order to be" (Rahner 1966e, 348).

Ochs identifies Rahner's second approach to death as an act as "existential." Whereas the "finality" approach claims that death is active since human freedom requires consummation, the "existential" approach says that every human being chooses the basic attitude with which they face their own impending demise. The posture towards death can be one of despair or trust, either of which can be manifested in many different ways. Looking forward to the apparent extinction of our own selves, we must either view death as an empty end or as fulfillment. From the perspective of human value, death is a pure loss. Viewing death as something other than pure loss is therefore an affirmation of a larger scale of meaning that rests on divine value. Death confronts us with this existential question about meaning and demands an answer. Attempts to evade or ignore the issue are futile—we cannot escape this question.

For Rahner, facing the question is a necessity for saying "yes," because it is a recognition and affirmation of human freedom. Human beings find themselves in the middle of an already ongoing freedom that demands decision and action. We have been burdened with an imposed freedom that we cannot discard. Yet we can choose how we regard and enact this freedom. A person "may prefer to be like drift-wood, and in a cowardly, lazy manner he may regard himself as but the product of his age and environment. But his real duty is to accept his freedom willingly and without force, to love it and to have the courage to face it" (Rahner 1964, 94). In facing our own death, we must decide how to understand and live out our own freedom, either as "forced freedom or free liberty" (106).

Ochs asserts: "Rahner's second approach to death as act comes from a conviction that everything in a person's existence should ul-timately be act, should be freely affirmed. Man is basically defined by freedom…Even man's freedom, which he discovers as a fact, must be freely assumed. It has to be taken up as a task. The imposed freedom must become a free freedom" (Ochs 1973, 133). This does not simply mean acknowledging the fact of inevitable death as a brute fact that cannot be avoided (133). Rather, it means freely accepting the fact as meaningful. Thus Rahner writes "free liberty to die has to be … a lib-erty which says 'yes' not only to death itself, but also to its meaning, to the meaning of human existence" (Rahner 1964, 95).

While such free acceptance of death does require an affirmation of meaning, it is not a calculation and articulation of what the meaning of human life and death is in human terms. On the contrary, it is the trust in mystery, the hope that beyond all human striving there is a meaning that is outside our comprehension and yet, nonetheless, given to us. It is precisely because the meaning of death cannot be calculated in human terms that it is an act of faith, a way of saying "yes" or "no" to God.

Although death is a universal experience, a part of everyday life with which we all have contact, it is also something about which we know very little. Our loved ones who pass away do not explain the specifics of the experience. In fact, they fall silent to our ears (Rahner 1997c, 145). In any given instance, we cannot ascertain if death is nothing-ness or plenitude (Rahner 1964, 49). Rahner states, "Death is, indeed, hidden from the experience of man" (50). It is, for us, exactly the dark-ness and hiddenness of death that demands and enables our decision to accept or reject God's offer of salvation. If we knew exactly what happened next, death would neither tempt despair nor require trust. The hiddenness of death is the silence that creates space for our freedom. Rahner writes:

> But it is precisely because death is concealed from us in this sense that it is (to reiterate) the situation *par excellence* in which we can make the most radical and absolute option possible between faith and despair…The dying man passes into a state of silence and solitude which engulfs everything in its own stillness. It is a state to which he has been drawing ever closer throughout his life, the situation in which he is faced with a question, an option to be taken, in which a decision is demanded of him, the situation either of the faith that redeems or of the despair that kills. The fact that death is concealed from us in this way makes it possible for us to choose either of these alternatives. (Rahner 1971b, 292)

Rahner does not claim that the moment of death is the exact time that a person says "yes" or "no" to God.[2] Instead he asserts that the reality of our own death is something about which we cannot remain neutral. It forces us to take up a posture that either affirms or denies the love of God. This is Rahner's "existential" approach to death as an act of the human person.

The two approaches to death as act that Ochs identifies in Rahner's work are deeply bound together in a single view of theological anthropology. Human freedom requires culmination in death, while approaching death demands the decision of human freedom. Furthermore, both of these ways of understanding death as an act imply that death is something that is present throughout human life. All of our lives, we are moving towards that final consummation of our freedom. All of our lives, we are facing our impending death and thus the demand of an existential question of meaning. Thus Rahner states, "Dying takes place throughout life itself, and death when it comes is only the ultimate and definitive completion of the process" (Rahner 1971b, 290).[3]

Furthermore, given the underlying vision of the relationship between time and eternity, this means that in those moments of life when we make free decisions that affirm meaning beyond human cal-

2 Rahner rejects this view in Rahner (1975a, 85). Some readers tend to elide Rahner's view with that of Boros (1965). See also Kelly (1984).

3 See Rahner (1964, 51, 70).

culation, in some manner we participate in and experience the eternal. This truth can never be seen from the outside. But Rahner argues that for the person acting, within an action of moral decision or love, there is an awareness of the eternal validity of the action and of the person's own immortality. When we can manage to act out a full affirmation of moral love—in ways momentous or minuscule—we know that the meaning of human life is not abolished in death. Rahner writes, "where such a free act of lonely decision is done, in absolute obedience to the higher law or in radical love of another person, something eternal happens, and man becomes immediately aware of his validity as something born of time but taking place outside its mere onward flow" (Rahner 1966e, 350).[4]

Thus the human person creates the character of her own eternity throughout a life imbued with death as both final consummation and existential choice. In Rahner's words: "the death of man is the moment at which the whole of his history as a free being, now consummated and completed, is brought into immediate confrontation with the mystery of God, encountering this either as its consummate blessing or as judgement" (Rahner 1974c, 318). Rahner describes these two possibilities through the rubric of dying in sin and dying in Christ.

## DYING IN SIN AND DYING IN CHRIST

Although the human freedom of Adam and Eve would have required consummation and therefore would not have continued indefinitely in time, Rahner states that death as we know it is a manifestation of sin. Without sin, this definitive finality could have been reached through a transformation that glorified the physical reality of the human person without the relinquishment of the body that happens in death now (Rahner 1971b, 288). While some form of consummation or death is natural, death as we know it is unnatural in that our physical reality "falls away...as though it were of no permanent significance" (289). Rahner describes original sin in relation to original justice, which is "a union with God through grace which transformed man's whole spiritual being, penetrating even his bodily life." Due to the loss of original justice in original sin, death has become "a visible demonstration of the fissure between God and man which cleaves man's being to its very

4 See also Ochs (1973, 129).

essence" (Rahner 1964, 41). Also, if sin were not in the picture, death would not be hidden in darkness. Adam could have had "a pure, apparent and clearly experienced maturing of man from within" (55; see also 50).[5] Death as we know it is a consequence, manifestation, and expression of the rejection of God, and as such is a penalty for sin (56, 57).[6] Dying in sin remains a possibility for each of us and we cannot know with certainty whether or not we are dying this death, saying "no" to God.

However, the death of Adam has been redeemed in Jesus Christ, creating the possibility that death can be an act of saying "yes." In understanding the significance of Jesus' death, Rahner is, in typical fashion, working within the framework of an inherited tradition in regards to which he positions his own view. On this subject, Rahner carefully criticizes two traditional ways of understanding Jesus' death. The first of these is sacrifice. Rahner questions several elements of sacrificial views of Christ's death, including the idea of changing God's mind, its helpfulness for contemporary Christians, and its relation to Biblical accounts of Jesus. However, he focuses on issues concerning freedom. If Jesus freely took on the role of sacrifice, then God's love is the cause of the reconciliation, not an expiatory sacrifice, simply understood. Further, Rahner maintains that "all real salvation can only be understood as taking place in the exercise of each individual's freedom," in which case it is difficult to determine how Jesus' free sacrifice liberates human freedom (Rahner 1982, 282, 283). Rahner then addresses inadequacies with traditional satisfaction theories. In particular, he claims that they do not make clear why Christ's death, rather than some other moral act, is redemptive. While Rahner eschews both sacrifice and substitution, he finds Scripture compelling in its insistence that redemption is wrought precisely in Jesus' death (Rahner 1964, 67, 68).

For Rahner, the death of Jesus, like the death of any other person, marks the finality and consummation of his personal history, and his acceptance or rejection of God's offer of salvation. As discussed in the

---

5 This raises the age old question of why or how Adam could sin, especially given that Rahner identifies the darkness of death as part of why it demands freedom's decision.

6 See also Rahner (1964, 41).

previous chapter, Rahner presents God's offer of self-communication in the supernatural existential in a relationship of mutual causality with the Incarnation and cross of Jesus.[7] Both the offer of God's self-communication and humanity's acceptance of this offer are actualized in the personal history of Jesus Christ, and thereby become irrevocable and eternally valid in his death. The victory of this acceptance, as itself accepted by God, is manifest historically in the resurrection. In Jesus, the giver, offer, recipient, acceptance, and final triumph of salvation are all one.

This again displays a pattern of mutual causality between Jesus and God's salvific will. Rahner writes:

> The pure initiative of God's salvific will establishes the life of Je-
> sus which reaches fulfillment in his death, and hence this salvific
> will becomes real and becomes manifest as irrevocable. The life and
> death of Jesus taken together, then, are the "cause" of God's salvific
> will (to the extent that these two things are regarded as different)
> insofar as this salvific will establishes itself really and irrevocably
> in this life and death, in other words, insofar as the life and death
> of Jesus, or the death which recapitulates and culminates his life,
> possess a causality of a quasi-sacramental and real-symbolic nature.
> (Rahner 1982, 284)

Within this view of mutual causality, it is fair to say that in Jesus Christ, God's salvific will and offer of salvation become actualized in history. In his death, humanity's acceptance of this offer is actualized and made eternally valid. In his resurrection, this victory, through God's acceptance, is made historically manifest. In the sending of the Spirit, God's offer to humanity is made to each person, creating and enabling the freedom for her to say "yes" or "no" to God, to her own beatitude within humanity's corporate salvation. In this way, the birth, life, death, resurrection, and sending of the Spirit of Jesus are all held within the one, loving, saving act of God.[8]

---

7  See also Rahner (1982, 317).

8  For example, Rahner portrays the death of Christ as, in some sense, the completion of the Incarnation, for in death Christ takes on all of what it is to be human. Philip Endean notes that Rahner stresses "how Christ's death demonstrates his full and unreserved sharing in the human condition, in all its vulnerability," and comments that Rahner's view "more or less consciously echoes Ignatius's *Exercises*, where the Incarnation appears as a process cul-

This act takes place in history. Rahner's understanding of history and death, wherein only that which is lived historically and consummated in death is fully finalized and actualized, is applied to Jesus and, thereby, to the salvific act of God. Rahner credits the death and resurrection of Jesus with the irrevocability and irreversibility of God's offer of salvation, as well as for its victory and success (Rahner 1982, 195). He writes that through Jesus' "death and his resurrection a situation for decision is present which, with respect to the *irreversibility* of God's offer of salvation, was not present before" (251). More boldly still, he states:

> In the absolute event of salvation God must live out its history as his own history and retain it permanently as something done in freedom, for otherwise it would remain something inconsequential and provisional for him. Only if this event is his own history, a history which, as lived out in divine and of course also in created freedom, determines him once and for all and hence becomes irrevocable, only then can we speak of an absolute and "eschatological" event of salvation. (301)

This is in keeping with Rahner's affirmation of eternity as the mature fruit of time and indicates the significance of the history of Jesus. He thus describes the death of Jesus as "that unique occurrence in the history of mankind for the sake of which God in his eternity has once and for all determined to keep mankind for ever enfolded in his compassion and love" (Rahner 1971b, 285).

Note also that Rahner's view of Jesus' death relies on an understanding of both humanity and salvation as corporate. Rahner asserts "that human history is a *single* history, and that the destiny of one person has significance for others" (Rahner 1982, 283).[9] This presupposition of human solidarity grounds Rahner's claim that "we are saved because this man who is one of us has been saved by God, and God has thereby made his salvific will present in the world historically, really and irrevocably" (284). The death of Jesus creates the context for

---

minating in the Cross" (Endean 2001, 191). Also, as discussed in Chapter Two: Silence, creation is a moment within this loving act of God. See Rahner (1982, 261).

9 See 211, and 198, where Rahner states "all men form one human race in mutual intercommunication,"

our existential decision of freedom and makes it possible for us to die in Christ rather than simply in sin. Jesus has changed death itself through his own dying. In part, this is because, without diminishing the reality that one who dies is unmastered and passive, Jesus made death his own activity.

Jesus encounters human death in all its horror. Rahner emphasizes that Jesus' death is unexceptional. He is not spared the "darkness" and "unmastering" (Rahner 1964, 69), "the agony of the body" (Rahner 1974c, 321), or "the horror of divine abandonment" (Rahner 1964, 78). And while Jesus' death did have additional elements of injustice, hatred, and mockery, Rahner does not elevate this death into something beyond what other people face. He writes, "Certainly it was a particularly agonising and unjust death. But death is every bit as terrifying as it occurs in the gas-chambers of Buchenwald or the mudholes of Vietnam" (Rahner 1971c, 140).

Yet as Jesus experienced the powerlessness and radical passivity of his own death, he also acted. Rahner exhorts Christians to believe that, "he was not only put to death, was not only swallowed up and engulfed by the absurdity of existence, but that he himself died. In other words he has made death into his own act, in which he accepts the inconceivable which is beyond all human control, and himself acts out what has to be endured" (141).[10] Rahner uses many traditional terms to describe this act, including acceptance, obedience and submission. He indicates that even in powerlessness, Jesus accepts his death with faith, hope, and love—trusting in the absent God who abandoned him. Jesus acts precisely in his powerlessness and passivity.

Rahner explains his view of the relation between passion and action in death clearly in one passage that is worth quoting at length:

> The freedom which is exercised on the physical plane is, in fact, that freedom by which man lays himself open to intervention from without, submits to control by another power or powers. They physical side of man's nature constitutes the sphere in which the interplay takes place of action from within himself and passion as imposed from without. As a physical being endowed with freedom man has to take cognizance of the fact that he occupies an intermediary position. He is neither wholly self-directing nor wholly subject to control by another, but half-way between these two. The mysteri-

---

10   See also Rahner (1974c, 320).

ous interplay between action and passion in the exercise of human freedom appears above all in the fact that it is precisely at the very point at which man freely achieves his own perfection that he is, at the same time, most wholly subject to control by another. The ultimate act of freedom, in which he decides his own fate totally and irrevocably, is the act in which he either *willingly accepts or definitively rebels against* his own utter impotence, in which he is utterly subject to the control of a mystery which cannot be expressed—that mystery which we call God. In death man is totally withdrawn from himself. Every power, down to the last vestige of a possibility, of autonomously controlling his own destiny is taken away from him. Thus the exercise of his freedom taken as a whole is summed up at this point in one single decision: whether he yields everything up or whether everything is taken from him by force, whether he responds to this radical deprivation of all power by uttering his assent in faith and hope to the nameless mystery which we call God, or whether even at this point he seeks to cling on to his own autonomy, protests against this fall into helplessness, and, because of his disbelief, supposes that he is falling into the abyss of nothingness when in reality he is falling into the unfathomable depths of God. (Rahner 1971b, 289, 290)

It is the situation of acknowledging powerlessness that creates the possibility of Christian hope. Rahner offers a theological vision of "hope" as a paradoxical combination of both activity and passivity. When we truly hope, in a Christian sense, we long for something beyond what we can create for ourselves, something that we can only accept as pure gift. In this sense, that which is hoped for must come to us in our passivity. At the same time, it is only within the activity of hoping that what is hoped for can even be imagined. The activity of hope makes the object of hope present and conceivable to us. As long as we have our own resources to fall back upon, Rahner argues, we will content ourselves with planning and calculation. It is only when we are deprived of the possibility of acting on our own behalf, when the materials at hand provide no possible leverage or foundation upon which to build, that Christian hope is truly possible (Rahner 1975b, 177, 178). Therefore, the situation of death, the unmastering and powerlessness of the human person, "constitutes precisely the true and necessary situation of Christian hope" (181).

In this situation of death, Jesus hopes for eternal life, making the Passion his own act. He has created the situation in which we die, such that we can face the prospect of our own powerlessness in death and trust that our fall into the abyss is a fall into the loving hands of God. Given the darkness of death, we cannot know enough to retain any control. But we can choose if that control will be wrenched from us or willingly surrendered.

Again, it is important to remember that Rahner is speaking of death at a high level of abstraction. He is not talking about seeking one's own death concretely, or being careless with one's life, let alone about cheerily submitting to the existence of death camps and needless wars, to Buchenwald and Vietnam. The surrender, obedience, and self-abandonment in death that he advocates are always directed to God, not to the injustices of human culture. He states that death "is faced rightly when it is entered upon by man as an act in which he surrenders himself fully and with unconditional openness to the disposal of the incomprehensible decision of God" (Rahner 1964, 52).

This kind of surrender is what Rahner understands to be the meaning of dying in Christ. Rahner is clear that dying in Christ is not limited by the confines of the confessing church. Rahner writes, "the death of Jesus is died by many who do not explicitly believe in him at all, or know him by name, yet who, by remaining faithful to the end, let themselves be received by death without thereby pronouncing a curse upon life…[f]or to accept one's death is in itself a way of knowing him and entering into communion with him" (Rahner 1971c, 143).[11] This is in keeping with Rahner's theory of anonymous Christians, especially in its insistence that the very act of dying in this way is possible only because of Jesus. In Rahner's words, "Death is a downfall, and only by faith can this downfall be interpreted as falling into the hands of the living God" (Rahner 1964, 95).

The surrender to the mystery of God is something that the Christian undertakes not just in the death that occurs at the end of her life, but also in the dying that is present within and throughout her life. This

---

11   Gerard Mannion (2004, 167, n. 4) notes that Rahner "foreshadows" his theory of anonymous Christians in Rahner (1964, 94-95). See also (1964, 95-96).

dying in Christ throughout life takes visible form in the sacraments, especially in Baptism, the Eucharist, and Extreme Unction (86). The conditions of this dying—the darkness that confounds human comprehension, the powerlessness that is the situation of hope, the abandonment by God that Jesus experienced and yet still trusted—mean that "the everyday and banal occurrence which we call human death, and which awaits each one of us also, has been elevated to a place among God's mysteries" (Rahner 1971b, 293). The moment of God's absence—no, God's abandonment—is, in Rahner's theology, "the ultimate mysticism" (Rahner 1978a, 21).[12] This is what death is (Rahner 1971b, 293). When we can surrender to God in death, in the company of Jesus, then this is the purest moment of faith, in which the God who is loved is surely not an idol of our own construction, but the God of mystery. Abandonment of the self to this mystery is not a negation of the self, but rather the path to the individual's unique and eternal validity. Rahner is concerned with the God of mystery, "in whose incomprehensible fire we are not, in fact, burnt away but become ourselves and of eternal value....if we allow ourselves to be taken up by him, we are not destroyed but given to ourselves truly for the first time" (Rahner 1978a, 17).

Thus far Rahner's depiction of death reiterates several important points that were covered in my analysis of his use of silence and his theology of love. Rahner repeats his emphasis on God as mystery and the portrayal of Christian life as a participation in that mystery. Jesus, again, makes it possible for human beings to say "yes" to God and is, therefore, the central logic of salvation. The dynamism between self-possession and openness to the other is stated anew in this context, as Rahner declares that the self is actualized in her unique individuality precisely in opening to the mysterious, unknowable other. There is, repeated, a sense that Christian faith involves the person accepting the conditions of human existence. Yet one element important to Rahner's discussion of love is less discernible here, that of interpersonal relationship. Up to this point, Rahner has described death in individualistic terms, focusing almost exclusively on the free act of death as the task of the person viewed in isolation. He states bluntly, "Everyone must

---

12   For discussion of this passage within a larger exploration of Rahner and Ignatius, see Endean (2001, 15).

die his own death for himself in supreme loneliness" (Rahner 1967d, 264). Can this be seen in some continuity with Rahner's elevation of interpersonal love? Does it indicate Rahner's thoroughgoing individualism, and therefore mitigate his statements about love? Where does the rest of humanity fit in?

## SANCTIFIED HUMANITY

Part of the individualistic slant of the preceding account of Rahner's theology derives from the focus of this study, which is how we say "yes" to God's offer of salvation. This leads to a discussion of death as a way in which we say "yes," rather than to a more general exploration of Rahner's eschatology. Rahner explicitly aims to hold together individual and collective eschatologies (Rahner 1982, 436). Tensions between the two arise not only from his own theological anthropology, but also from various aspects of the Christian tradition that speak both in terms of individual salvation and in terms of general resurrection, a new heaven and a new Earth.

The collective aspect of Rahner's view of death was briefly mentioned above; one of the presuppositions for Rahner's assertion that Jesus' death is salvific is the corporate nature of humanity. His death matters for each of ours because he is one of us. Or, narrated from a different perspective, what happens in Jesus is not, first and foremost, about the free decision, salvation or damnation, of any individual human being. Rather, it is about the success of God's self-communication. In Jesus, God's self-communication to humanity is accepted and is victorious. Humanity receives and accepts God's offer; the dialogue between God and humanity is one in which each party says "yes" to the other; the salvation of humanity is secured in Jesus and made manifest in his resurrection. Indeed, the resurrection of Jesus is the beginning of the general resurrection, the final consummation of the world.

Jesus' resurrection indicates the relationship between individual and collective eschatologies. Each human being who says "yes" to God is saved within Jesus' resurrection, as a person included in the consummation he inaugurates. At the same time, the faith of all believers, of each person who says "yes," is essential to the full realization of Jesus' resurrection (267, 268). Rahner states repeatedly that Christian hope for eternal life—and recall his theological understanding of hope described above—is primarily a hope for the salvation of humanity. It is a hope that God's grace succeeds, that the history of the world is held in the triumphant arms of a redeeming God. At base, it is hope that God *is*. As we live in this hope, within it we can begin to envision the possibility we hope for, can begin to imagine that the void ever surrounding human life is the mysterious and loving God of Jesus Christ. Such hope, Rahner says, "constitutes the basic dimension of the Christian understanding of existence as such" (Rahner 1975b, 177). Clearly hope thus perceived is not a narrow hope of self-preservation amidst destruction. Rahner writes, "hope is present only in him who first and foremost hopes on behalf of *others*—hopes in the responsibility he takes for them, hopes in that love for him whom we call God, and in the face of whom even authentic hope must in its turn forget its own nature" (176). Only secondarily and derivatively can any one of us look with hope towards our own salvation as an instance within the corporate salvation of humanity. Rahner sees "the salvation of an individual as one which is not achieved fully except within the absolute future of the whole of mankind, as the ultimate result of the love of all the others in the absoluteness of God. In other words, the salvation of an individual soul does not consist in escaping from the history of humanity but in entering into the latter's absolute future, which we call the 'kingdom of God'" (Rahner 1972b, 189).

Furthermore, the way in which human beings say "yes" to God and accept salvation is primarily described by Rahner as taking place in interpersonal relationships of love. While the decision to accept or reject God's offer is a lonely decision, a burden of individual freedom that cannot be passed on to another, it is also a decision made within community and by a person who is formed in community. Again, Rahner attempts to hold individuality and community together, such that each is necessary for the other. This applies even to salvation. Rahner writes:

> Intercommunication in all its tenaciousness, according to which the other person is necessarily always present, sustaining and making demands upon me, would be a mere surface appearance if I could withdraw to a region where I was simply alone, where no-one could follow me or was necessary for me any longer, and where there was no-one for whom I was partly responsible. If, therefore, the ques-

138 Silence, Love, & Death

tion of salvation is an unavoidable element of human existence, intercommunication is also a factor of existence, whether for or against salvation. Here too no-one is alone; each one supports every other person, in the matter of salvation everyone is responsible and significant for everyone else. The commandment to love one's neighbour was not given to make our social or private lives bearable or agreeable, but to proclaim everyone's concern in everyone else's possibility of salvation. It goes without saying that concepts like 'people (of God)' in salvation-history, 'covenant,' 'Body of Christ,' 'Prayer for one another' etc., presuppose this kind of intercommunicative existence. The reality and experience of this intercommunicative existence which is so important for salvation is made concrete in the absolute quality and unfathomable depths of the love of one's neighbour, in the puzzling experience that in the fate of any individual we are confronted and put face to face with the fate of all human kind, and that this experience cannot be explained away rationalistically as abstraction, induction or the seeing of all 'cases' in a single 'case.' (Rahner 1972c, 176, 177)

The individual who says "yes" or "no" to God in such a way that this free decision is consummated in death thus achieves her own eternal validity within the larger context of corporate humanity, in a way that cannot be accurately seen by focusing on her alone. Therefore in discussing what it means to say "yes" to God in death, it is necessary to briefly address more traditional eschatological themes of heaven, hell, and purgatory. Before doing so, it is important to note that Rahner places clear boundaries around such eschatological statements. The last things are, for us, in the future of history, and therefore can only be known through God's revelation in salvation history. He is wary both of reducing eschatology to merely the present and of imagining that we can know its content so clearly in advance as to produce, in effect, a travelogue of heaven and hell. Furthermore, he aims to distinguish between the form and content of eschatological statements, such that the metaphors and analogies accumulated throughout the centuries of Christian tradition are not understood in simplistic and overly literal ways. We can know about eschatology, in Rahner's theology, based on our present experience of grace and salvation in history and always within the revelation of Jesus Christ (Rahner 1966d).[13] Rahner there-

---

13   Peter C. Phan gives a detailed, concise summary of Rahner's view on this matter in Phan (2005, 177-179).

fore understands eschatology as projecting human experience of self, God, and Jesus into our visions of the future. He writes, "eschatalogical statements are a transposition into the future of something which a Christian person experiences in grace as his present" (Rahner 1982, 433).

In Rahner's view, the final state of blessedness or despair is not an external reward or punishment inflicted upon the person from the outside. Rather, it is the person's own choice: "eternity as the fruit of time means to come before God either to reach pure immediacy and closeness to him face to face in the absolute decision of love for him, or to be enveloped in the burning darkness of eternal god-lessness in the definitive closing of one's heart against him" (Rahner 1966e, 351). God's attitude towards the individual human person does not change, indeed does not depend upon that person's freedom at all. In Jesus Christ, the love of God for humanity is irrevocably decided, guaranteed and secured. Our freedom cannot change this. However, each human person is burdened with the freedom to either accept her own identity as one who is created, redeemed, and consummated by the incomprehensible God, or to reject this given identity in the vain hope of constructing a new one that is not dependent on this abandoning other, this ungraspable mystery. Ironically, those who accept their identity as given become partners in their own self-creation, while those who reject it become twisted with self-contradiction, refusing to allow themselves to become who they most truly are. In death, these choices are brought before God, whose "judgement is the unveiling of what we are" (Rahner 1967c, 144). Heaven and hell, then, are not external reward and punishment, but the inherent consequences of decision freely made.

Given this, it is clear to see that heaven and hell do not have equal status in Rahner's theology. The success of God's self-communication to humanity is a primary point of Christian faith. Heaven, as the eternal communion of humanity and God, is therefore a tenet of faith, a point of revelation, a truth to claim. In contrast, hell is a possibility that must be acknowledged while we hope that no one ever manages to completely close themselves off to the love of God. Indeed, given that Rahner understands hope as primarily for the collective salvation of humanity, our very hope for heaven includes a prayer that hell is an unrealized possibility.

Many readers assume that Rahner's emphasis on the universal salvific will of God, along with his depiction of God as irrevocably saying "yes" to God in Jesus Christ, means that he believes in universal salvation, or apocatastasis. However, this is not what his written texts assert. Rahner clearly hopes for universal salvation; indeed, he claims all Christians must. But he does not teach it as known and true for at least three reasons. First, as Phan notes, "[t]he Church's magisterium has condemned the *positive* assertion of an apocatastasis as heretical" (Phan 1988, 153). Second, an assertion of universal salvation would undermine Rahner's emphasis on human freedom and the dignity of humankind. Appreciating the enormity of the burden and gift of human freedom requires acknowledging the possibility that a person could choose to deny themselves, to contradict their own ordination to God, and that God would allow such a choice to achieve eternal validity in death. Freedom plays too large a role in Rahner's theology for it to be so diminished, reduced to a choice between "yes" now and "yes" some other time. Rahner states, "the dogma of hell means that human life is threatened by the real possibility of eternal shipwreck, because man freely disposes of himself and can therefore freely refuse himself to God" (Rahner and Vorgrimler 1981, 205). Third, on a pastoral level, given that death is hidden in darkness and we cannot report back from the other side, the stakes are too high to teach a doctrine of universal salvation. Each of us must reckon with the possibility of absolute loss; we cannot avoid that reckoning through theological and theoretical maneuvers that deny the risk (Rahner 1982, 443, 35). The purpose of the doctrine of hell is precisely to remind us of this risk and to "bring us to our senses and to conversion" (Rahner and Vorgrimler 1981, 206).

While Rahner once commented that he would like to write about "a possible orthodox teaching on apocatastasis," to my knowledge he never produced such a document (Rahner 1986b, 194). His written work speaks of both heaven and hell, although always in an unequal, asymmetrical relationship. Heaven is the ultimate success of God's sanctification of corporate humanity, while hell is the possibility that individual human persons may reject God's grace. He states, "we profess that the world and the human race as a whole will find a blessed and positive fulfillment in Jesus Christ by the power of God's grace. In the doctrine of hell we maintain the possibility of eternal loss for every individual, for each one of us, because otherwise the seriousness of free history would be abolished" (Rahner 1982, 444).

Heaven must be discussed in both corporate and individual terms. It is the collective salvation of humanity; the success of human history as a dialogue with God; and the reality of beatific vision conferred upon those individuals who, through their unique personal histories, say "yes" to God. For Rahner, self-abandonment into the mystery of God is the most important moment of self –constitution. It is precisely in openness to this divine other (an openness enacted throughout our lives in love of the concrete others of our neighbors) that we step into full self-possession. As Phan notes, "according to Rahner... the creature's genuine autonomy and radical dependence on God are simply two sides of one and the same reality, and therefore they grow in direct and not in inverse proportion" (Phan 1988, 139). For this reason, Rahner's conception of heaven is intensely corporate and intensely individual in equal measure. Each person achieves salvation by accepting God's grace in his own lonely decision and his individuality is not subsumed into a mass of redeemed humanity. He is not "consumed into universality, but rather he becomes for the first time someone absolutely unique" (Rahner 1982, 308, 09). The particularities of a person's relationships and history are not lost, but drawn into the presence of God. Rahner writes of heaven:

> this abiding of personal creatures in the presence of God essentially means the gathering of mankind into the definitive Body of Jesus Christ, into the "whole Christ," to commune with God who is made (and remains) man; hence it is that we shall "see one another again," that the human relationships of this world continue in heaven. This union of man with God and with his fellows means no loss or absorption of individuality; rather the closer man approaches to God the more his individuality is liberated and fortified...the individual who is finally saved by God's grace alone...remains conditioned by what he has done and what he has become in history, and it is in this historical measure and "mould" that God wholly fills and loves him. (Rahner and Vorgrimler 1981, 204, 205. Emphasis removed.)

As the individuality of each human person is not discarded in eternity, neither is the humanity of Jesus Christ. Even in the beatific vision, "[t]he human reality of Christ must always be the abiding mediation of the immediacy of God to us" (Rahner 1982, 308).[14] All of this—in regard to all persons and to Jesus—is in keeping with Rahner's view of eternity as the mature fruit of time, with his insistence that human beings know God in and through the world around them, and with his understanding of eschatology as reading theological anthropology into the future.

Furthermore, it is consonant with Rahner's claim that the beatific vision does not mean the final "comprehension" of God by humanity, the clarity of sight and knowledge in which mystery is abolished and all that was once hidden is brought forth. Rahner affirms that God's mystery and incomprehensibility remain intact in heaven. Rahner's assertion of incomprehensibility of God is not a regretful statement about humanity's limited intellectual capacity. Instead, it is a proclamation about God, about the mystery which grounds and enables human knowing. Therefore the beatific vision is not the overcoming of incomprehension, but rather intimacy with the incomprehensible. For Rahner, beatific vision means "grasping and being grasped by the mystery" such that "the supreme act of knowledge is not the abolition or diminution of the mystery, but its final assertion, its eternal and total immediacy" (Rahner 1966c, 41).

As a Catholic theologian discussing eschatology, Rahner addresses purgatory as well as heaven and hell. This is a complicated doctrine for Rahner, since it comes with centuries of descriptive language he regards as metaphorical; it implies development of the person after the finality of death; and it raises issues of the possibility of temporal progression after death. Without ever making a strong pronouncement about what, precisely, he sees purgatory to be, Rahner strives to conceive of purgatory in a way that is coherent with the rest of his theology.

Having repeatedly claimed that death marks the finality and consummation of a personal history of freedom, in which a human being definitively answers God's call to beatific vision, what is Rahner to make of purgatory? He offers a number of suggestions. One is that,

---

14   For a discussion of this, see Phan (1988, 138-42).

due to the complexity of the human person, a final decision can be made without being immediately integrated fully into all aspects of the human being. While the basic attitude of the person is achieved before death, the perfection of all dimensions of the human person may be fulfilled "after" death in some sense (Rahner 1966e, 353). He states, "Purgatory can be conceived absolutely as the integration of all the manifold dimensions of man into the one basic decision of man (which no longer changes after death)" (Rahner 1967c, 153). Rahner clearly does not want to simply apply temporal categories to purgatory, seen in this light. He does not want to imagine the human person changing horses after death, continuing a temporal existence. However, he sometimes links this view of purgatory, as the full integration of a basic decision, with the notion of an interval between death and the bodily fulfillment of the human person in the resurrection, or an 'intermediate state.' (Rahner 1982, 442; 1966e, 353). Much of the Christian tradition assumes there is an intermediate state in which the individual who has died is already saved or damned and yet not yet fully glorified, awaiting the general resurrection of the dead. In one essay, Rahner imagines that purgatory might take place in this interval. In another, he suggests that the traditional temporal imagery of purgatory could be transposed onto the process of dying, such that the duration of time in purgatory would "be identified with the (diverse) depth and intensity of the pain that man experiences in death itself" (Rahner 1983e, 186).

Rahner restates these views of purgatory as integration in the voice of one member of a dialogue between two theologians that he constructs in an essay called "Purgatory." The second theologian in this essay offers a view that Rahner develops in his later years, here constructed explicitly in conversation with other religions. He suggests that while, in principle, the death of the human person marks the finality of her life of freedom, there may be cases in which a real history of freedom has not even begun and therefore "death in the full theological sense as freedom made definitive" has not yet been achieved (191). Such a history of freedom might then happen either as "postmortal" or perhaps in another lifetime. Rahner suggests that the doctrine of purgatory could, in this way, be seen in continuity with a modified version of reincarnation or the "migration of souls." Of course, in a Christian framework, such migration could not be seen as going on infinitely, as freedom seeks its definitive and eternal end (191, 192).[15] Rather, it would be an opportunity for a true history of freedom, a real and definitive death. In "Purgatory," Rahner raises these issues in regard to traditional "marginal" cases in Catholic theology, including unbaptized infants (190, 191),[16] but the theory is obviously open to much broader application, a possibility that will be discussed in the next chapter. Christianity presumes, says Rahner, that the choice of freedom is normally made in the course of one life, so while he discusses the possibility of this form of purgatory, he does not speculate on how common or how rare it might be (Rahner 1983e, 192-193).

Rahner's statements about purgatory show a movement away from assuming that there is an intermediate state between individual death and the glorification of the body towards one of interpreting traditional Christian statements about such an interval in different ways. This movement can be seen most clearly in Rahner's discussion of the human soul as all-cosmic, which includes another possible interpretation of the doctrine of purgatory.

## AN ALL-COSMIC SOUL?

This theory is articulated in Rahner's early work, *On the Theology of Death*. Here, as elsewhere, he rejects understandings of death that include a sharp duality between body and soul or envision the immortal soul shuffling off a dispensable mortal coil. Body and soul are united. Furthermore, Rahner reasons, the soul is thereby related to "that 'whole' of which the body is a part, that is, to that wholeness which constitutes the unity of the material universe" (Rahner 1964, 26). He suggests that the separation of body and soul in death does not mean that the soul is no longer connected to the material cosmos at all, but

---

15    Rahner rejects the possibility of eternal migration of souls or reincarnation in Rahner (1971b, 289).

16    Rahner (1982) briefly mentions this view of reincarnation as a way to reconceptualize the traditional notion of an "interval," linking it to the view of purgatory as integration. Both cases seem to require a particular reading of other statements by Rahner, namely that all lives are worthy of eternity such that a "life" is understood as a person. See Rahner (1982, 441; 1966e, 351).

rather that the relationship between the soul and the cosmos is radicalized. Instead of becoming "a-cosmic," the soul becomes "all-cosmic" (28). In death, the soul's relationship to the world "is not abolished, but is rather, for the first time, completed, giving way to a fully open, world-embracing relationship, no longer mediated by the individual body" (32).

No longer connected to the world through the limited location of one human body, the soul takes on a more intimate relationship with the world as a whole. Rahner is careful to note that this should not be interpreted such that the cosmos "becomes the 'body' of this particular soul," or such that the soul is thought to be omnipresent (30). Yet in this newly-radicalized relationship, the all-cosmic soul might become "a co-determining factor of the universe precisely in its character as the ground for the personal life of other spiritual-corporeal beings...might come to have, through the actions performed in this world, a real ontological influence on the whole of the universe" (31). This view of the communion of the saints is gestured towards in another essay, where Rahner states that the existence of those who have died is "embedded" in the "silent, secret ground of our own existence" (Rahner 1966e, 353).

Within this theoretical framework, Rahner suggests that purgatory means that the person who achieves, through death, this new level of relation to the universe experiences "her own harmony or disharmony with the objectively right order of the world" and contributes to "the establishment of that right order" (Rahner 1964, 33). While this understanding of the "all-cosmic" soul is formulated as a possibility for the interval between death and the resurrection, or the intermediate state, it also casts new light on the glorification of the body in resurrection. In light of this theory, "the glorified body seems to become the perfect expression of the enduring relation of the glorified person to the world as a whole" (34).

Rahner's theory of the all-cosmic soul is based on a number of presuppositions, two of which I wish to highlight. First is "the basic oneness of the world...by which all things in the world are related and communicate anteriorly to any mutual influence upon each other" (27). This corporate aspect of creation is why the soul has a relation to the cosmos, and not just an individual body, to begin with. Second, "the spiritual soul is an open system towards the world" (30). This view of human spirituality plays a crucial role in Rahner's early, philosophical works, primarily worked out in epistemological terms. Here we see Rahner employing this theme in a fairly early, theological work in a way that emphasizes the soul's connection to materiality and the interrelationality of the cosmos. He states that it is "almost impossible to restrict the idea of the human 'body' to what is covered by the skin. The spiritual soul, moreover, through her essential relationship to the body, is basically open to the world in such a manner that she is never a monad without windows, but always in communication with the whole of the world" (30). Building on these two presuppositions, Rahner's provocative portrayal of the communion of saints through the theory of the all-cosmic soul highlights the interconnection of all persons and the abiding relation between spirit and matter.

This theory also does some theological work for Rahner, in that it provides a framework for understanding how the death of Jesus changes the situation in which each of us will die. Rahner's theology emphasizes the humanity of Jesus. While he is clearly more and other than the rest of us, he is also profoundly *one of us*. This is important for Rahner in avoiding extrinsic understandings of grace, in providing an intellectually defensible account of Christian faith, and in that—as mentioned above—the unity and solidarity of humanity is necessary to his view of salvation. The theory of the all-cosmic soul asserts that when any human dies, she becomes a "co-determining factor of the universe" and has "a real ontological influence on the whole of the universe" (31). In this context, Jesus' death is unique in the kind of influence it has on the universe, but not in the very fact that it does have an influence. His death is understood within Rahner's theological anthropology, not in stark distinction to it. This repeats a pattern seen throughout Rahner's Christology.[17]

Later in his career, Rahner appears to discard the theory of the all-cosmic soul. In one article, "The Intermediate State," Rahner refers to it as something he postulated earlier, and then goes on to admit that

17  See Mannion (2004, 181) in this regard, where he suggests that "Rahner's thoughts on the changed relation of every human person to the world through death actually developed out of such reflections upon the changed and definitive relation of Christ to the world through his death on the cross."

there is an easier and, he implies, better way to understand what happens to the human person after death. In this essay, Rahner suggests that there is no intermediate state between individual death and resurrection (Rahner 1981a, 119, 120).[18] His reasons for doing so involve the difficulty of attributing some sort of temporal interval 'after' death, when he takes such pains to articulate a relationship between time and eternity that cannot be seen this way. As mentioned above, in Rahner's view time and eternity are not linearly contiguous. They might better be imagined as parallel, such that eternity is borne of time. Furthermore, this bearing of eternity is not a single birth at the end of time (either for the individual's life or for the collective history of humanity) but rather throughout time there are moments and acts that bear eternity. The history of freedom is not just something that happens to take place in time. No. Time comes to be for this freedom; freedom is the essence of time (Rahner 1981a, 119). Within this view, it makes little sense to imagine that a person completes her free history, yet remains temporally bound as she awaits bodily resurrection.

In addressing this difficulty, Rahner does not reject his earlier thoughts about the relationship between body and soul, but takes them further. He continues to bring together scholastic understandings of the soul as "informing" the body with contemporary scientific and philosophical approaches to the body that discern the ways in which each individual's body is—when seen in its smallest components—radically interconnected to the rest of the universe. A fuller appreciation of the connection between the soul and all matter, which earlier helped generate the all-cosmic theory, later supports Rahner's claim that it is not necessary to envision a material connection between the resurrected body and the corpse of the deceased. He writes:

> Indeed, probably no metaphysically thinking theologian would continue to maintain today (for either philosophical or theological reasons) that the identity of the glorified body and the earthly body is only ensured if some material fragment of the earthly body is found again in the glorified body. For this kind of identity cannot even be found in the earthly body, because of its radical metabolic processes. (120)

---

18  See also Phan (1988, 114, 115, 236, n. 102).

Rahner's loss of the theory of the all-cosmic soul, therefore, stems from struggles to understand Christian traditions about individual and collective eschatology within a coherent view of eternity as the mature fruit of time. He claims we are not "absolutely forced to posit a temporal interval between the death of the individual and that which we really mean when we speak of the 'resurrection of the flesh'" (Rahner 1975b, 176).

While Rahner's dismissal of the intermediate state leads him to let go of the all-cosmic soul theory, many of the ideas within this early theory remain active in his theology. He continues to perceive the world as a fundamental unity. As noted above, his view of the relationship between spirit and matter is not altered in its central aspects. Given that these ideas are still operative, it is unclear how much is actually lost when Rahner drops his earlier theory. Also, it is still conceivable to see the resurrected human being as a perfected soul in unity with a glorified body that is not restrained to a particular spatio-temporal location, but rather permeates the whole of the cosmos. As Phan notes, Rahner's "basic ideas concerning the relationship of the soul to matter after death remain unchanged" (Phan 1988, 114). Considering such continuity, one could ask if Rahner's conception of the communion of the saints could still function, understood as abiding in eternity instead of an intermediate state. In other words, could actualized free histories, consummated in death and perfected in the presence of God, become eternal co-determining factors of the universe?[19] Such a Rahnerian view of the communion of the saints would have the benefit of (re-)placing the salvific work of the death of Jesus Christ in a context of a general understanding of human death in which lives of freedom come, through death, to influence the universe as a whole.

In the same volume of the *Theological Investigations* as "The Intermediate State," Rahner published an essay that was first written in 1967, titled "The Body in the Order of Salvation." Here Rahner rehearses several familiar themes, including the human being as an open system, understood materially, such that "[t]hrough bodiliness the whole

19   The issue of how the actions of others influence people will be addressed in the next chapter. Here, it is important to note that such influence would be mediated through God, in whose presence the dead are perfected. This is analogous to Rahner's understanding of how we can influence one another's freedom temporally. See Rahner (1967d).

world belongs to me from the start" (Rahner 1981c, 87). He states that modern science prevents an understanding of the body as self-contained within skin. He then offers a brief reflection on this that contains much of his understanding of death—both in regard to individual freedom and in regard to humanity as communally sanctified. He writes:

> In a certain sense—and I am exaggerating here, in order to make what I want to say clearer—we are all living in one and the same body—the world. And because that is so (and this is really the metaphysical, theological premise) something of the nature of original sin, and something of the nature of redemption can exist too. This one total physical existence as the common space which makes intercommunication between individual spiritual subjects possible from the start—this one concrete space can of course be accepted by the individual spiritual subject in various ways: it can be loved, put up with, or hated.
>
> Let me draw attention to one small result of this, although it really takes us too far. The transfiguration of the End-time, therefore, means the resurrection of the individual, and a new earth and a new heaven. And let us just ask ourselves whether what we call blessedness, heaven and hell, might not be thought of as being distinguished for us in a matchless way by the manner in which a particular person accepts this common reality. Since everyone, as spiritual person, lives essentially in the space of existence that is common to all, into which he continually acts—and acts into the whole—and from which he continually receives, he is continually active and continually passive. What he specifically experiences as himself is always the unity of the act suffered, committed by everything towards him, and the self-fulfillment from within, which he actively expresses outwards. We can see in this way what the communion of saints really means. This one 'concrete' existence in which we consummate our own spiritual, final liberty, is itself involved in a dynamic history which sometime ends in transfiguration, in a reality not only of the spiritual person, but also of his common sphere of being. (88)

Throughout Rahner's theology, there is an affirmation of the unity of humankind that includes the material as well as the spiritual and that is fundamental to his understanding of sin, redemption, and eternal life. Exploring his theory of the all-cosmic soul reveals that these traits were present in his theology early in his career. While the perception that Rahner's theology moves from the more individual to the more interpersonal certainly bears weight, it is also important to note here, as in Chapter Two: Love, that elements of the interpersonal are present and important in Rahner's theological work from early in his career.

Furthermore, in Rahner's theology of death there is more than a concern for interpersonal relations. There is a theological affirmation of humanity as corporate, such that our sin and our redemption can only be understood in this light, and such that our eternal vocation is primarily a call to communal glorification. Rahner presents death as the consummation of individual free decision, made in interpersonal relationships in community. This lonely decision can be a "yes" to God because of the faithful death of Jesus and the corporate nature of humanity. Thus individual death opens into a communal eternity, in which individuality and interpersonal relations are preserved within a profound intercommunion.

What is seen in Rahner's use of silence and his discussions of love is cast into clearer relief in his work on death: individuality and community are deeply intertwined, each requiring the other for its own actualization. We only become who we are as individuals in opening ourselves to others in community. And community requires persons who have a sturdy individuality, or else it is something less than community, a mere amalgam of humanity. Similarly, the salvific possibility of our individual decisions rests upon the communal sanctification of humanity, while the actualization of this sanctification in the salvation of humanity relies upon our individual decisions.

## SILENCE, LOVE, AND DEATH

How does death connect with silence and love in Rahner's theology? Recall his prayer concerning the silence of the dead discussed in Chapter Two. He struggles with the awful stillness of loved ones who have died and demands that God answer for their silence as well as God's own. From this, Rahner moves to affirm the silence of God as the space offered for his own free decision of faith. He concludes: "Your Love has hidden itself in silence, so that my love can reveal itself in faith" (Rahner 1997c, 147). The silence of the dead and of God is part of the darkness and hiddenness of death, which is why death demands the commitment of our freedom.

This is clearly an iteration of Rahner's major point concerning death, that it is an opportunity and demand for human freedom to accept or reject the offer of God's grace. While Rahner acknowledges the reality that death is passively suffered, he emphasizes the activity of human freedom in death. Ultimately, this is a freedom to accept our humanity as one in which we are finite creatures, powerless in the face of death, and yet called to communion with God. Thus while passivity is vital in Rahner's view of death, activity is the focus. In this prayer, the death of loved ones is seen as yet another call to free decision.

It is also more than this. Given Rahner's understanding of love as opening the self to the other, the loss of a loved one is more than an opportunity for faith. It is also a loss of part of the self. Rahner writes earlier in the prayer about those people he loves who have died and the emptying out of his own life through these deaths. He laments:

> There is no substitute for them; there are no others who can fill the vacancy when one of those whom I have really loved suddenly and unexpectedly departs and is with me no more. In true love no one can replace another, for true love loves the other person in that depth where he is uniquely and irreplaceably himself. And thus, as death has trodden roughly through my life, every one of the departed has taken a piece of my heart with him, and often enough my whole heart.
>
> A strange thing happens to the man who really loves, for even before his own death his life becomes a life with the dead. (144, 45)

So Rahner describes his own life of loving people who then fall silent in death as "a dying life" (147). In such a life, he cannot expect the superabundant life that his dead now experience. This is part of their silence—the gulf between a life that is emptied as loved ones depart and a life that overflows in communion. Rahner then interprets the silence of the dead as a call to him, to join them in eternal life in the presence of God. The silence of God is seen as an opportunity for faith through a fairly existential lens. The silence of the dead is quite similar, but in more relational terms. It is the challenge to believe that love conquers death; that human, temporal relationships endure for all eternity. It is the call to a man, heart-broken and alone, to join his departed friends again in love. Rahner writes:

Their silence is their loudest call to me, because it is the echo of Your silence. Their voice speaks in unison with Yours, trying to make itself heard above the noisy tumult of our incessant activity, competing with the anxious protestations of mutual love with which we poor humans try to reassure each other. Against all this, their voice and Yours strive to enwrap us and all our words in Your eternal silence.

Thus Your word summons us to enter into Your Life. Thus You command us to abandon ourselves by the daring act of love which is faith, so that we may find our eternal home in your life. And thus I am called and commanded by the silence of my dead, who live Your Life and therefore speak Your word to me, the word of the God of Life, so far removed from my dying. They are silent because they live, just as we chatter so loudly to try to make ourselves forget that we are dying. Their silence is really their call to me, the assurance of their immortal love for me. (147, 148)

For Rahner, part of the reason why unconditional love between persons is so very risky, and makes no sense apart from Jesus Christ, is that people die. When someone opens himself up to another, risking changes to his own worldview and identity, he makes himself vulnerable to incredible loss—including loss of part of himself—when the beloved dies. Choosing to love is choosing "a dying life," is dying with Christ throughout life.[20]

When we manage to love someone, it is an implicit affirmation that the meaning of human life is held within a larger, greater framework—that the darkness and void that surrounds us ultimately sustains, rather than negates, the meaning of human life. This, for Rahner, is the act of faith, enabled by Jesus Christ. In the same way, when we love a mortal human being, we implicitly affirm that the meaning of human life is not extinguished in death. We affirm the eternal validity of the beloved and, in so doing, we experience our own eternal validity. This pattern repeats itself in regard to our own deaths. When we die a death of free liberty, we lay claim to the truth that the meaning of our lives is not abolished by death. It is therefore an act of faith, explicit or implicit, when any person accepts her own powerlessness in the face of death without despair. For this reason, death and love are both de-

---

20  Rahner also makes an unusual case for death being an act of love, in that through death we make room for other people and affirm God as absolute future (1972b, 198, 199).

scribed by Rahner as the central act of human life, through which the person says either "yes" or "no" to God.

In silence, love, and death, there is an acceptance of the blunt realities of human life—of inescapable distance between persons and our unavoidable intercommunicative existence; of encroaching death; of the hiddenness and darkness that surrounds human life. When someone loves and dies faithfully, she acknowledges these realities and goes beyond that, not merely accepting the brute facts of the matter (Ochs 1973, 133), but hoping and trusting that within these very conditions of human life, there is ultimate meaning. Both love and faithful dying happen when a person opens herself up to the mystery of the unknown other, a posture that is often marked by images of silence in Rahner's work. He writes: "The death that is accomplished in life, therefore, must be really the act of that loving and therefore trustful faith which gives man courage to allow himself to be taken up by another" (Rahner 1971b, 291).

In his use of silence and his writings on love and death, Rahner portrays the faithful act of saying "yes" to God as a choice to fully inhabit a divinely-gifted identity marked by both self-possession and openness to the other. We become ourselves most fully when we open ourselves to the other, both human and divine. We say "yes" to God through such openness. In this way, human identity is depicted in Rahner's theology as both gift received and task accomplished.

# CHAPTER 5

# A MODERN MEDIEVAL IN
# POSTMODERN TIMES

*"Ostensibly we seek the clarity of a faith that never falters, but in reality we want only a freedom from doubt that waters down our faith and its decision. We think we are seeking the Spirit of faith; yet instead of the certainty of the Spirit, who dwells in the darkness of faith, we are seeking only the clarity of earthly truisms."* (Rahner 1993a, 213)

## INTRODUCTION

Few would argue against the statement that Karl Rahner is one of the greatest Christian theologians of the modern era. Yet it is precisely his modernity that leads many contemporary theologians to question Rahner's continued relevance for constructive Christian theology. The intellectual context has changed; postmodern criticisms of all things modern now deeply influence theological discourse. In the previous chapters, I have offered a particular interpretation of Rahner's work centered on the question of how Christians say "yes" to God's offer of self-communication. With this in mind, I will now address some of the common current arguments against the ongoing vitality of Rahner's thought, focusing on those related to theological anthropology. I do not, thereby, implicitly accept postmodernism as a valid standard for Christian theology. Rather, I point out that the interpretation of Rahner's work that I have offered makes it clear that many current criticisms of his theology as irretrievably modern oversimplify his thought.[1] Postmodernism is my conversation partner not because it is the measure of theology, but because it is an important trend in contemporary intellectual life. As Rahner consistently engaged the

---

1 Such is the inherent weakness in arguments that dismiss particular thinkers by subsuming them within types to be rejected. Few influential authors submit to typologies without resistance.

current ideas and movements that were influencing Christians in his lifetime, I seek to engage today's ideas with his work.

To do this, I begin by offering a brief description of the amorphous and multiple perspectives, methods, and strategies that are loosely categorized as "postmodern." This is undoubtedly a mere sketch, and surely unnecessary for many readers, yet I believe it provides a useful starting point. I then rehearse a number of the prominent criticisms of Rahner's theological anthropology that are rooted in postmodern sensibilities. After addressing these criticisms specifically from the interpretation of Rahner provided above, I provide a broader assessment of Rahner's theology in a contemporary context. I argue that while Rahner is not postmodern, he also cannot be flatly characterized as a modern thinker whose insights and methods have been superseded.

## MODERNITY, POSTMODERNITY, AND HUMAN KNOWING

Postmodernism is a sustained critique of modernity, focused on exposing the unstated, repressed conditions and assumptions of modern cultural and intellectual discourse. This critique happens in various ways, in many different fields and disciplines, from architecture and theater to philosophy and theology. In this brief sketch, I use "postmodern" as an umbrella term to indicate the work of several disparate authors who could be more specifically termed deconstructionist or post-structuralist, thus generating an appearance of singularity that sacrifices specificity for clarity. Also, I focus primarily on postmodern concerns that serve to critique and question Rahner's theological anthropology.

While many of modernity's unacknowledged assumptions have deep roots in Greek thought going back to Plato, several of these assumptions gain new importance beginning with René Descartes. Descartes wrote in the 17th century during a time of tremendous social and cultural upheaval: there had been nearly a hundred years of religious warfare in Europe; there was an explosion of scientific knowledge in areas including chemistry, biology, anatomy, astronomy, and physics; religious and ethnic diversity was becoming more a part of daily life; and the governmental and economic structures of European countries were in transition. In this context, Descartes wanted to find certainty, to locate some touchstone of truth that could be both universally applicable and universally accessible.

Descartes' famous epistemological conversion took place in 1619, when he sat in a stove-heated room and attempted to doubt all things in order to find some sure foundation upon which to build human knowledge. He wanted to abstract himself from all cultural prejudices and bodily sensation. Descartes' method aimed at certainty, accepted the indubitable, and did not question clear and distinct ideas. He found his indubitable starting point in his own self-presence, declaring, "I think, therefore I am." By using this method, Descartes attained what he considered to be certainty concerning the existence of the soul, the existence of God, and the proportions of a triangle within his own mind. He writes:

> I saw clearly that, if we assume a triangle as given, its three angles would have to be equal to two right angles; however, for all that, I saw nothing that convinced me that there was any triangle in the world. In contrast, when I returned again to examine the idea I had of a perfect being, I found that existence was included in it in the same way as, or even more evidently than, the idea of a triangle includes its three angles being equal to two right angles or the idea of a sphere includes the equidistance from its centre of all its parts [on the surface] and that, consequently, it is at least as certain as any geometrical demonstration could ever be that God, who is this perfect being, is or exists. (Descartes 1999, 27)

Descartes stove-side epiphany had a deep influence on modern thought. He bequeathed to modernity an understanding of knowledge that focuses on the self-presence of the subject; that seeks certainty; that presupposes a dualistic understanding of the human person as individual, autonomous, and essentially rational; and that believes in the possibility of knowledge untainted by cultural prejudice. David Tracy writes:

> René Descartes spoke for the entire modern era when he pleaded for certainty, clarity, and distinctness. He spoke again on behalf of modernity when he pleaded for a method grounded in the subjects' self-presence, a method, in principle, that would prove the same for all thinking, rational persons. The drive to clarity, the turn to the subject, the concern with method, the belief in sameness—mod-

ern thinkers embraced and embrace all these ideals in modernity's working out of its unique history. (Tracy 1994, 104)

These principles and presuppositions, exemplified and strengthened by Descartes, continue through modernity in various forms and guises.

Postmodernism has its roots in thinkers throughout modernity and gained significant momentum in the works of authors such as Wittgenstein, Hans Georg Gadamer, and Martin Heidegger. It became more of an identifiable (although not easily circumscribable) intellectual movement in the final quarter of the twentieth century, notably with writers such as Jacques Derrida, Emmanuel Levinas, and Luce Irigaray. Postmodernism includes a wide range of works in a plethora of different disciplines. It coheres, however, as an attempt to identify the unacknowledged, forgotten, or repressed conditions of modernity. To use Heidegger's phrase, it is an effort to "think the unthought of modernity" (Tracy 1994, 108).

## BEING

One way of approaching this complex bundle of criticisms is through ontology, or the philosophical understanding of being. Postmodern thinkers point out that modern ontology and metaphysics are actually deeply theological.[2] Western metaphysics has understood being as that property common to all entities (Chauvet 1995, 26, 27). It further follows a pattern of logic focused on causal relationships, such that the being that is present in all entities must have its source in some foundational Being or source of being which is itself uncaused. Thus Western ontology posits an uncaused Being (unmoved mover, first cause, the Good, the One, etc.) as both the source of all being and the ultimate rationale and telos of all being. "This," says Heidegger, is the equivalent to naming the metaphysical concept for God" (quoted in Chauvet 1995, 27). The philosophical discourse about being is thereby already invested in a theological concept of God; it is from the beginning an onto-theo-logic.

---

2 This analysis was spearheaded by Heidegger (1968, 294). I am here relying on Louis-Marie Chauvet (1995, 27). Chauvet's description is impressively clear, straightforward, and helpful. The focus on Thomas Aquinas and Heidegger is particularly useful to students of Rahner.

By this critique, metaphysics functions with an unquestioned logic of foundation and causality that drives it to affirm a God who guarantees stability, presence, and similarity. Everything comes from the same foundational, causal source, and therefore everything can be compared, ordered, and ranked within a closed system (Chauvet 1995, 27). Louis-Marie Chauvet writes:

> Because of its exclusive fixation on the being of entities, metaphysics is to be placed at the level of a "technique of explanation of reality by means of ultimate causes." The god it posits appears only in the perspective of a *causality* working as a foundation. The entire discussion is distorted by the passion to master the truth. Such an ambition inevitably degrades the truth into an unfailingly available foundation, a substantial permanence, an objective presence. This need for a reassuring plenitude is symptomatic of a visceral *anthropocentrism*: the need to begin with the certitude of the self, with the presence of the self to the self, by which everything else in the world is ultimately to be measured. In this manner, everything "is ordered," everything is justified, everything has good reasons to be and to be there as present. From the notion of being-as-substance as present permanence to the notion of the subject-substance as permanent presence, it is the same logic at work, a logic of the Same unfolding itself: a utilitarian logic which, because of fear of all difference, of what is by its nature permanently open, and finally of death, reduces being to its own rationality and, unknowingly, makes of it the glue that bonds a closed totality. (28)[3]

While this pattern was already deeply embedded within Western thought long before Descartes, the quest for certainty, which took definitive modern shape in the turn to the subject he articulated, fortifies the onto-theo-logical pattern of thought that both relies on a concept of God and denies that it does so. Recall that Descartes felt he was able to logically deduce—in a fashion claiming to be divorced from all cultural and societal prejudices—the existence of the human soul, of God, and of the proportions of a triangle within his own mind. The existence of a triangle outside of his mind proved more difficult to establish since sense perceptions were always subject to doubt. In fact, in order to attain certainty on this matter, Descartes makes a small

---

3 Chauvet quotes Heidegger, *Lettre sur li'humanisme*, Q. 3, 80.

detour, anchoring his affirmation of objective knowledge of external reality on the trustworthiness of God. He writes:

> the very thing that I had accepted as a rule above—viz. that the things we conceive clearly and distinctly are all true—is guaranteed only because God is or exists, that he is a perfect being, and that everything in us derives from him....But if we did not know that any reality or truth in us comes from God, then no matter how clear and distinct our ideas might be, we would have no reason that would convince us that they had the perfection of being true. (28, 29)

According to Descartes, we can know that such a triangle exists and has certain proportions because God does not deceive us. The theological character of this particular originary moment of modern epistemology does not take center stage. Postmodernism claims that even, and perhaps especially, when it is not acknowledged, modern understandings of knowledge rely on an unexamined theological affirmation of a particular view of God for stability and completeness.

It must be acknowledged that modern epistemology and the presuppositions that undergird it have a lot of benefits. The ideals of equality and freedom are part of the modern legacy. The assumption of a common, essential humanity can enable strong ethical and normative claims. However, there are costs to this kind of epistemology as well. Many postmodernists explore the ways in which difference has been denied in modernity. The stability and certainty that modernity seeks is found in a hierarchical ordering of beings who are all, at bottom, the same. This abstract pattern of thought plays out, many claim, in concrete political, economic, military, and social realities that have difficulty acknowledging, and are often actively engaged in suppressing, real difference. Difference can only be understood, within this system, as a lesser or defective form of the same. Modern epistemology's privileging of the disembodied, rational knowledge of the individual renders many other forms of knowledge (including those that are embodied and/or communal) illegitimate. Furthermore, the combination of modernity's desire for sameness and its focus on the rational, autonomous self has made the systematic exclusion (in varying degrees of severity and violence) of whole groups of people (who are seen as lesser, defective, less rational, more bodily, etc. etc.) thinkable and possible within a worldview that understands itself as upholding the principles of freedom and equality for all.

## LANGUAGE

In connection with an analysis of metaphysics as onto-theo-logy, postmodernism also focuses on an analysis of language. Often modernity operates with an assumption that the human person has pre-linguistic knowledge and experiences that are then expressed through language. Language serves this instrumental function by referring: a word makes sense by pointing towards a thing or experience that is fundamentally outside of language. Language is a tool made up of signs that have meaning insofar as they refer to that which is signified.

In this view, language is a useful instrument for communicating meanings that already exist before language. However, it is not entirely adequate. There are times when language cannot fully express what is intended, such that language is both an instrument and an obstacle to communication. "The ideal," writes Chauvet, "impossible in this world, would thus be to *dispense with* language altogether—just as to dispense with the body—in order to benefit directly by the light of the immanent meaning" (33).

Note that this understanding of language is also anchored and stabilized by an underlying, often unacknowledged, view of God. God is the source of meaning, foundation for knowledge that is universally true, the single arbiter of singular Truth. God is the "transcendental signified," that which is never a sign for something else but rather is the anchor that holds the whole system together. God—that which is the ultimately real, the highest Good, which defines pure reason and thought—exists outside of language, time, matter, and culture.

Postmodernists offer differing views of language. Many share certain similarities, including the claim that meaning does not pre-exist language, but is rather generated in and through discourse. This generation of meaning does not happen through reference to that which is signified so much as through the interplay of signs. It is in the relationship between words within the complexities of discourse that meaning takes shape. Clearly, in this kind of view, language is not an instrument used by human persons to express their pre-linguistic knowledge. On the contrary, knowledge is constructed in language, as are human persons.

What we know, how we know, and who we are as knowers all come to be in language. We come into a world that is already a world of language, in which the ways of knowing and patterns of thinking are already established in the discourse we inhabit. It is an indication of how thoroughly we are shaped by and in language that we cannot simply choose to think otherwise. Instead, the reality that cultural meanings have been discursively produced over time is forgotten—the way the world appears to us is seen as natural, as the only possible way of seeing the world. From a postmodern perspective, truth and meaning are culturally and discursively produced over time. The triumph of modernity is that it has forgotten this, generating an onto-theo-logy that declares truth, meaning, and thought to be prior to language and history. Chauvet states:

> Metaphysics thus reveals itself, according to its most characteristic tendency, as the logic of a discourse which conceals the original moment of its own knowledge, forgetting…that the subject who does the enunciating is never completely separate from the linguistic subject of its statements—in short, that humans never utter their judgments from a distant height and with a sovereign neutrality, but rather start with a concrete language in which a universe is already structured into a "world," that is, from a place that is socially arranged and culturally organized. (36)

One postmodern author I find compelling on issues of language and identity is the French feminist theorist Luce Irigaray. She paints a picture of the Western world where the language we think in is organized around apparent binary oppositions that are hierarchically ordered. Thus, in common thought and practice, "stop" is the opposite of "go," "dark" is the opposite of "light," "no" is the opposite of "yes," and "women" are the opposite of "men." Irigaray argues that while the difference between these binary terms is needed to stabilize the identity of each term, Western language and metaphysical thinking quickly suppresses real difference. If there were real difference, we would have apples and oranges that could not be compared. But we do not really think that way. In each binary opposition one term is clearly known to be an absence, negation, or inferior version of the other—to stop is not to go, dark is the absence of light, women are inferior men. While these pairs are identified by our culture as opposites, in reality Western culture will not allow that much difference. The "lesser" members of each pair are really inferior reflections of the "better" members.

The hierarchical ranking in each binary pair coordinates with a larger view of the world in which everything can be hierarchically ranked— such that rocks are less than grass and trees are less than squirrels and dolphins are less than humans. In turn, this great hierarchy of being is based on a larger binarism between creation and creator, between everything else and God. All of creation is a kind of inferior reflection of God. In Irigaray's analysis of the Western world, difference is needed to create and shore up identity, but difference must be suppressed so everything can be compared and ranked from best to worst. This entire system is anchored by a picture of God, understood in traditional Western terms as single, unchangeable, all-powerful, fount of all knowledge.

Irigaray contends that this view of the universe is so pervasive, and so permeates the way we communicate through language, that as infants we start learning this from our first breath. It shapes our ways of knowing the world and constructs our identities such that we cannot imagine something radically different. Even our most creative and disruptive visions of utopia will always bear the marks of this system in which our minds were formed. Any attempts to radically change the world—for example, to create gender equality—would need to somehow subvert or disrupt this whole huge system. The first step in subverting the system is to remember and recognize that the system is a human production, generated culturally and discursively over time (Irigaray 1985, 243-364).[4]

## BEING AND LANGUAGE

Another important author who addresses similar issues in language is Jacques Derrida. His works highlight many of the interconnections between postmodern discourses about being and about language. He recognizes that modernity understands language as gaining meaning in the process of a sign referring to that which is signified. "For the

---

4 Irigaray offers more essentialist views of the self and the possibility of utopic visions in other writings, such as Irigaray (1993).

signification 'sign' has always been understood and determined, in its meaning, as sign-of, a signifier referring to a signified, a signifier different from its signified" (Derrida 1978, 281). Further, language as a whole is seen as a coherent system, organized around a central, stable, grounding point of presence. This central point provides the possibility of language and also its limits. Derrida deconstructs this view of language, in part by noting that the center of the system—the point of pure presence—must also be thought of as outside the system of language altogether. He writes: "Thus it has always been thought that the center, which is by definition unique, constituted that very thing within a structure which while governing the structure, escapes structurality. This is why classical thought concerning structure could say that the center is, paradoxically, *within* the structure and *outside it*" (279).

However, Derrida points out that the idea of a center that is both at the center of the system and escapes the system is a contradiction. He writes, "The concept of centered structure—although it represents coherence itself, the condition of the *epistémé* as philosophy or science—is contradictorily coherent" (279). This understanding of language as a coherent system governed by a stable center is, Derrida argues, produced by human desire for certainty, by a desire to alleviate anxiety through the identification of a ground and goal that is fully present. The center has received different names throughout the history of Western thought, all of which have indicated "an invariable presence," all of which have participated in a "determination of Being as *presence* in all senses of this word" (279). These names include: "essence, existence, substance, subject…transcendentality, consciousness, God, man, and so forth" (280).

Derrida continues by describing this center as:

> a central presence which has never been itself, has always already been exiled from itself into its own substitute. The substitute does not substitute itself for anything which has somehow existed before it. Henceforth, it was necessary to begin thinking that there was no center…that the center had no natural site, that it was not a fixed locus but a function, a sort of nonlocus in which an infinite number of sign-substitutions came into play. (280)

This same idea can be approached from a slightly different direction. Understanding the meaning of language not to be produced by a process of referring, Derrida instead sees it as produced by a process of play between and among signs that are not anchored to a stable center, a function of the differences among signs. In this view, the traditional distinction and opposition between signs and signifieds breaks down. Every sign is also a signified and every signified is also a sign. There is no signified that does not participate in the play of signs—there is no signified that is "absolutely present outside a system of differences" (280).

Both ways of approaching this idea—that the center is in exile and that every signified is also a sign—indicate that the "transcendental signified," that point of pure presence to govern the structure while remaining outside it, is absent. This, as a point about language, is also a point about being. For Derrida, the uncovering of the absence of the transcendental signified necessitates a critique of understanding being in terms of presence. This implies a theological critique of understandings of God as a supreme being or pure presence that guarantees language without ever being contained within it.

Again remembering that there are many different postmodern perspectives, it is possible to note certain concerns common among several of them, certain ways of thinking typical of modern onto-theo-logic that raise postmodern suspicions. These include, predictably, any conception of a natural, stable, unitary foundation of truth and/or being that can serve as an anchor and guarantee of human knowing. Given postmodern analysis of how pervasive onto-theo-logic is, there is a suspicion both of engaging in traditional metaphysics and of imagining that one can escape or avoid traditional metaphysics. As postmodernists are wary of any account of being that re-inscribes a logic of the same, so they are wary of any account of history which attempts to apply a singular goal or pattern universally, any "grand narrative." In regards to human persons, postmodernity tends to avoid any description of a universal essence of humanity, since such essentializing views presuppose a human subjectivity prior to language, culture, and history. Also, essentialist pictures of humanity portray everyone as ultimately the same, a logic that participates in the degradation of those who are or appear different. Instead, many postmodernists speak of the self as socially constructed, as coming to be in society over time.[5] Others de-

---

5 This will be discussed in more detail later in the chapter.

scribe the self as "performative," focusing on the ways in which who we are is not a pre-set essence but rather a series of improvisational enactments that take place within cultural situations, expectations, rituals, and traditions (Butler 1990).

## POSTMODERN QUESTIONS REGARDING RAHNER'S THEOLOGY

Many contemporary criticisms of Rahner's work are directed at his theological method. If Rahner is seen as a philosophical foundationalist whose work reinscribes the modern turn to the subject, this starts a domino cascade of criticisms. Rahner's anthropological starting point sounds like an echo of Descartes' stove-side epiphany at the beginning of the modern period. He begins with the individual subject and investigates how he knows. It is in the course of this epistemological query that Rahner finds, within the subject's own presence to himself, the infinite horizon which will later be called God. Fergus Kerr describes Rahner's picture of the human person as a "mentalist-individualist self," in whom "the capacity for self-presence in acts of knowledge is tacit apprehension of the absolute" (Kerr 1997a, 22). Kerr doubts that any theologian beginning in a place so similar to Descartes' could possibly avoid replicating the problematic elements of Cartesian thought. He writes:

> Consider the work of Karl Rahner, whom nobody would dispute is by far the most influential Roman Catholic theologian of the day. The speed with which he charms the reader into his system, and the immediate rewards in theological assurance, conceal, from readers who are philosophically unwary, the problematic character of the first step. The obsession with epistemological preliminaries, which should at once indicate how Cartesian his theological constructions are likely to prove, only persuades students that they are on the right track....It is always as the cognitive subject that people first appear in Rahner's theology. Students alerted to the bias of the Cartesian legacy would suggest that language or action, conversation or collaboration, are more likely starting points...[y]et consciousness, self-awareness in the cognitive act, is always his favoured way into theology. (10)

Thus it can be argued that Rahner's anthropological starting point, his turn to the subject, necessarily shapes the rest of his theology such that it can only retrace the familiar steps of modernity. In such a reading, the experience of knowing, including the elements of transcendence and the supernatural existential, become the foundation, the universal touchstone upon which knowledge is built in the pursuit of certainty.

One of those steps understands humanity primarily in terms of the individual subject, instead of in terms of intersubjectivity or community. Many scholars claim that Rahner narrates a problematically individualistic account of personal identity. Reading Rahner's early philosophy as foundational to his theology makes any claims for the importance of intersubjectivity that come later in Rahner's work, such as in his description of love of neighbor, appear unconnected to the structure and system that undergirds his thought. After describing how Rahner's theology unfolds from his Cartesian understanding of knowledge, Kerr writes, "other people remain marginal to his epistemology" (12). Mark Lloyd Taylor gives a helpful summary of many critiques and rebuttals on this issue by Rahner interpreters. He notes that even those scholars who defend Rahner as aiming "to integrate an understanding of the importance of the interpersonal aspect of human being into his anthropology," also admit "this integration is not fully successful" (Taylor 1986, 65).

Rahner's individualistic account is often understood to apply to all of humanity by describing all persons as essentially the same. This can be broken down into two separate criticisms. The first is that Rahner universalizes, assuming that one picture of humanity fits all persons. Not only postmodernists, but also feminists, womanists, and mujerista theologians have all identified the difficulties that follow such presumption. Any author who attempts, from his own particular standpoint, to describe what is universally true about humanity, runs a strong risk of merely generalizing from his own experience and assuming everyone else is fundamentally like him. If this is presented as an adequate account of humanity, then everyone who does not fit within this description is implied to be less than fully human. This is another appearance of the modern logic of the same.

Rahner gives an account of humanity that is based on his own experience of being an educated, middle-class, religious white German

man. Is it not quite likely that there are people, all over the world but also, perhaps, on the other side of any given town in Germany, who do not experience themselves in the same way Rahner does? Perhaps a mother of three young children, constantly involved in fiercely embodied and radically communal ways of being in the world, does not spend the quiet moments of her day when she is nursing a child at her breast in reflections that can be captured by Rahner's existentialist description of the human person as a free question. Such different ways of being—and more importantly for Rahner, of knowing, willing, loving, and experiencing grace—are ignored or marginalized in an universal account of humanity.

The other problematic element in Rahner's single description of all human persons is that he gives an essentialist account of humanity. This means that Rahner describes the human person by attempting to identify those characteristics that are definitive of humanity, those essentials without which we would not be human. Such a description assumes that what it means to be human is given at birth—inborn and innate before the influence of culture, society, and language. Humanity's essential identity is a pre-given factor that remains unchanged, not something that is shaped and constructed over time.

Essentialism entails the same problems as universal description and then some. It assumes a logic of the same that disallows real difference among persons, just like universal description. Additionally, essentialism goes one step further in concretizing the degradation of those who are different by claiming that those who are different (remember that within the metaphysical logic of the same this means "inferior") are essentially so. Concretely, essentialism has played and continues to play a significant role in the oppression of women, people of color, and others.[6] Philosophically, it is built upon an understanding of the self as having a preset identity, thus minimizing or negating the importance of culture, history, and language.

Rahner's theological anthropology is most often read as clearly essentialist. Rahner's approach to theological anthropology attempts to

---

6 See Jones (2000, 24-31) Jones presents an excellent and accessible discussion of essentialism and constructivism. While she uses essentialism and universalism interchangeably, I find it pragmatically helpful to treat them separately in discussing Rahner's work.

identify the structures of the human person that make knowing, loving, willing, and the experience of grace possible. This approach certainly seems to indicate that there are certain structures of humanity that are hardwired. Rahner's language concerning these characteristics of humanity is often couched in essentialist terms. He writes about the *a priori*, necessary and inalienable structures of the self and at times refers to "man's essential being" (Rahner 1982, 25).

The existential of transcendence is particularly central to Rahner's understanding of the human person. He says that the human subject is "fundamentally and by its very nature pure openness for absolutely everything" (20). This transcendence is so definitive of what it means to be human, in Rahner's writings, that it is hard to understand this description as anything other than an essentialist claim.

These criticisms all claim that Rahner's method and theological anthropology pay inadequate attention to differences among persons and to the influence of culture and history. On such a reading, Rahner's theology is incompatible with an understanding of human identity as socially constructed, and participates in modernity's dismissal of many ways of knowing beyond the individual, rationalistic, and speculative.

A related criticism of Rahner's theology bears specifically on the issue at hand, namely, how we say "yes" to God. While Rahner often talks about saying "yes" in relationships and in actions, many scholars perceive him as starting with such a deeply individualist and subject-centered anthropology that this must be understood in expressivist terms. The freedom Rahner speaks of as enacted throughout a whole life is actually a radically individual, internal freedom that is only expressed historically and interpersonally. David Kelsey writes:

> Rahner construes these "acts of free decision" as interior and subjective or, we might say, "mental" acts. As such they are quite "private." Our public action, bodily and overt, is not so much the effect of these internal acts as the manifestation or expression of our interior and subjective acts. Further, Rahner is well known for insisting that the relation of our overt and public behavior to our inner and private acts of decision is highly ambiguous. (Kelsey 1997, 367)[7]

Another way of putting this criticism is to say that at times it seems that humanity's real freedom takes place transcendentally and is only

---

7  See also Rahner (1983g, 72, 73).

then played out categorically. This concern is related to the issues of expressivism discussed earlier in relation to language and experience and in conversation with Lindbeck. Many of Rahner's statements sound expressivist. For example, he writes, "By its very nature as an act of the subject, therefore, freedom does not take place in the individualizing, isolating and so observable, empirical world of the individual sciences....For whenever I act freely as a subject, I always act into an objective world, I always, as it were, leave my freedom and enter into the necessities of this world" (Rahner 1982, 96, 97).[8]

An expressivist view makes it quite difficult to describe what happens categorically and historically to human persons as having any great effect on their transcendental freedom. Freedom seems not only essential, but inviolable. While Rahner does infrequently address questions about how human freedom can be affected, the bulk of his theology does not directly address these issues. One more often encounters statements that emphasize human freedom. For example, in a list of examples of experiences of the Holy Spirit, Rahner includes, "where a man experiences and accepts his ultimate freedom, which no earthly compulsions can take away from him" (Rahner 1992a, 83).[9]

Christian ethicist Jennifer Beste launches a similar criticism of Rahner in concrete terms, evaluating Rahner's theological anthropology in the light of victims of long-term incest and the trauma they experience. She argues that Rahner's claims about personal freedom and his call to interpersonal love do not adequately account for the harm done to incest victims (Beste 2003a). Looking closely at the physical and psychological effects of long-term sexual abuse on the embodied human person, Beste argues that the ability to enact loving openness to the other, which Rahner identifies as the primary way in which humans say "yes" to God's offer of salvation, can be profoundly damaged and possibly destroyed by such trauma. She states, "In many of his writings, Rahner implies that a person's capacity to receive and accept God's grace is invulnerable to earthly contingencies" (10). Beste contends that the experiences of incest victims "testify to the damage that

---

8 See also Rahner (1971b, 287, 288).

9 See also Rahner (1967c, 151, 152), where he states that "one must not overrate the significance of the difference in external situation for the proper achievement of man's existence."

interpersonal harm can have on one's capacity to receive God's grace in any active sense at all" (10). It is, in her view, ethically irresponsible to deny the depth of the harm that we can inflict upon one another by positing an aspect of the self that somehow remains immune.[10]

These various, related criticisms claim that Rahner sees the human subject as basically given—a stable, autonomous, individual subject who has inviolable personal freedom and whose embodiment is secondary to his identity. Language is a tool for such a subject, and culture is a context in which his stable identity can play itself out. Rahner does not, according to the most stringent criticisms of his work, have a way to account for human subjectivity coming to be in and through culture, language, history, and society.

These contentions are connected to a well known criticism of Rahner's work, which comes from his student, J.B. Metz, and was briefly mentioned in Chapter Three. Metz argues that Rahner's theology does not take adequate account of history, in two different, related ways. First, Metz claims that Rahner's presentation of salvation does not offer enough focus on the concrete realities of salvation history. Rahner narrates the salvific action of God primarily in terms of offering grace to humanity in the supernatural existential, present always and everywhere, instead of describing God's historical relation with the Hebrew people and the salvific import of the concrete, historical birth, life, crucifixion, and resurrection of Jesus. Thus Metz voices the concern that Rahner's speculative thought and transcendental method describe Christianity such that "the historical identity of Christian faith" might be understood as "fixed, in this theory, to a basic anthropological structure, according to which man is 'always already,' whether he wants to be or not, 'with God.'" (Metz 1980, 172). Second, and more importantly, Metz claims that concrete history is not fully attended to in Rahner's presentation of how human beings accept God's offer of salvation. This is the heart of his critique of Rahner. Metz states, "[m]y criticism, then, is principally directed against the attempt to explain the historical identity of Christianity by means of speculative thought (idealism), without regard to the constitutive function

---

10  I have learned a great deal from conversations with Beste concerning these issues.

of Christian praxis, the cognitive equivalent of which is narrative and memory" (173).

His favorite way of explaining this criticism was to tell a German fairy tale about a hedgehog and a hare. The slow hedgehog challenges the speedy hare to a race in a furrow of a field. The hedgehog's wife, who looks exactly the same as her husband, then stands at one end of the furrow while her husband stands at the other. The hare runs back and forth, at each point seeing the hedgehog already ahead at the end of the furrow, until the hare dies of exhaustion. The hedgehog and his wife have outsmarted the hare and can win by standing still. Metz worries that Rahner's transcendental approach to Christianity works a bit like the hedgehogs' trick. He writes, "Is not...the threatened historical identity of Christianity guaranteed for a too high price: the price of confusing identity with tautology?" (174). This account of Christianity, he fears, negates the necessity of running the furrow, entering the risky field of historical identity. Instead, it declares "one hedgehog is exactly the same as the other, the beginning is like the end, paradise is like the end of time, creation is like the fulfillment and at the end the beginning repeats itself. History itself—with its forms of identity that are constantly threatened and in danger of being overcome—cannot intervene" (175).

Other scholars who, like Metz, acknowledge the importance and positive influence of Rahner's work, also note this problem. Miguel Díaz, author of a book that explores theological anthropology from both U.S. Hispanic and Rahnerian perspectives, writes, "While Rahner recognized readily that as spirit-in-the-world the person encounters self and God in and through his or her concrete ordinary communal life experiences, Rahner did not go far enough in terms of exploring the particularities of such encounter" (Díaz 2001, 131). Díaz' critique moves directly to the most concrete difficulties with this view, stating that Rahner's understanding of the human subject, "though *theologically* indispensable, comes across as being ethically neutral and lacking sufficient historical specificity" (131).

Metz is not a postmodernist. However, it is perhaps telling that the most prominent criticism of Rahner's work is that he does not adequately address historical identity. Many of the questions that arise from a postmodern consideration of Rahner's theology are, in a sense,

radicalizations of this critique. In general, postmodernists view meaning and identity as historically produced. If one reads Rahner as performing a version of the hedgehogs' trick, it seems that he neglects
such historical and cultural production of meaning and identity.

Another form of this critique is given in contemporary terms by
John Milbank.[11] His book, *Theology and Social Theory: Beyond Secular Reason*, provides a sweeping rejection of modern secular reasoning
from a Christian perspective deeply influenced by postmodernism.
Milbank contends that a number of assumptions inherent to modern
secular discourse arise in conflict with orthodox Christianity. Christian theology allows its own secularization and limitation either by
participating in some form of natural theology, such that it "connects
knowledge of God with some particular immanent field of knowledge," or by consigning the holy to a realm "beyond representation"
and thereby accepting the concept of an autonomous, rational, rep-
resentable secular realm (Milbank 1990, 1). For Christian theology
to reclaim its rightful place as a metadiscourse, it must resist both of
these forms of secular positioning, neither subsuming itself within a
secular, rational discourse or confining itself to a distinct sacred realm
and abdicating its larger role.

Within this larger analysis of Christian theology and social theory,
Milbank's general interpretation of Rahner combines several of the
criticisms mentioned above. Rahner's method is flawed because it sub-
mits to secular reason. This leads to an ahistorical and overly individualistic theology. Milbank deems Rahner's conception of the supernatural existential a failed attempt to avoid extrinsicism that results
in the naturalization of the supernatural and effectively "*denaturalizes*
history, and so ignores actually constituted human nature altogether"
(223). Milbank's version of the critique first offered by Metz is that
"Karl Rahner fears to entrust the supernatural to the merely historical,
to the succession of human actions and human images" (223).

Milbank goes on to denounce political and liberation theologies
that bear Rahnerian influence, asserting that because of their debt to
Rahner, these theologies remain "trapped within the terms of 'secular

---

11   While I draw connections between Milbank's critique and that of Metz,
it should be noted that Milbank criticizes Metz as well as Rahner. See Milbank (1990, 238-40).

reason' and its unwarranted foundationalist presuppositions" (207).
He claims that Rahner's thought leads to theology in which

> the social is an autonomous sphere which does not need to turn
> to theology for its self-understanding, and yet it is already a grace-
> imbued sphere, and therefore it is *upon* pre-theological sociology
> or Marxist social theory, that theology must be founded. In conse-
> quence, a theological critique of society becomes impossible. And,
> therefore what we are offered is *anything but* a true theology of the
> political. Theological beliefs themselves, however much a formal or-
> thodoxy may still be espoused, tend to become but a faint regulative
> gloss upon Kantian ethics and a somewhat eclectic, though basically
> Marxist, social theory. (208)

While political and liberation theologies involve further emphasis on
human sociality and ethics, Milbank declares that their Rahnerian
categories effectively either reduce human transcendence to secular
ethics or to individual ethical motivation, viewing salvation either as
a liberating social process or as an individual surmounting of human
finitude. He writes:

> For political and liberation theology therefore, the ethical belongs
> to the social, but both remain essentially apart from the 'religious,'
> which is either their anonymous secret, or else a categorically sepa-
> rate dimension of 'experience.' But the belief in a 'natural' morality,
> essentially unaffected by religious belief, and shared in common
> with all humanity, goes along with a thoroughly unhistorical view
> of ethics. (230)

Thus Milbank argues that salvation remains relegated to a particular,
separate religious dimension for political and liberation theologians,
and within this it remains an asocial concept that applies to the experience of the individual.

Due to these criticisms and others, some scholars influenced by
postmodern analysis of modernity dismiss Rahner as an outdated
theologian whose work is no longer relevant. Much of this dismissal
is ultimately rooted in particular views of Rahner's methodology. As
discussed in Chapter One, it is not necessary to interpret Rahner as
a philosophical foundationalist. I have offered a different reading of
Rahner that does not view him as such. Does such a shift in interpretation change the impact of the specific criticisms leveled above?

## READING RAHNER IN A NEW KEY

To address these questions, note the historical situation in which Rahner is writing and some of his major intellectual and spiritual influences. Rahner is part of the second generation of Roman Catholic thinkers self-consciously trying to bring traditional church theology into conversation with modern philosophy.[12] Thus he is deeply engaged with the very tenets of modernism, which profoundly affects the shape and substance of his theology. Rahner's modern influences include the whole of modern German philosophy and specifically Kant, Idealism, and Existentialism. Rahner's influences also include pre-modern figures who, while participating in traditions of Greek metaphysical thinking that postmodernism would identify as a problematic foundation of modern thought, are not in themselves modern, specifically Thomas Aquinas and Ignatius of Loyola. Perhaps especially in their spiritualities, these figures cannot be subsumed into the world of modernity. Finally, Rahner is a student of Heidegger, whose work can be seen as early postmodernism, particularly his work on being (Tracy 1994, 107).

Rahner is quite aware of both the problems and possibilities of modernity's turn to the subject. He sees "modern philosophy's transcendental anthropological change of direction since Descartes" as "[w]ith few exceptions…profoundly un-Christian in so far as it pursues a transcendental philosophy of the autonomous subject, who stands aloof from the transcendental experience in which he experiences himself as continually dependent, with his origin in and orientation towards God" (Rahner 1972e, 38-39). At the same time, he recognizes this tradition of philosophy as being "most profoundly Christian" in understanding that humanity "is not ultimately one factor in a cosmos of things…but the subject on whose freedom as subject hangs the fate of the whole cosmos" (39). With such a view of both the costs and benefits of modern philosophy's anthropological approach, Rahner writes that theology can neither return to a pre-modern approach, nor jump beyond modernity directly into whatever is to follow (38, 39).[13]

---

12   See (Vorgrimler 1986, 52 ff).

13   Rahner's sense of the necessity of bringing Roman Catholic church theology into conversation with modernity is seen clearly here. He writes,

Rahner begins with the human subject, in part, in order to address the modern tradition from Descartes onwards, perhaps most particularly from Kant, Maréchal, and Heidegger. However, he does not simply reiterate modern philosophy. It is important to note that Rahner also has spiritual and pastoral concerns guiding his choice of entry into theology. Spiritually, Rahner begins with affirmation of the experience of God, an affirmation Rahner credits to Ignatius.[14] Rahner turns to the subject, in part, in order to affirm that God is involved with the human subject (Kerr 1997a, 7; Rahner 1972e, 38). He wants to portray grace as something connected to everyday life and relevant to ordinary existence. Grace is not, for Rahner, an object or event foreign to mundane reality, the existence of which the Church might either succeed or fail to convince us of, but rather is something we can learn to recognize as an integral part of our run-of-the-mill experiences. Thus Rahner's turn to the subject takes place in a context of internal apologetics, with a concern to articulate carefully the relationship between nature and grace.[15] Rahner writes, "If what 'grace' is must not merely be expressed in a mythological-sounding verbalism which communicates no experi-

> But this does not alter the fact (even if the kind of philosophy studied in the Church has only taken notice of it in the last forty years or so) that philosophy today and hence theology too *cannot* and must not return to the stage before modern philosophy's transcendental anthropological change of direction since Descartes, Kant, German Idealism (including its opponents), up to modern Phenomenology, existentialism and Fundamental Ontology. (1972e, 38)

And:

> If it is the case that Christian Neo-Scholastic Philosophy, together with theology, have been mostly asleep during the modern period, they cannot be spared the task set by modern philosophy on the grounds that perhaps this philosophy is declining in its contemporary form: the lost ground must be at least made up if theology is really to do justice to the spirit of the age which is to *follow* the 'modern period.' (39)

14   For in-depth analysis of Rahner's use of Ignatius, see Endean (2001). On the subject of immediate experience of God, see particularly 21.

15   Kerr, in a later book that takes a more positive view of Rahner's theology, summarizes this nicely (1997b, 178-180). Another useful summary is given in Dych (1992, 32-46). See also Reno (1995).

ence, it can only be understood from the point of view of the subject…"
(Rahner 1972e, 36).

In order to understand grace in a non-extrinsic fashion that will
resonate with people in the contemporary world, Rahner concludes,
theology must participate (albeit critically) in this modern turn. However, as I have maintained throughout this book, in keeping with other
contemporary scholarship on Rahner, it is not necessary to understand
Rahner's turn to the subject as a philosophically foundationalist move.
Rahner has no intention of spinning out the truths of Christianity
from within the mind of the human subject, nor does he imagine that
indubitable clarity is the goal in regard to religious truth and spiritual
knowledge.[16]

While this nuances Rahner's choice to start with the human, what
about his choice to start with the individual? The sting of this particular criticism—that Rahner gives an individualist account of the self to
which other persons always remain marginal—is much abated when
one refuses to simplify Rahner's theological method into an elabora-
tion of his early philosophical works. The recognition that his theology
was written in an unsystematic, occasional, mystagogical, and apologetic manner undercuts the contention that since he starts with the
individual human subject, he can never fully integrate intersubjectivity
into his theology. As Mark Lloyd Taylor writes, "If Rahner's view of
human intersubjectivity is inadequate because of the occasional style
of the essays in which it is elucidated, then Rahner's theology as a

---

16  Rahner writes:

> Of course one cannot demand (and it would be heretical Mod-
> ernism to do so) that the attempt must be made simply to deduce
> strictly all theological statements *from* man's experience of him-
> self as if they were the latter's objectifying conceptualisation and
> articulation. That is not what is meant, although this problem is
> more difficult than the traditional opponents of Modernism mostly
> think, for there *is* also an *experience* of grace, and this is the real,
> fundamental reality of Christianity itself. If we leave this question
> here, it must be remembered that the connections between man's
> experience of himself and the content of the statements of dogma
> must be conceived otherwise than simply as logical connections of
> deduction or explication. (1972e, 41, 42)

whole must be judged to be inadequate for the same reason" (Taylor 1986, 67).[17]

There are several essays, written throughout Rahner's career, in which he describes social relationality as integral to the human subject. As mentioned in Chapter Three, he portrays human transcendence as transcendence to the other. In an essay that was published in 1954, Rahner writes:

> The personal spirit is a spirit referred to others. An absolutely lonely spirit is a contradiction in itself and—so far as it is possible at all—is Hell....Where there is man, there is necessarily—not only in fact—*human* community, i.e. bodily personal community, personally spatio-temporal community. (Rahner 1961b, 287)

In at least one essay, Rahner responds directly to the charge that he neglects human intersubjectivity. He concedes that intersubjectivity was not "sufficiently prominent" in his account of humanity. However, he contends that "the criticism in its usual form is inaccurate and unjustified" (Rahner 1981c, 87 n.20).

Rahner's theology, while occasional, is consistent in its insistence that we become who we most truly are, most fully human, in saying "yes" to God's offer of self-communication, and that the primary way in which we make this response is by loving our neighbor. While Rahner's narration of the human person often does not begin with intersubjectivity, loving openness to the unmanipulable other forms the summit and goal of his account of human subjectivity. The human person becomes most fully herself in the act of loving her neighbor, which is also always an act of loving God. Thus the picture Rahner paints of the human subject is not a modern vision of solitary certainty in self-presence, but rather one in which the subject's relations to self, neighbor, and God are always interwoven and mutually interdependent.[18]

To the degree that Rahner's theology does follow a pattern that moves from the individualistic to the communal (even in narration), Miguel Díaz offers an insightful form of criticism. Díaz contends that the pattern of "movement from individual to community" is a perspective that does not resonate with the theological anthropology of Hispanic

---

17    Taylor gives a brief assessment of this type of criticism and his own defense of Rahner in 64-70.

18    See Rahner (1975c, 128). Taylor also notes this passage (1986, 68).

theologians. Díaz argues that Rahner "undoubtedly conceives person-hood and freedom in communal terms," and yet the movement of his theological anthropology contrasts with "U.S. Hispanic anthropology [that] accents the organic constitution of reality and underscores the individual as a unique expression of the whole" (Díaz, 2001, 132).[19] This analysis acknowledges the intersubjectivity in Rahner's work and does not reject his theology as a type of modern thought that has been surpassed. Instead, Díaz brings his work into constructive dialogue with Hispanic theologians, furthering both Rahner scholarship and Rahnerian theology.

In regards to the criticism that Rahner thus gives a universalizing description of humanity, I concur. Rahner explicates human existence as if it were always and everywhere the same. Furthermore, it is clear that the content and form of his theological anthropology are not shaped only by his method, particular historical concerns, and spiritu-al and apologetic commitments. They are also a reflection and exten-sion of Rahner's own experience, profoundly conditioned by his social and cultural location. Rahner's anti-elitist inclination and concomi-tant desire to articulate the experience of God in everyday, mundane existence, while admirable in many ways, also reveal his basic sense of a "normal" Christian life. He assumes that he can locate the ordinary and that such location requires no analysis of race, class, or gender. His view of which aspects of humanity deserve discussion indicates not only the theological traditions he works out of, but also his own biases.

I would like to add two comments to this view of Rahner's univer-salizing tendency. First, like many aspects of modernism, it has sig-nificant theological benefits. Milbank laments that modern theology abdicates the role of metadiscourse by positioning its own statements in relation to the authority of secular reason. While he includes Rah-ner in this analysis, the condemnation is unpersuasive. Rahner offers a sweeping vision of humanity and God, making theology the broader discourse that questions all regional discourses that arise. The genera-tion of a large framework for understanding the relationship between God and humanity allows Rahner to address many theological issues clearly and well. Contemporary theologians who try to avoid univer-

---

19   See also Nancy Pineda-Madrid (2005).

salizing and essentializing are finding that such avoidance comes at a cost of limiting the scope of theological claims that can be made.[20] Rahner's universalizing picture of humanity helps him to make normative claims regarding ethics, to declare unequivocally that every human being is called to a future with God, to rhetorically narrate a compelling vision of the relationship between God and humanity.

Second, insofar as this criticism is about the suppression of difference, it should be acknowledged that Rahner is open to, and appreciative of, many of other ways of doing theology. His openness to theological pluralism mitigates, to some extent, the totalizing power of his descriptions. His enthusiasm about Vatican II marking the beginning of a world church, his support of emerging Latin American liberation theologies, his support of the ordination of women, his support for theologians with whom he strongly disagrees, and his hope that the theology of the church could begin to build from the bottom up—all of these things show Rahner encouraging strong and different voices in the church. Rahner's own bold declaration of theology from his point of view is coupled with concrete efforts to help other people boldly declare theology from their points of view. Such practice is in keeping with what feminist theologian Beverly Wildung Harrison calls an *"academic-political practice of inclusion"* and shares many of the ethical concerns for difference are often expressed theoretically in postmodern texts (Wildung Harrison, 1999, 158).

Rahner understands both the benefits of a universalizing account of humanity in relation to God and the importance of multiple Christian theological perspectives. Endean relates that Rahner suggests a pluralist world might require "two forms of theology running parallel." One would "try to call on, to bring into play, and to answer in faith ('redeem') only that experience of existence which is nevertheless still common, and permanently so." The other form of theology would "courageously let itself disintegrate into a plurality of theologies" (Endean 2001, 257, 258).[21] Interestingly, Rahner's theology, as it fits within the prior form, helps to fund liberation and feminist theologies that often move toward the latter form. The broad framework of Rahner's the-

---

20  See Jones (1997, 33-53).

21  Endean quotes Rahner (1972d, 82) and (1981d, 99). See also Kilby (2004, 91-98).

ology provides, in Nancy Dallavalle's words, "a theological scaffolding that has proven fruitful for feminist constructive theology" (Dallavalle 2005, 268).[22] Dallavalle also notes that "Rahner's assertion of the human capacity for the self-communication of God opened the door for women to claim their experience as a starting point for theological reflection" (265).

Some scholars understand universalizing and essentializing as being the same thing, such that whenever someone describes what is always and everywhere true of humanity, they are describing elements of human nature that are essential (Jones 2000, 26). Traditional wisdom among Rahner scholars views his work as essentialist (Kerr 1997b, 174), and many scholars accept his "existentials" as being basically a list of essentials. However, while it is certainly possible to read Rahner as an essentialist, I contend that it is important to nuance this significantly.

Throughout his career, Rahner understood himself (and was understood by others (Vorgrimler 1986, 22, 23)) as addressing and reflecting on the average, normal person. Indeed, Rahner states clearly that a theological account of humanity must concern itself with the normal human experience.[23] While one may certainly question the categories of average and normal, and recognize the limited society in which Rahner's conception of these categories was formed, such criticisms of universalizing can be seen as significantly different from the charge of essentializing. One can read Rahner's description of humanity not as delineating essentials that exist prior to the exercise of freedom, but rather as general characteristics that mark human beings. The difference is that such a universalizing (but non-essentialist) view would

---

22  Dallavalle mentions, in particular, Anne Carr, *Transforming Grace: Christian Tradition and Women's Experience* (San Francisco: HarperSanFrancisco, 1988); Catherine M. LaCugna, ed., *Freeing Theology: The Essentials of Theology in Feminist Perspective* (San Francisco: HarperSanFrancisco, 1993); and Elizabeth A. Johnson, *She Who Is: The Mystery of God in Feminist Theological Discourse* (New York: Crossroad, 1993). Susan Abraham, *Identity, Ethics, and Nonviolence in Postcolonial Theory: A Rahnerian Theological Assessment* (New York: Palgrave Macmillan, 2007), models yet another form of dialogue with Rahner.

23  See Rahner (1983a, 237; 1982, 106).

not necessarily assume that intrinsic traits are hardwired into human nature. They could be the results of social construction.

One could see Rahner's existentials as descriptions of the constants exhibited by the process of social construction.[24] The products of social construction are fundamentally open to other persons. They are social beings who are finite, mortal, and marked by time. They have the freedom to decide—in their social contexts—to accept or reject their orientation to mystery. This includes the possibility that—in the context of corporate guilt and its objectifications—they might reject the most constitutive element of themselves, namely, that they are called to a future relationship with mystery.

Does viewing Rahner in this way undermine his intentions in addressing the nature/grace debate with his understanding of the supernatural existential? If so, then it would seem that understanding his work as non-essentialist would have multiple repercussions that would have to be examined further. However, I think that the supernatural existential is, perhaps, the best argument for my interpretation. To fulfill Rahner's desiderata regarding the nature/grace debate, the supernatural existential must be understood as not belonging to created nature as such but as a further gift from God, as intrinsically related to created human nature, and as always and everywhere present as the innermost constitutive element of human nature as it actually exists. As a gift from God that constitutes who we most truly are and is present always and everywhere, the supernatural existential certainly sounds "essential" to human nature. However, Rahner is clear that although it is, in the actuality of creation, what is most constitutive of our humanity, we could have been human without it. If it is an "essential" of our humanity, without which we could not have been human, then Rahner's point in the nature/grace debate is lost and the freedom of God's gracious offer is compromised. Furthermore, recall from the discussion of the Holy Spirit in Chapter Three how Rahner describes the causality behind the supernatural existential. The efficient cause is the universal salvific will of God. This exists in a relationship of mutual conditioning with the final cause, which is the concrete reality of Jesus Christ, enacted in history. Rahner writes,

---

24   I am grateful to David Kelsey for this idea, which we discussed in conversation on January 13, 2002.

"God's self-communication in grace comes to man not from 'Adam,' not from the beginning of the human race, but from the goal of this history, from the God-Man Jesus Christ" (Rahner 1982, 114). This means the final cause of the innermost constitutive element of human nature comes to be in history (185).

Another question to be raised is whether or not Rahner's language requires an essentialist interpretation of his work. He does write about "man's essential being" and he makes a list of existentials. However, some of the statements where Rahner writes explicitly in essentialist terms serve to complicate these terms and undermine any simplistic reading of them. For example, in *Foundations*, when he is first describing his hybrid transcendental methodology, Rahner explains that the Christian message presupposes certain things about the human subject and, at the same time, "the Christian message itself creates these presuppositions by its call" (24). He continues, "The presuppositions which are to be considered here refer to man's essential being. They refer to his essential being as something which is always historically constituted, and thus as existing in confrontation with Christianity as grace and as historical message" (24, 25).

In several ways, Rahner's appreciation for the historicity of Christianity produces theological grounds for not viewing the human person in a strictly essentialist way. He writes:

> Christianity is not the ideological creation of a religious enthusiasm, nor of the religious experience of an individual. It comes to the individual rather by the same route from which he receives the rest of his life, including his intellectual and spiritual life: it comes from history. No one develops and unfolds from out of the purely formal and antecedent structure of his essence. Rather he receives the concreteness of his life from a community of persons, from intercommunication, from an objective spirit, from a history, from a people and from a family, and he develops it only within this community, and this includes what is most personal and most proper to himself. This is also true for salvation and for the Christian religion, and for the Christianity of an individual. (389)

Traditional readings of Rahner as a pure essentialist neglect the many ways in which he acknowledges the effects of social construction on the self, not only as an observable occurrence but also as a theological reality of the Christian faith. His understanding of Christianity as historical and ecclesial undermines any movement towards identifying the essential elements of humanity as innate and inborn.

Finally, I mentioned in my summary of this criticism that transcendence is such a defining element of humanity for Rahner that it would be difficult to conceive of humanity without it. It would seem that this, at least, must be an essential feature of the human person. However, as was discussed in Chapter Three, Rahner's further explication of human transcendence is that it is primarily openness to the human other. Thus the two existential elements of Rahner's theological anthropology that seem most essential—our transcendence to the other, both human and divine, and our vocation to union with God—seem incompatible with a simple, modern essentialist reading of the self. Both our transcendence and its elevation in the supernatural existential mark the human person as profoundly formed in relation and marked by history.

Far from offering a standard modern, essentialist view of the human person in which an identifiable inborn characteristic constitutes what it is to be human, Rahner portrays the human person as, paradoxically, being called to co-create herself over time by acknowledging and embracing that she is someone profoundly open to the unknown and mysterious other. For Rahner, the human person is "one who does not possess within himself what he essentially needs in order to be himself" (Rahner 1967e, 31). He states: "[i]nsofar as human beings...are willing to see their center as outside themselves, they truly find themselves" (quoted in Kelly 1992, 40).[25]

Rahner clearly makes universalizing claims about what is most central to our humanity; therefore, it is not inaccurate to characterize him as an essentialist. But it is a very particular essentialism, quite distinct from mainstream modernity. For Rahner, each and every human being is essentially a person who has been called to a future with God, who must in freedom accept this vocation by opening himself in love to the unknown other, both human and divine. Rahner writes, "In his *essence*, in his nature, therefore, man himself is the mystery, not because

---

25    Karl Rahner, "Anthropozentric," in Josef Höfer and Rahner, eds., *Lexikon für Theologie und Kirche* (Freiburg: Herder, 1957-67), 1:634. Kelly relies on a translation by Anne Carr, *The Theological Method of Karl Rahner* (Missoula, MT: Scholars Press, 1977) 181. See also Rahner (1977, 250).

he is in himself the infinite fullness of the mystery which concerns him, which fullness is inexhaustible, but because in his real essence, in his original ground, in his nature he is the poor, but nevertheless conscious orientation to this fullness" (Rahner 1982, 216).

Rahner certainly participates in the modern turn to the subject, yet this, too, in a distinctive manner. Rahner looks to the human person to make it quite explicit that we cannot understand humanity without reference to God. We begin with the human, but cannot stay there:

> Man can be expressed only by talking about something else: about God, who he is not. It is impossible to engage in anthropology without having first engaged in theology, since man is pure reference to God. Thus he himself is a mystery, always referred beyond himself into the mystery of God. This is his being; he is defined by the indefinable which he is not, but without which he is not even (nor realizes) what he is. (Rahner1967e, 31)

This is a far cry from Descartes' essentializing assumptions about autonomous, rational, "reasonable men"—indeed it is a criticism of such views. Rahner does turn to the subject, but in a way that turns the subject inside out.

The charge that Rahner presents an expressivist view of the self, related to the discussion of expressivism and language in Chapter Two, is less easily answered. It can be further broken down into two questions. First, does what we do in the world shape who we are, or are our actions mere expressions of a fundamental decision made at a transcendental level? Second, do the actions of others, and the circumstances produced by them, affect who we are on the deepest levels? Do they influence our freedom or is it inviolable?

Rahner's works contain a number of possible ways of answering the first question, regarding the degree to which human beings are shaped by their own concrete actions. It is possible to understand Rahner as articulating a fairly Kantian view, in which the transcendental realities of the self are expressed, fulfilled, or objectified in concrete categorical actions.[26] One could also understand Rahner as trying to articulate a more Thomistic view, in which what a person does concretely and profoundly shapes who they are. Andrew Tallon reads Rahner in this manner, understanding love as a virtue or habit. Tallon writes:

---

26   See Rahner (1992b, 258; 1982, 96, 97).

Love as a habit (*virtus*) and love as act *mean* person: person is at
once the "nature" (essence, source) whence issue these acts of love
and the essence constituted by these acts of love. This saying is not
so paradoxical as it may seem, not more paradoxical nor difficult
than the question how a habit can be both a source of actions and
the result or product of these actions. (Tallon 1982, 148)

Rahner presents human bodies and human acts within his theology
of the symbol, such that "the bodily reality of man, and so his acts in
the dimensions of space and time, history and society, are conceived
of as symbolic realities embodying his person and its primordial decisions" (Rahner 1966f, 242, 243). Recall from the previous discussion
of language as symbolic that for Rahner, it is only through symbolization that that which is symbolized comes to be fully itself. He states,
"The symbol strictly speaking (symbolic reality) is the self-realization
of a being in the other, which is constitutive of its essence" (234). This
view asserts the necessity of embodied action in saying "yes" or "no"
to God. Given that Rahner's primary examples of a symbol are saying "yes" in a wedding ceremony and Jesus Christ, there is significant
evidence that it would be an oversimplification to ascribe to Rahner
a straightforward expressivist understanding of the self in relation to
bodily actions.

Our moral choices have, at least, a corralling effect—limiting the
scope of future choices and driving our lives forward to a culminat-
ing goal. As Beste writes, "Aquinas' insight that individuals' acts leave
traces in their being resonates throughout Rahner's reflections about
how persons' present acts shape and circumscribe the range of their
future options and decisions. Each free action, then, simultaneously
affects who one is becoming and one's fundamental option towards
God" (Beste 2003a, 4, 5).

It is precisely in accepting such a view of Rahner that a second question arises for Beste as a Christian ethicist: If what we do in history
shapes who we are, what about the effects of what happens to us? If
our free actions in space and time truly do affect our eternal destinies,
then the ability of circumstances and the actions of other people to
limit our actions is quite significant.

Rahner repeatedly affirms that human subjects are dependent and
historical, such that our freedom is actualized in history and is not ab-

solute freedom. However, his theology functions with the assumption that this freedom is universally present. This can be seen as problematic to the extent that it disregards the blunt, bodily realities of how freedom is limited in situations of oppression and abuse. If human freedom is inviolable, then the influence of history is limited, and this one existential appears to be an essential element of human nature. Furthermore, we again have a view of the self that cannot account for social construction, a variant of expressivism.

Rahner addresses this question specifically in an essay titled, "The Consecration of the Layman to the Care of Souls." Here he deals directly with the question of how another person can influence an individual's free decision to accept or reject God's grace. While he begins by discussing human community, he affirms the loneliness of personal decision. Each person must say "yes" or "no" alone. For Rahner, this is because the choice is not separate from the identity of the person involved. There is no pre-existent, fully realized human being who then opts for or against God. Rather, precisely in saying "yes" or "no," each person participates in her own creation. Rahner understands freedom as an act of self-creation; therefore, it cannot be passed off to another person. He writes:

> This is the case with man's liberty, where with the whole force of his nature he gives its ultimate meaning and character to his whole being, where he forms his own existence into what he wants to be. Here he is essentially alone. For the doing and what is done are inalienably his, they are as much his own as he is himself. For his action is the forming of his eternal physiognomy, it is himself in his eternal uniqueness. And hence only he himself can ever perform this act of eternal destiny. Everything that is done to a man, everything that happens to him, remains subject to the ultimate pronouncement of his liberty, in which he is still capable of understanding and accepting his lot (what is done to him, what is allotted to him); so everything that remains on this side of that ultimate personal verdict is not yet what finally counts in man. Only to a being that is not free is its 'lot' really its destiny; for the free being his destiny lies in himself. The choice which God has put into our hands we cannot confide to the care of any other. (Rahner 1967d, 265)

Since Rahner views salvation as necessarily "the fruit of a personal decision," any salvation that could be gained for another person or on his behalf would not truly be salvation at all (266).

At the same time, Christian traditions affirm that we are to care for each others' souls. Rahner handles this by relying on his understanding of love. One Christian can influence the freedom of another through love. If we try to love one another directly in the full, unconditional sense of the word, we will always find that our love has reservations that prevent penetration into the heart of another person's freedom. Yet we can love God unconditionally, and love others "for the sake of" God. This "for the sake of" means something different with God than it would if applied to another person, for "God is not another 'alongside' man. He is what is most intimate, the essential kernel of the beloved being, he is within even the inmost, the least relative, the ultimate enclosure of man in himself" (270, 271). Through love, we have a union with God that allows us to reach the innermost center of the other. Pastoral care, then, bears the characteristic marks of love of God ("adoration, surrender of one's own will to God, confidence") and ultimately takes the form of prayer (271). Thus even in reaching the soul of the other, pastoral care does not apply force or take over freedom, but rather "remains humble and pure and leaves the other alone with the living God in spite of the loving proximity with him thus discovered" (271).

By relying on his theology of love, Rahner explains that we can influence one another's freedom by loving God and neighbor, holding one another in prayer. This is an abstract and indirect vision of the care of souls that maintains the basic loneliness of personal decision while affirming that we can affect one another profoundly in a positive way. Perhaps the more pressing question, however, is whether or not we can affect one another in a negative way. Can sin, harms done to us, and the circumstances created by sin affect human freedom?

Rahner states that because of original sin, the concrete situations in which human freedom is enacted are altered, such that our free actions are always co-determined by the guilt of others. In Chapter Four there is quoted a passage in which Rahner discusses intercommunication, particularly the partial responsibility and concern everyone has in everyone else's salvation. That paragraph continues:

> Everyone is aware [of the significance of intercommunicative exis-
> tence for salvation] in the experience of his being weighed down by
> a guilt which is not merely his own, in the experience of his own
> historicity. This historicity is on the one hand a co-determinant of
> the most ultimate aspects of one's own existence, and on the other
> hand it is itself partially the result of the historical decisions of oth-
> er people. (Rahner 1972c, 177)

The material of our decisions is part of a concrete situation of sin, and
this material is not merely the context of our free decisions, it also
becomes part of those decisions.[27] Rahner constructs his description
of the human person such that the objectifications of the guilt of others necessarily become part of her free decisions. Given what has been
said above about actions as the symbols of the person, in and through
which she constitutes herself, it is possible to understand this in such
a way that the objectifications of the guilt of others become a part of
the self as she enacts herself. Thus Rahner can refer to "negative experiences with life, with society, with people, and so on" as connected to
"temptation" of human freedom (Rahner 1985, 110).[28]

In an essay titled, "The Body in the Order of Salvation," Rahner explains that embodiment entails vulnerability, an openness to "break-
through from outside." He illustrates the obvious nature of this claim:
"For whoever doubted that since I have a cheek, someone else can

---

27  See Rahner (1982, 109), where Rahner states:

> All of man's experience points in the direction that there are in fact
> objectifications of personal guilt in the world which, as the mate-
> rial for the free decisions of other persons, threaten these decisions,
> have a seductive effect upon them, and make free decisions painful.
> And since the material of a free decision always becomes an intrin-
> sic element of the free act itself, insofar as even a good free act which
> is finite does not succeed in transforming this material absolutely
> and changing it completely, this good act itself always remains am-
> biguous because of the co-determination of this situation by guilt.
> It always remains burdened with consequences which could not re-
> ally be intended because they lead to tragic impasses, and which
> disguise the good that was intended by one's own freedom.

28  See also Rahner (1966g), where he claims that the human person "is
continually being affected by powers and forces from outside himself, which
affect him *contrary* to his free decision and so make him 'suffer'" (393).

smack my face? And that since I have a head, a brick can fall on it?"
Rahner then reflects:

> There is no 'inwardness' which does not also stand open, as it were,
> to what is without. The ultimate, most personal freedom, which is
> to be found where man is inevitably himself, without any substitute
> or any excuse, at the heart of his being (or however we like to ex-
> press it)—the place, that is to say, where he is virtually the absolute
> and irreplaceable subject—is where he still has something to do
> with Christ, and with all other men and women too. For there are
> no spheres which can be cleanly separated from one another in an
> existential cleavage. (Rahner 1981c, 86, 87)

In this passage, Rahner reiterates claims addressed in Chapter Four,
namely, the unity of body and spirit in the human person and the significance of humanity as corporate for redemption in Jesus Christ.

Rahner also addresses issues of how human freedom can be im-
paired in terms of "peripheral" cases, such as those who are in extreme
pain, who die in infancy, or who are mentally handicapped. For example, Rahner writes:

> [I]t can be said that in the last resort we do not know how or whether
> this doctrine [of human freedom to say "yes" or "no" to God's offer]
> is to be applied to those who die *before* the moment at which...we
> would be inclined to ascribe to them an actual decision of freedom
> in the radical sense; nor do we know whether in fact everyone who
> is 'adult' in the sense generally understood really makes *that* decision
> of freedom...From the Christian standpoint, all that we can really
> say must be about the 'normal case' of humans and Christian life.
> (Rahner 1983a, 237)

And elsewhere:

> At this point we cannot go into the question whether and how
> this freedom can be accounted for in those peripheral cases where
> a person exists on a merely biological level, cases in which we do
> not recognize any concrete possibility of accounting for subjectivity,
> for example, the mentally handicapped who, at least by our normal
> standards, never seem to come to the use of reason. But we can-
> not understand something fundamental which is experienced at the
> center of existence in terms of such peripheral cases. (Rahner 1982,
> 106)

Here Rahner is avoiding the brunt of the question, refusing to speculate about persons whose embodied reality might mitigate against
their freedom to say "yes" to God.[29] However, the way he is avoiding
the question is telling. He describes his own method of approaching
theological anthropology as one that is generalizing rather than essentializing. When pressed for theological comfort on such issues, Rahner trusts in the goodness and grace of God to be operative in such
situations, rather than asserting that human freedom must somehow
remain intact in a way that we do not recognize. Elsewhere Rahner
has such "peripheral" cases—and perhaps cases of oppression—in
mind when he suggests that traditional doctrines of purgatory might
be understood in terms of a modified form of the migration of souls.
Another lifetime might provide "an opportunity for *those* who did not
reach a final personal decision in this earthly (or, first) life" (Rahner
1983e, 192). In this suggestion, as well, Rahner avoids declaring that
human freedom is inviolable within a given life. Rahner does consider
human freedom to be quite sturdy. Furthermore, sturdy human freedom plays an important structural role in Rahner's theology, particularly in the distinction and difference within the intimate relationship
of God and humanity. Yet when facing challenges to his universalizing
account of freedom, Rahner does not resort to an account of human
freedom as immune to the dangers of history.

This is seen even more clearly when Rahner addresses questions of
how what befalls us affects our freedom in the context of oppression.
In the midst of one discussion of the radical freedom to say "yes" or
"no" to God's offer of self-communication, Rahner writes:

> I feel bound however, to say this. The idea that man, as a Christian
> or as the philosophical subject of freedom, is still free, even when
> he is born in chains is extremely dubious and may be fundamen-
> tally wrong. This is clear from the fact that one man can deprive
> another man by murder (of his biological or psychological reality
> as a human being) of the possibility of freedom, even in the theo-
> logical sense. It is possible to dispute this and argue that no man
> can completely deprive another of every possibility of expressing his
> religious freedom, because the other can always have an attitude of
> freedom towards such an attempt. Even if this is asserted, it cannot
> be denied that there is an essential relationship between religious

29   See also Rahner (1979c, 201).

and social freedom as the conditioning factor of the possibility of the former. (Rahner 1978b, 38)

In a different essay, Rahner speaks more boldly on this subject: "From the Christian point of view it is not enough to say, as an abstract idealism usually does, that even in chains man is still free" (1966g, 405). He contends that it is "precisely because" the human person is free "that he absorbs into himself these presuppositions of his freedom which another has brought about, and for this very reason the free person is marked for ever with the traits imposed on him by force" (405). Because the human person constitutes herself freely in history, the decisions and actions of others shape her, even to the extent of influencing her "eternal destiny" (405).[30]

In several different texts, Rahner addresses the ways in which historical and embodied realities can limit and possibly negate human freedom in a given life. In these discussions he does not defend an essentialist view of human freedom or a view of human freedom as a transcendental, inviolable reality that is only expressed in actions. His explicit view is optimistic, accounting for the effect of one person on another primarily in a positive direction through love of God.[31] On the negative side, he admits that freedom might be tempted, temporarily foiled, and even marked forever, but he does not assert the most extreme position Beste explores, wherein the damage we do to one another could have eternally damning consequences.[32] He does

---

30   Rahner describes the conditions under which someone could rightly "impose on others, as their eternal destiny (or a component of it), a contingent and accidental concrete element which the free use of his power has brought into being and inserted unasked as something definitive into the sphere of another's existence" (405).

31   A rather Schleiermachian optimism.

32   See Beste (2003b). Beste herself is somewhat stronger that Rahner's boldest statements on this issue, without claiming that one person can damn another:

> I am obviously not arguing that interpersonal harm can damn a person *qua passive victim*; I affirm that God's grace can ultimately save persons if their freedom has been impaired by interpersonal harm to such an extent that they die before effecting a fundamental option. (2003a, 20, n. 37)

not envision the horrors that persons inflict upon on one another as eternally destroying the individual's freedom and ultimately overriding God's salvific will. One can see in Rahner's anthropology a form of social construction, but one in which the primary agents of that construction remain God and the individual person.

I began this discussion of postmodern criticisms of Rahner by describing a postmodern suspicion of any kind of pre-given meaning or identity, and a corresponding proclivity to understand meaning and identity as culturally and discursively produced over time. I then argued that Rahner can be understood as not offering an essentialist account of the human subject, but rather generalizing about what he (no doubt problematically) perceives to be the normal or average human existence. His writings indicate a significant appreciation for the ways in which the human person comes to be in and through social and cultural relations, in and through the contexts in which she acts and the actions she performs, in and through her own engulfment in a particular linguistic world. These considerations make it possible to understand Rahner as having a constructivist view of the self. At the same time, his willingness to universalize and his strong view of freedom mitigate against interpreting Rahner as holding a purely constructivist position. Therefore, I think it is most helpful to see Rahner's theology as occupying a different space, between the purely essentialist and the purely constructivist.

Serene Jones explores the problems and benefits of both essentialist and constructivist positions in her book, *Feminist Theory and Christian Theology: Cartographies of Grace*. After describing both positions, Jones offers three ways of identifying middle ground between them. "Weak constructivism" describes the view of people who have a commonplace understanding of the large role that social contexts play in shaping who we are, and yet believe that these cultural forces work upon an essential self that is already given. Jones writes, "Like the clay of a potter, the raw material of personhood can be formed by culture into different figures, but it never ceases to be clay" (Jones 2000, 35). The second position, "strategic essentialism," accepts constructivist critiques regarding how normative descriptions of human nature are socially constructed instead of being hardwired. At the same time, strategic essentialists recognize the pragmatic and political values of being able to make normative claims, and therefore deploy essentialist language for strategic ends (45). Because strategic essentialists understand such normative visions as also being formed in society, culture, and language, they are free to critique and revise current views of what is essential to human nature as political and pragmatic concerns warrant (45-47). The third position Jones describes is a theological position she calls "eschatological essentialism." This form of strategic essentialism is shaped by a vision of an eschatologically redeemed humanity, which forms a normative account that is both already valid and not yet fully realized. "This normative perspective looks ahead to a model of identity yet to be realized and not back to models of personhood that remain rooted in an essentialized nostalgia for the natural and the given" (54). In outlining these three positions, Jones makes clear that a strict theoretical division between constructivism and essentialism is inadequate to the variety of views that coherently fall between them.

It is possible to argue that Rahner's theological anthropology fits in each of these three middle positions between essentialism and constructivism. His description of freedom, transcendence, and the universal human experience of grace are strong enough to suggest that he does hold some things to be essential to humanity, while his comments regarding knowledge, language, and historicity affirm that we cannot have any access to our freedom or experiences of grace that are not always mediated by our interactions with the world. One could read Rahner as a weak constructivist who says that the essence of humanity lies in our experience of the grace of God and our unavoidable freedom to respond to that grace, while both experience and response are profoundly shaped by the cultural contexts in which we live. This designation is not an exact fit, however, since the giving of the grace of God has, as its final cause, the historical reality of Jesus Christ. Therefore, what could be called most essential to humanity in Rahner's view is neither natural nor pre-given.

A case could also be made that Rahner is a strategic essentialist, making broad normative claims about the structure of human nature while also being aware that such claims have a history and genesis of their own. This is resonant with his willingness to generate such a universalizing account of humanity, while not arguing that exceptions to this account are either impossible or inhuman. Rahner holds his own description of humanity seriously enough to reap the sizeable theological benefits (an apologetic approach starting with the human subject, the structure to support strong ethical norms, etc.) that such a broad framework generates, yet also loosely enough to admit that there may well be concrete circumstances in which it does not apply. Also, there are instances where Rahner's universalizing appears quite intentionally deployed to respond to certain situations. For example, his account of anonymous Christianity uses universal claims to concretely argue for salvation beyond the institutional church, a position with political and practical implications.

It is perhaps most easily argued that Rahner is an eschatological essentialist, given that the two elements most constitutive of human nature in his account are the call toward a future with God and the freedom to say "yes" to that vocation. This description of what it means to be human, more than any other, guides and shapes Rahner's theological vision and spiritual sensibility. However, neither of these two latter categories fits exactly for I suspect that this is not a strategic deployment on Rahner's part, but rather a profound theological conviction—formed within church tradition and practice—that the deepest, now unchangeable truth about all human persons is that we are called to a future of beatific vision, to eternal communion with enduring mystery in love.

Whatever term is applied to Rahner's view of the self, I believe that it is most appropriate to try and situate his anthropology within the range of middle views that share some aspects with both essentialism and constructivism.[33] Rahner can be seen as presenting a picture of the human person as communally, historically, and socially constructed. Our experiences and knowledge are always mediated and shaped by our cultural and discursive settings, such that some pure, untainted knowledge—of either ourselves or of God—given outside the confines of our corporeal and historical realities, is not part of Rahner's vision.[34] At the same time, the assertion in some postmodern views that

---

33  Within a different context, one could also choose to understand Rahner in terms of relational ontology.

34  As discussed in Chapter One, Rahner does allow for this type of extraordinary mystical experience, in what appears to be deference for the traditions and accounts of Christian mystics, but he is clear that this is rare, is not

all meaning is discursively and culturally produced cannot be found in Rahner's work. There is more to the human person than can be explained away by regional discourses. No amount of appreciation for how we are shaped by culture allows us to be unburdened of ourselves or our freedom. While our enactment of ourselves is conditioned by society and discourse, we cannot be reduced to the performances of culture itself. Our spirituality and our agency cannot be entirely accounted for as cultural productions.[35]

The final postmodern criticism offered above was that Rahner does not pay due attention to history. The comments made in regard to theological method and theological anthropology all go some distance towards mitigating this concern, as they prevent an overly-transcendental interpretation of Rahner and note the ways in which Rahner addresses the historical and social construction of the human person. Furthermore, the fact that Rahner's later writings incorporated criticisms concerning history have been much remarked. However, all of this does not erase the ahistorical criticism completely, especially in the forms offered by Metz and Milbank.

Recall Milbank's critique: Rahner's attempt at understanding the relation between the sacred and the secular is a failed integralism that capitulates to the standards of secular reason and thereby naturalizes the supernatural. In trying to blur the boundaries between sacred and secular, Rahner grants the secular priority and states that nothing is present within Christianity that is not also present outside it as an anonymous secret. Secular life is baptized and the sacred remains a separate sphere, albeit one now contained within the individual in an ahistorical way. Thus the particular character and history of Christian life—especially church life—is lost. Finally Milbank argues that liberation theologies, due to their reliance on Rahner's flawed attempt at bringing sacred and secular together, are inadequate both in that they are too Marxist and because they do not place enough trust in history.

---

better or more pure than the experience of God in ordinary existence, and is probably attributable to psychological differences among persons.

35  Hogan asserts that Heidegger was concerned to avoid the illusion of a "worldless subject" (1998, 184). Rahner does not describe a worldless subject, but neither does he describe a subjectless world.

Clearly the reading of Rahner that I have offered above differs from Milbank's considerably. The significant interpretive shift away from viewing Rahner as a philosophical foundationalist, towards viewing his theological and spiritual writings in a non-foundationalist frame, provides a different perspective on Rahner's theology. Instead of understanding the supernatural existential as a ground for Christian theology, philosophically gained, I view it as a particularly Christian interpretation of existence that is apologetically deployed. I do not see the supernatural existential solely as an answer to the nature/grace debate. Instead, I see it as a proclamation of the universal scope of the grace of God in a context wherein religious truth and divine grace where unduly constricted by religious institutionalism,[36] as well as an affirmation that the claims of Christianity pertain to the everyday experiences of human persons.[37] Thus in my reading, Rahner's emphasis on the pervasiveness of grace is not a baptism of the secular that abdicates Christian theology's role as metadiscouse, but rather a claim that no part of human life falls outside the realm of theological questions and interpretation. The assertion that the world outside the explicit church is already imbued with grace is not a claim based upon, or leading to, pre-theological discourses. It is a theological, Christological claim that leads to further reflection on the grace of God and Christian responses to it.

Furthermore, this does not entomb the sacred within an inner aspect of individual experience. Given that human transcendence is the obediential potency for the supernatural existential, and that human transcendence is transcendence to the other, such an individualistic view is inadequate. Social history is not a separate sphere from the sacred. Rather, concrete intersubjectivity in personal history is where the transcendental offer of grace is actualized, that is, comes fully into being.

Finally, my interpretation highlights several ways in which Rahner recognizes the importance of history in relation to the human person and to language, and underscores the deep Christological commitments that provide the inner logic of Rahner's theology. Rahner's entire theology is driven by something historical: the event of God's self-

---

36   See Adams (2005, 219).

37   See Endean (2001, 226).

communication in Jesus Christ. In Rahner's work this event is grand in scope, including creation; the birth, life, death, and resurrection of Jesus Christ; the sending of the Holy Spirit; and the ongoing life of the church. He understands this event to be historical to such extent that human belief and performance are "constitutive" of it. Consider two comments on Christian faith: "If the resurrection of Jesus is to be the eschatological victory of God's grace in the world, it cannot be understood without faith in it as something actually and freely arrived at, and it is only in this faith that its own essential being is fully realized" (Rahner 1982, 267, 268). Similarly, he writes:

> [T]he church was founded in the first place by the fact that Jesus is the person whom the believers professed to be the absolute saviour and to be God's historically irreversible and historically tangible offer of himself, and by the fact that he would not be who he is if the offer of himself which God made in him did not continue to remain present in the world in an historically tangible profession of faith in Jesus. This is true *because of the very nature* of God's offer. Abiding faith in Jesus is an intrinsic and constitutive element in God's offer of himself which has become irreversible in Jesus. (329, 330)[38]

One particular statement by Milbank, quoted above boils down perhaps the deepest division between Rahner and some postmodern critics, while also hearkening back to the concerns expressed by Metz and other modernists. He writes: "Karl Rahner fears to entrust the supernatural to the merely historical, to the succession of human actions and human images" (Milbank 1990, 223).[39] For all the differences between our interpretations of Rahner, I agree with this remark. However, unlike Milbank, I think it does not spell the end of Rahner's relevance in a postmodern era, but rather indicates why Rahner continues to be pastorally compelling to Christians in confusing times.

Rahner does not entrust the supernatural to the *merely* historical. While I argue that Rahner is more attuned to the historical than he

---

38   See also Endean's view of this: "In Rahner's Christology, our response to Christ is an aspect of Christology itself, because Christ's relationship with us is part of his identity" (2001, 234).

39   While I am pointing out an affinity between Metz and Milbank in criticisms of Rahner, please note that Metz has a far greater appreciation of Rahner than Milbank and that Milbank criticizes Metz as a part of the larger Rahnerian trajectory in modern Christian thought. See 237-240.

has often gotten credit for, at the end of the day Rahner is adamant that there is more than the historical. There is the eternal and there is God. These are not strictly separate from history, for eternity is the mature fruit of history in the presence of God, and God has made history God's own and has a human history in Jesus Christ. But neither can eternity and divinity be contained, accounted for, or produced by history alone.

Rahner rather notoriously commented that nothing extraordinary happened in his own personal history. Some people have been affronted by that comment, given that Rahner saw the horrors of the Shoah and was himself exiled from Germany during World War II. Some have interpreted this as further indication that Rahner did not understand the importance of history. However, this statement can be read quite differently. Rahner was not unaware of the suffering around him, or that it had reached a new extent in his lifetime. He writes, in "On Martyrdom," of "devilish modern techniques that murder the person, taking man completely from himself before the life of his body is extinguished," of people "whose personalities had been so crushed by inhuman practices, undreamt of in past ages, that they were physically unable to profess their faith" (Rahner 1964, 125, 89). Yet even though the scope and extent of suffering might be new, the reality of sin, evil, and suffering is a constant in human history. Genocide must always be considered an exceptional atrocity, but we can also recognize—to our own abject horror—that it is neither a unique nor a rare event. *Mere* human history is a long account of pain, loss, loneliness, and desolation.

I think that Rahner does fear to entrust the supernatural to the *merely* historical, to the succession of human actions and human images alone. If the supernatural were entrusted entirely to the merely historical, I think we would have destroyed it long ago. Christian hope, for Rahner and for many faithful Christians trying to survive in a difficult and deadly world, consists in acting as if the mystery surrounding human life is not a neutral territory awaiting human determination, but rather is filled by the love of God into which we can surrender. Such a conviction cannot be logically or rationally arrived at based on the evidence around us. Thus while this hope takes place in history, it is also funded by a transcendental offer of God's grace, an offer that we understand and experience within the practices, traditions, and language of the Christian faith (Rahner 1975b, 177). The supernatural is entrusted to the historical, but it is not contained within the historical alone.

For postmodernists who wish to talk about human beings as socially constructed, meaning as a human creation, and the holy as a result of human performance, there are resources in Rahner for productive discussions with Christian traditions and doctrine. But Rahner refuses to locate human identity, meaning, and the supernatural only within mere history. As slim as the line between God and humanity may sometimes be, as thoroughly permeated as the world is by grace, there is more to the otherness and mystery of God than what can be accounted for by human history.

## TURN TO THE OTHER

These considerations of postmodern perspectives on Rahner's theology have not yet addressed the areas in which his work is most consonant with postmodern concerns. Several scholars have noted Rahner's attention to the other—both to the otherness of God and to the concrete human other (Tallon 1982, 167; Taylor 1986, 67)[40]—and some have explored the deep resonances with the works of postmodern authors.[41] If postmodernity in general is understood as a critique of the logic of the same in modernity, then attention to otherness is an important characteristic of various postmodern perspectives. David Tracy writes, "Beyond the early modern turn to the purely autonomous, self-grounding subject, beyond even the more recent turn to language (the first great contemporary challenge to modern subjectism) lies the quintessential turn of post-modernity itself—the turn to the other" (Tracy 1994, 108). In so far as Rahner describes Christian faith as a posture of radical openness to the unmanipulable other, his work moves beyond the confines of modernity strictly understood and

---

40   See also, for a much briefer sketch of Rahner that looks first to the philosophical structure of his theology, Brinkman (1984, 259). For a discussion of otherness in relation to Rahner's Christology, including a fascinating translation of one provocative paragraph of Rahner's work, see Endean (1996, 288).

41   See especially Purcell (1998). Also Hogan (1998).

pushes towards the sensibilities that have become prevalent among postmodern authors.

The turn to the other becomes more obvious in Rahner's work as his career progresses. This means that the choice to read him primarily through the lenses of his theology and spirituality, instead of focusing on his earlier, more philosophical works and understanding his theology as an outgrowth of this, already serves to highlight the turn to the other in Rahner's writings. Furthermore, choosing to address the three themes of silence, love, and death, each of which represents a way of saying "yes" to God's offer of salvation, constructs a view of Rahner focused on the appropriate human response to grace. This places additional emphasis on Rahner's turn to the other since, as I have argued throughout this book, his description of faithfulness is one of openness to the mysterious other.

Rahner uses images of silence to mark and evoke a posture of openness to that which is beyond the scope of our manipulation and control. In describing saying "yes" to God with images of silence, Rahner presents such openness to the other as central to Christian faith.

Rahner writes more explicitly about openness to the other in terms of love. He begins his explication of the human person by describing the individual subject in her transcendence, in her radical openness to the infinite. He continues by identifying this transcendence as primarily an openness to the human other. Each human act of knowing, willing, and loving is ascribed a threefold structure—each act involves the self in relation to the self, to God, and to the human other (Taylor 1986, 68). As the human person enacts her own identity in contextualized freedom, she becomes most truly herself only in and through loving other persons, with loving understood to be adopting a posture of openness to the unknown and unmanipulable other, risking the reconfiguration of the self, and refusing to see the other as a means for one's own self-assertion. While Rahner's discussion of openness to the other remains at a highly abstract level, such that it does not concretely address difficulties of openness to hurtful others, there are resources for discussing such necessary boundaries in Rahner's insistence that the norm of neighbor love is acknowledgement of the beloved as other, not to be used, constrained, or defined by the lover.

This posture of openness to the other is developed more fully in relation to God in Rahner's use of silence and more fully in relation to human persons in Rahner's discussions of love. The relationship between the two comes into focus in Rahner's examination of the unity of love of God and love of neighbor. Michael Scanlon, comparing Rahner and Derrida, notes that "radical alterity is also at the center of Rahner's religion in which love of God *is* love of neighbor" (Scanlon 1999, 227).

Faithful death, for Rahner, is the free acceptance of the risk of self-loss in the face of the unknown. This acceptance happens both when a person approaches her own biological death without despair and all throughout life, when she loves other mortal persons with an unconditionality secured by Jesus Christ. Such love is dying with Christ in life. In both instances, faithful death is the enactment of self-possessing openness to the mysterious other, and all Christians are called to this as they are part of a communally sanctified humanity. Our redemption depends on our human solidarity, and our salvation flourishes in an eternal intercommunion in which individuality, and loving relationships forged in our earthly lives, are preserved.

## SELF-EVIDENT MYSTERY

These comments on otherness point to another place where Rahner escapes the bounds of modernity: he is not driven to certainty. By this I do not mean that Rahner is unsure of the reality of God or of the reliable assurance of God's presence.[42] Clearly, he makes strong theological claims that every human being is continually experiencing God. Rahner's faith—for which even the silence of God is indication of God's presence—does not lack this kind of deeply committed security. I mean something quite different. The modern period is marked by the desire for a particular kind of stable comprehension and unequivocal sure knowledge, indubitable and universal. This kind of cer-

---

42  Kilby discusses Rahner's theology—particularly in a non-foundationalist interpretation—in relation to statements from Vatican I that affirm that God can be known with certainty by reason (2004, 100-104). See also Rahner (1982, 181), where he states: "The clarity and the finality of Christian truth lies in the inexorability of man's deliverance into this mystery, and is not the clarity of comprehending a partial element in man and in his world."

tainty, which offers the illusion of human mastery, is not Rahner's aim. Rahner's theological goal is not to find a touchstone of certainty upon which to anchor a comforting view of a stable world. He does not attempt to build a certain structure of knowledge through which humanity gains progressive control over creation. In fact, he often writes about how it is precisely our experience of God that de-centers and destabilizes our world. Our bright little huts would be so peaceful if only we could content ourselves with them. But we cannot, for the engulfing darkness calls us out to face the incomprehensibility of God. When Rahner begins his theology with the turn to the subject, he does not find there an indubitable self-presence that serves as a foundation of sure knowledge. Instead, he finds a fundamental openness to the other—both human and divine—that has been radicalized into a vocation to beatific vision. At the center of the self is an offer, to be accepted or rejected in freedom in history, of God's own self. This is a call to abandon oneself into the mystery that shatters human knowing.[43]

One issue has come up repeatedly in the above consideration of Rahner in the light of postmodernity. While Rahner affirms that all of our knowing takes place in and through our encounter with the categorical, he also insists that part of this experience of knowing—the secret ingredient within it—is transcendental knowledge. This transcendental knowledge of God cannot be accessed directly, cannot be brought into immediate conceptual focus, and cannot be adequately thematized in language. To some, Rahner's description of transcendental experience looks like a trap door allowing escape from the confines of language, culture, and history. It appears to be another attempt to locate the epistemic touchstone of certainty that so fascinates modernity. However, I have argued above that Rahner's transcendental experience is not such a trap door facilitating escape. It is not a route to certainty outside the world, but an affirmation that there is more to this world than we can begin to calculate and quantify. Implicit in this understanding is that the experience of transcendence is not primarily or finally about knowledge.

---

43  Purcell offers a discussion of Rahner's work in relation to postmodernity that is very different from my own, but which also highlights the importance of mystery for Rahner (Purcell 2005, 195-210).

As mentioned above, Rahner criticizes common understandings of mystery and knowledge as they appear in School theology. Traditionally, the concept of mystery is formed in relation to that of reason and understood primarily as "the property of a statement" (Rahner 1966c, 38). Something mysterious is merely a statement that cannot be fully comprehended by reason at the present time, but which is accepted on faith and will eventually come under the purview of reason. Mystery is a "provisional" deficiency of knowledge and therefore, there are many mysteries (39, 40).

Rahner argues for alternative understandings of both mystery and reason. He contends that *ratio* should be understood in terms of the human person as spiritual and transcendent. In this light, mystery is not a gap in knowledge, but rather the infinite horizon that makes human knowledge possible. Rahner writes of the infinite mystery of God, "this nameless region beyond all categories, on which the transcendence of the spirit lays hold without comprehending, is not an accessory or a preliminary sphere of darkness which is to be gradually lit up. It is the primordial and fundamental which is the ultimate transcendental condition of possibility of knowledge" (42). Again, he describes mystery as

> the horizon which cannot be mastered and which masters all of our understanding, and which allows the other to be understood by being present itself in its silence and in its incomprehensibility. Mystery, therefore, is not something provisional which is done away with or which could in itself be non-mysterious. It is rather the characteristic which always and necessarily characterizes God, and through him characterizes us. (Rahner 1982, 217)

There are not multiple mysteries, Rahner asserts. The term mystery applies to God and to humanity as referenced to God (Rahner 1966c, 47).

Rahner defines mystery not as a limitation of human reason but as the condition of human spirituality, that is, as the abiding and eternal incomprehensibility of God. This incomprehensibility is vital to Rahner's theology and presents a real challenge to the modern ideal of knowledge. This ideal understands knowledge in terms of domination and appropriation. It deals in clear ideas, in what is unquestionable and obvious. This ideal of modern knowledge cannot approach the question of God's incomprehensibility. Indeed, it views divine incomprehensibility as a death sentence to the question of human meaning (Rahner 1983b, 95-96). Modern views of knowledge and reason find God's incomprehensibility to be a "nonconcept," such that all talk of it "falls on deaf ears" (97).

Rahner offers a different description of human reason than the one tacitly embraced by modernity's quest for certainty. He depicts reason as "the capacity of incomprehensibility" and "the perception of the ineffable." It is not about "mastery and subjugating," but rather a matter of "being seized by what is always insurmountable" (97). Within this description of reason, Rahner provides a picture of human knowing in transcendence towards the incomprehensibility of God that cannot be mistaken for a modern appeal. He writes of reason:

> For when it grasps and understands any object, it has already transcended the latter into an infinity that is present as unexplored, precisely as such and not otherwise; it always seizes the individual object by being tacitly aware of the fact that the object always is and remains more than what is grasped of it. It locates the individual object within reference systems which themselves are not precisely fixed and determined and in which such an individual reality has a place without being absolutely and forever settled there. It always has a bad conscience (which, if admitted and accepted, becomes a good conscience) that it has itself never adequately understood and authorized its own assumptions, although to do this would enable it to rely absolutely on its individual perceptions. It perceives, and every perception that gives expression to an individual reality is accompanied by a terrible awareness of its provisional character. It is only because we do not know that we can attempt to know something, only because we direct our questions to what is unanswered and thus in the last resort to the ineffable, that we can hear answers which, the better they are, the more they raise new questions. (9798)

Rahner declares the modern view of reason and knowledge to be inadequate to the Christian claim of the incomprehensibility of God. He further claims that such knowledge is not the ultimate aim and goal of humanity or of Christianity. It is in love that humanity can accept God's incomprehensibility "without being broken by it" (100). The unknowing experienced in facing mystery "forces knowledge either to be more than itself or to despair" (Rahner 1966c, 43). Knowledge becomes more than itself—preserves and transforms itself—when it becomes love. Rahner states, "in Christianity the last word is with love and not knowledge" (43).

This can be seen in Rahner's more spiritual writings, as well. In a prayer to the "God of Knowledge," Rahner sings the praises of forgetting. He claims, "I have learned much because I had to, much because I wanted to, but in either case the end result was always the same: I forgot it again" (Rahner 1997b, 15). Rahner does not lament this loss, but instead declares that he learned "in order to" forget, for it is in the forgetting that the poverty of knowledge is made clear:

> O God, it's good to forget. In fact, the best part of most of the things I once knew is precisely the fact that they could be forgotten. Without protest, they have sunk gently and peacefully out of sight. And thus they have enabled me literally to see through them in all their inner poverty and ultimate insignificance.
>
> It is said—and how am I to dispute it, Lord?—that knowing belongs to the highest part of man, to the most properly human of all his actions. And You Yourself are called "*Deus scientiarum Dominus*," the Lord God of all knowledge. But doesn't such high praise contradict the experience of Your holy writer? "I applied my mind to a new study: what meant wisdom and learning, what mean ignorance and folly? And I found that this too was labor lost; much wisdom, much woe; who adds to learning, adds to the load we bear"(Ecclus 1:17-18). (15, 16)

In this passage, Rahner protests the modern understanding of the human person as primarily rational. He stages this protest not from the grounds of postmodernity, but from a spirituality rooted in a tradition going back long before Descartes, a spirituality that does not grasp for certainty. Later in the same prayer, Rahner describes knowledge as "a kind of pain-killing drug" that cannot satisfy. He writes, "Truly, my God, mere knowing is nothing.…How can we approach the heart of all things, the true heart of reality? Not by knowledge alone, but by the full flower of knowledge, love" (16, 17).

Rahner's understanding of the relationship between God and humanity is not one in which knowing God is the goal. The goal, rather, is the posture of openness that steps beyond what the self can grasp or control, the self-surrender and self-abandonment that trusts mystery precisely as mystery, and the experience of God that undoes the opposition between presence and absence. In our openness to the other, human knowledge breaks. It is precisely in this breaking that Christians encounter God most fully.

Rahner is not enamored with an illusion of certainty, and does not incorporate Christian theology into a larger mission of securing indubitable knowledge. Acquisition of stable, clear knowledge is of little interest to Rahner. He scoffs at "clear ideas" and prefers primordial words that "perhaps obscure because they evoke the blinding mystery" (Rahner 1967b, 296, 298). He speaks of the "banality" of clear knowledge and declares that only mystery is self-evident (Rahner 1983b, 91-92; 1982, 22). Indeed, he asserts that a person experiences the Holy Spirit when he "entrusts all his knowledge and all his questions to the silent and all-sheltering mystery which is loved more than all our individual perceptions that turn us into petty lords" (Rahner 1983c, 203). Again and again, Rahner alludes to the modern drive for stabilizing, certain human knowledge, only to indicate that this is neither the ground nor the goal of Christianity.[44]

Declan Marmion identifies the central tenet of Rahner's theology as "the God of incomprehensible mystery, who cannot be explained with rationalistic clarity" (Marmion 2003, 212). He writes: "In effect, Rahner understands theology as the 'science of mystery,' which ultimately transcends the formulation of mere human words and which calls for an attitude of trembling and silent adoration" (Marmion 1998, 98).[45] Rahner's mystagogical approach, his description of God as the holy mystery that can only be surrendered to *as mystery*, his upholding of openness to the other as integral to Christian faith—all of these aspects of his thought and more indicate that his intent is not the drive for stabilizing certainty that permeates onto-theo-logy, but rather the spiritual vocation to a love of the incomprehensible God. Rahner's theology precludes any attempt to grasp and master God, instead moving to an understanding of openness and love as fundamental to Christian theology. Rahner writes:

> My Christianity is therefore, rightly understood, the act of letting myself go into the inconceivable mystery. My Christianity is conse-

---

44   See, for example, Rahner (1975a, 18-19).

45   Rahner refers to theology as a "'science' of mystery" in Rahner (1974b, 102).

quently anything but an 'explanation' of the world and my existence:
it is rather the injunction not to regard as definitive, as completely
intelligible in itself, any experience or any understanding (however
beneficial and enlightening it might be). The Christian has less 'ultimate' answers which he could throw off with a 'now the matter's
clear' than anyone else. He cannot use his God as *one* discovered
signpost in the assessment of his life, but only in silence and adoration accept him *as* the incomprehensible mystery, and *that* as the
beginning and end of his hope and therefore as his sole definitive
and all-embracing salvation. (Rahner 1975a, 23)

## CONTINUING CONSTRUCTIVE VITALITY

In describing these aspects of Rahner's theology that resonate deeply
with postmodern concerns, I do not intend to portray Rahner himself as a postmodern theologian. Rather, I mean to make clear that
Rahner eludes easy categorization as an obsolete modernist. Rahner
constructs a theological anthropology that defies simplistic definition. His ad hoc, occasional, mystagogical, multi-genre approach suits
a theology in which his pre-modern spirituality encounters modern
philosophy in ways that leave doors open for postmodern concerns.[46]

Particularly, I find that insofar as his work is governed by a pre-
modern spirituality that is not about controlling knowledge, it moves
towards a postmodern appreciation of otherness. In both form and
content, Rahner's work resists easy classification, and thus manages
to avoid both the strict onto-theo-logic of modernity and the narrative of postmodernity, which carries its own universalizing tendencies.
In many ways, Rahner travels a third path, beside and often between
those of modernity and postmodernity.

---

46  Metz, identifying a somewhat different set of Rahner's disparate commitments, makes a similar point. He states that Rahner "brought together in
his theology what has been divided for a long time. For Catholic theology in
modernity has been…stamped by a profound schism between doctrine and
life, between theological system and religious experience, between theology
and religion, between dogmatics and mysticism, between the doxography and
biography of Christian existence." The result, states Metz, is that Rahner's
"theology was a unique gesture of Christian existence in postmodern times"
(Metz 1998, 101).

Beside a modern grasping at certainty and a postmodern fascination with endless play, Rahner focuses on an abiding, unknowable mystery. This mystery is not the foundational truth claim upon which knowledge can be built, rising to the goal of indubitability, but rather is it is the enduring horizon that makes otherness possible, that demands that knowledge become love, and that calls not for a lack of doubt, but for an affirmation of faith.

Beside modern elevation of the individual and postmodern eclipse of the individual as an instance of communal production, Rahner presents a portrait of sturdy individuality that both comes to be within, and is necessary for, community. Individual and community are not oppositional terms in Rahner's theology.

Beside a view of language as bearing meaning through reference and one in which linguistic meaning is created in relation, Rahner offers a view of language as functioning symbolically, both pointing beyond itself and actualizing, in itself, that which it symbolizes.

Beside a modern emphasis on timeless truths and a postmodern picture of truth as historically and socially localized, Rahner claims that there is eternal truth which is grounded in mystery beyond the vagaries of human culture *and* which comes to be in history.

Beside modern essentialism that identifies the inborn characteristic of reason as that which makes us human, and postmodern views of the self as socially constructed in and through relation over time, Rahner portrays the human person as coming to be in a history that shapes her, while always being called into her truest identity as one who has been ordained to a future of beatific vision, one who is ultimately oriented to the mystery of God.

And beside modern obsession with the self and postmodern focus on the other, Rahner claims that the person, gifted with freedom in God's self-communication, is called to enact a self-possessing openness to the unknown other.

In all of these ways, Rahner's theology presents a critical engagement with modernity and, I believe, a productive conversation partner for theologians navigating the new and changing terrain of postmodernity. I think there are many people for whom the tropes of modernity—especially its depiction of the autonomous, rational subject—no longer ring true. They accept, with or without academic training and rigor, many postmodern critiques of modernity. At the same time, a purely postmodern depiction of the fragmentary, socially constructed, culturally determined person is also unpersuasive. Human persons still make choices, exercise freedom, think about themselves in fairly holistic ways, and aim for integrity of character. For the contingent of Christians (however large or small) who find themselves unconvinced by either modern or postmodern renditions of themselves, Rahner provides an insightful alternative theological anthropology. Furthermore, in part because his theology fits neatly into neither modern nor postmodern molds, Rahner offers a challenging and compelling depiction of faith to Christians who find that the enduring reality and radicality of Christian faith cannot be adequately represented by the generalized perspective of any era.

# CODA

## INTRODUCTION

In this book I have offered a particular way of reading the theology of Karl Rahner in a non-foundationalist frame, focusing on his portrayals of how human beings say "yes" to God, specifically on his use of silence, love, and death. I have placed Rahner's theology in conversation with postmodernism, explored current criticisms of his thought, and argued for the continuing vitality of his work. In these final pages I will gesture towards that vitality by briefly sketching ways that Rahner's work can contribute to three current conversations in feminist theology.

## SILENCE, LOVE, AND DEATH

In the beginning of *Foundations*, Rahner asks two questions: What are the conditions of the possibility of human knowing? And, what are the conditions of the possibility of the Christian message being heard? He declares that Christianity presupposes certain characteristics in the hearer of this message, while also calling these characteristics into being. In this brief introduction to a major theological text, Rahner signals to the reader that he will cross many methodological boundaries. He retraces familiar steps of modern intellectual inquiry, while also transgressing the rules of this pattern by asserting that we experience transcendence and by asking about the conditions of possibility of an historical happening. Rahner's theology intentionally engages modernity without ever agreeing to modernity's terms of engagement.

Rahner offers a Christian interpretation of the human person and of the meaning of human life. He aims to make his iteration of Christian faith compelling to the people of his era. To do this, he stresses that the grace Christianity proclaims is experienced in everyday life and that Christian faith has a recognizable coherence. By the strength of his argument and the enchantment of primordial words, Rahner paints a picture of the reader as understood by Christianity. When his rhetoric is successful, he brings the reader to accept a Christian interpretation of humanity, to recognize and even experience herself in terms of the faith Rahner has unfolded.

Rahner depicts the human person as finite infinity—a subject and person of sturdy individuality who at the same time transcends her own boundaries and moves outward to an infinite horizon of other persons, of mystery, and of God. She is dependent, historical, conditioned by her neighbors and her circumstances, and yet in her transcendence she is more than the sum of her parts or the specificity of her social location. She can imagine a new future, consider multiple possible paths to take, and ask about the meaning of her life as a whole. In all her finite limitation, she has human freedom. Human freedom is limited, conditioned, and opaque, yet for most of us, Rahner claims, it is also unavoidable. Our confrontation with the mystery that surrounds human life requires that we respond, either to hope that this mystery is ultimately the love of God, or to despair that our fleeting self-created meaning will ultimately perish in emptiness. This is the freedom to say "yes" or "no" to God's offer of self-communication.

This book has looked closely at how Rahner describes saying "yes." He often uses images of silence to invoke both the distance that separates persons and the act of accepting this distance in offering space and attention to the unknown other. This posture of self-possessing openness is vital to faithful response to God. Rahner explicitly equates saying "yes" with love, with opening the self to the other in a movement of trust supported by Jesus Christ. In death, human freedom comes into its eternal validity, as each individual either accepts or rejects her calling into an eternal intercommunion of humanity with God.

For Rahner, saying "yes" is a matter of freely accepting who we are called to be. We create our own identity as people of faith by acknowledging and freely choosing the identity that we have been given by God. We are created as self-possessing and open to the other. We say "yes" when we freely accept and enact this self-possessing openness.

The claim that saying "yes" is about accepting who we are as human beings is neither an accident nor an indication of unchecked modern anthropocentricism. Because Rahner is describing the human person from the perspective of Christian faith, his picture of humanity and his portrayal of Christian faithfulness are intertwined. If Rahner persuades the reader that this (self-possession and openness to the other) is what Christian faith looks like, he also convinces her that this is what the human person really is.

My focus on silence, love, and death has highlighted three balanced tensions in Rahner's theological anthropology.[1] The first is between self-possession and openness to the other as primary characteristics of human being. The second presents human identity as both gift and task. The third balanced tension is between individuality and community, as individuality comes to be in community and community requires individuality. These three balanced tensions are extremely relevant for contemporary theology, and Rahner's theology provides resources for addressing, maintaining, and further analyzing them.

For example, by making openness to the other—both human and divine—central to his understanding of the human person, Rahner's theology suggests a possible new deployment of apophatic language in relation to the human person. Rahner describes the human other as unknowable and unserveillable mystery, referenced to the mystery of God. He also universalizes this claim: all humans are unknowable mystery. One element of the apophatic strand within Christianity approaches and appreciates the otherness of God through a discursive strategy of affirmation and negation, such that the truth of either affirmative or negative claims requires the statement of both. One might imagine, then, a Rahnerian claim that humans are all the same and humans are each unknowably, mysteriously other. Within an apophatic discursive strategy warranted by otherness, the statement of human similarity is only true insofar as the statement of human otherness is also articulated, and vice versa.[2] Such apophatic theological anthropology would place valuing otherness and affirming human solidarity in necessary relation, drawing upon a traditional form of Christian

---

1 Note these three tensions do not correlate neatly with silence, love, and death, but they are brought to the fore by this interpretive lens.

2 Denys Turner writes about an apophatic anthropology in which the self is denied in the writings of a number of Christian mystics. See Turner (1995, 6, 167, 254). I am using the phrase quite differently, not to indicate a denial of self but rather a discursive strategy that employs paradoxical tensions between affirmation and negation in efforts to speak Christian truths. I am grateful to Denys Turner for conversations and encouragement on this matter.

discourse. This could address current feminist concerns to fund political unity while honoring difference.

## SILENCE AND LOVE

In addition to highlighting Rahner's continuing relevance as a conversation partner on theological anthropology, focusing on silence, love, and death also invites Rahner into dialogue particularly on the issue of silence in feminist theology. "Silence" has gained common usage among feminist theologians as a shorthand expression for the complex of oppressive practices that undermine women's subjectivity as expressed in the economy of language. Rebecca Chopp (1989), Betty Govinden (1994), Elisabeth Schüssler Fiorenza (1996), Margaret Farley (1992), and others use "silence" to indicate the oppression of women through limiting, dismissing, controlling or erasing women's ability to name and shape their reality through language. Anne Loades claims that "only half the story has been told" and explains: "The story about women has been thoroughly obscured by the ways in which women have been excluded from the processes by which cultures find meaning, interpret and explain their past and present, and orientate themselves to the future, as all this is expressed in *texts*, which may simply represent the views of the most privileged and atypical members of a given community of language users" (1990, 2). The category of "silence," used in this way to mean women being silenced within the context of a patriarchal society, has been important for feminists in helping to identify and resist this particular form of oppression.[3]

Rahner invokes silence in a very different manner, in conjunction not with oppression, but within the context of a divine/human dialogue. Recall from Chapter Two that in Rahner's theology silence is an interpersonal reality that enables discourse. The silence of God allows the voice of the human person to be spoken; the silence of the human

---

3 Similar negative understandings of silence appear in mainstream culture, through slogans such as "silence = death," used by the gay and lesbian community, and "break the silence," used as a call for victims of domestic violence to acknowledge their abuse to others and accept help in transforming their situations. In these instances, "silence" indicates the destructive lack of truth telling, enforced by shame and fear, which must be overcome for oppression to be resisted.

person allows the voice and the silence of God to be heard. Also, as silence marks the limits of language, it gestures towards all that cannot be adequately thematized, pointing towards mystery from within discourse. Analyzing silence in Rahner's writing, I argue that he uses silence to mark the distance and difference between persons which is painful and isolating and, at the same time, is the precondition of relation and love. Being silent in relation to the other is a recognition of otherness and an openness to hear the other's voice. It is an offering of time, space, and attention to the other precisely as other.

While Rahner employs silence quite differently in his writings than feminist, womanist, and mujerista theologians, there are some significant connections. In his depiction of the relationship between God and humanity, Rahner suggests that the silence of God is offered to humanity to enable human speech. Feminist, womanist, and mujerista theologians draw attention to a similar dynamic between human persons. The offered silence of one person can foster the speech of another.

This has two important implications. First, it allows for further analysis of sinful silencing, which can be understood as having two levels. On one level, people are oppressed by being denied the capacity to utter or inscribe their own words. On another level, people are oppressed by being denied the opportunity of being heard, denied a listening audience, denied conversation partners willing to hear their free voices, denied the respect of being acknowledged and accepted in their otherness and difference. In these instances, people are silenced by a lack of offered silence.

Sinful silencing of both varieties occurs on a small, intimate scale and on a huge, cultural scale. The triumphant monologue of the powerful requires, if it is to be accepted, the silence of the powerless.[4] Sometimes this silence is enforced with violence and brutality. History is replete with examples of noisy people who had different stories to tell disappearing into silence, being quieted by torture and death. Yet even this hideous silence could be eloquent if someone were to listen to it. One can read a history book with ears attuned to the stories that are not mentioned, can glean information about the power dynamics of the past by hearing what was not said. Those who are entirely, pro-

---

4 See Rahner (1966g, 406) in this regard.

foundly silenced are those for whom speech is inaccessible and silence itself is unheard.

Second, recognizing that offered silence can enable speech also suggests strategies of resistance. Offered silence can be useful in resisting sinful silencing. Listening to the other can help her to claim her own voice. The importance of listening in resisting sinful silencing has become, at least in theory, an accepted part of feminism in recent years. Serene Jones states that feminist theology has a "commitment to listening" to women in the church, women who have been harmed by the church, and women and men with many religious and non-religious perspectives (2000, 14).

In Nelle Morton's classic text, *The Journey Is Home*, she recounts the words of a woman who said, "I have a strange feeling you heard me before I started. You heard me to my own story. *You heard me to my own speech*" (1985, 205). Morton describes "[a] hearing that is a direct transitive verb that evokes speech—new speech that has never been spoken before" (205). She identifies a kind of "persistent hearing" that can break through silencing and evoke the speech of those to whom speech had previously been inaccessible (203). She recognizes that taking the time to hear the silence of the unheard and offering silence to those who are speechless may enable and empower their speech.

This sense of humans persons empowering the speech of others through offered silence resonates in many ways with the dynamics of silence in Rahner's portrayal of divine/human dialogue. To bring his work fully into the contemporary conversation about silence between persons, however, requires extrapolating from Rahner's discussions of silence between God and humanity to discussions of silence between human persons. Such extrapolation is warranted by the strong connections between silence and love in Rahner's theology. Love and silence occupy similar positions in Rahner's texts. Silence and love both indicate the space of saying "yes" to God, the space of self-abandonment to mystery, and the space of radical openness to the other. Rahner uses both silence and love to describe a kind of relationship that does not attempt to grasp, control, or fully comprehend the other but rather accepts them in their otherness.

In considering connections between silence and love in Rahner's theology, it is also helpful to remember that he uses silence repeatedly in descriptions of human transcendence. He writes about the term of our transcendence as the "ontologically silent horizon of every intellectual and spiritual encounter with realities" (Rahner 1982, 77). This horizon is "the ineffable and silent source and term of everything, which in fear and trembling and before the final silence could be called 'God'" (85). He states, "This infinite and silent term is what disposes of us. It presents itself to us in the mode of withdrawal, of silence, of distance, of being always inexpressible, so that speaking of it, if it is to make sense, always requires listening to its silence" (64).

Rahner also asserts that human transcendence unto this silent term can be described as a "transcendentality towards the other who is to be loved" (1969d, 243). The term of our transcendence is the silent mystery and radical otherness of God, which, through grace elevating our transcendentality into the supernatural existential, is present to us in mediated immediacy in our relationships with other human beings. The term of our transcendence is silent, and our acceptance of this term, our surrender to its mystery, also takes place in silence. At the same time, the term of our transcendence is our neighbor, and our acceptance of this term, our surrender to its mystery, takes place in love. Rahner connects what happens in silence and what happens in love:

> If we are silent, if we forgive, if without reward we give ourselves wholeheartedly and are detached from ourselves, we are reaching out into a limitlessness which exceeds any assignable bounds and which is nameless. We are reaching out towards the holy mystery which pervades and is the ground of our life. We are dealing with God. And something of this kind happens necessarily and always in the act of loving freedom of real, radical personal communication with one's neighbour. (1968, 112)

A Rahnerian view of silence between human persons, patterned on his depiction of love, can add to the on-going conversation about silence an appreciation for the risk involved in listening to the other. Rahner's use of silence makes it very clear that acknowledging and accepting the otherness and distance between persons is very difficult. His writings on love further emphasize that enacting self-possessing openness to the other involves risk to the self. To open the self to the unknown, flawed, and finite other is to risk the self, to venture into an unforeseen future, and to refrain from calculations of how to use the other for one's own benefit.

Feminist theology, at times, minimizes the radicality of listening and hearing by failing to recognize and enact this real risk. This can be seen in assumptions that feminists will listen. Morton writes that "[o]nce a person is heard to speech she becomes a hearing person" (1985, 210).[5] Rebecca Chopp states that "[c]laiming one's voice on the margins does not make one deaf; rather, it gives new ways to hear, new eyes to see, and new possibilities for solidarity" (1989, 16). While this is accurate in some instances, feminist theology as a whole must acknowledge that we have not lived up to this ideal. We have often allowed our own new voices to silence others and have not heard the silence of those who have yet to speak. Our openness to the other is often limited by unexamined dynamics of race, class, sexuality, etc.[6]

A poem by womanist ethicist and theologian Emilie Townes addresses the difficulties of hearing difference (Eugene et al. 1994). It begins:

> for years, there was silence
>     or more appropriately, few listened
> whole worlds were left outside dominant discourse and analysis
>     except as the occasional other
>     who served the needs of oppression and dehumanization (107)

Through the rest of the poem, Townes explores the nature of otherness and its role in the struggling conversation between feminist, mujerista, and womanist theologians engaging postmodernity. She warns against imagining that the difficulties of this conversation can be quickly or easily overcome when, too often, we refuse to hear difference and otherness. Part of her poem reads:

---

5  Morton 210. Note that the racial identities of the women in Morton's story about hearing into speech are not mentioned. Morton hints that hearing into speech employs a non-hierarchical power, but she does not develop this in the texts.

6  For a good introduction to these issues, in addition to the texts used in this chapter, see Williams (1994) and Cannon and Heyward (1994).

the voice is salient
   yet this is not a disembodied voice
   but one in which rich traditions and histories
   have shaped it
   (and continue to be renewed and transformed)
it is a voice from a particular culture
   whose integrity and worth must be respected
if we rush in too quickly
   with our tools of correct analysis
   and sisterly solidarity
the voice we will hear is our own echo
   a distortion of the original
   but dolby in sound (109-110)

The poem ends with Townes' awareness that while the womanist voice is new at the table, the voices of many others remain unheard. She writes in the final section:

   but I am also aware
that other voices have not yet joined
   (and there are those who are just pulling up to)
   our kitchen table
     the power to name and speak of native american women is a
      yawning silence
   and there are others…
the challenge for me
   is as more women join what has largely
   and ill-fittingly
   been a black/white dialogue
that i will take my words to heart
   and not interrupt them
   as they speak
but listen (112-113)

In this poem, Townes makes clear that not listening plays a role in sinful silencing. Further, she identifies a kind of listening that is not truly open to the other, but only hears that part of the other's speech that reaffirms the hearer's own identity. Townes contrasts this with the listening she intends, one which opens the listener to challenge, change, and transformation.

Townes, like Rahner, recognizes that openness to the other is difficult and risky. Both make it clear that the silence of which they speak is not the safety of non-involvement, even under cover of a politically correct reticence. The kind of silence and listening that emerges in this conversation is not a lack of speech in the face of suffering or injustice, but an active, powerful offering of space and attention to the unheard—a political act.

In a Rahnerian framework, the risk of opening the self to the unknown and unmanipulable other makes no sense apart from grace. The other person is finite and flawed, subject to death and sin, and therefore the risk of offering silence to the other is unwarranted. However, if, given the connections between silence and love in Rahner's theology, we see silence in the pattern of love, this suggests a unity between offering silence to God and listening to neighbor. Every offering of silence to another takes place within the silent horizon of the mystery of God and, as we are oriented towards this silent horizon, our silence offered to another human being is also offered towards God. We can know and love God in and through the mundane world around us, preeminently through interpersonal relationships. We can see and hear God that way, too (Rahner 1968, 200). Further, through grace, God has elevated our transcendentality towards our neighbor such that it becomes the possibility of immediacy to God.[7]

This Rahnerian logic relies on Christological claims, in two related ways. First, in and through the grace of the incarnation of Jesus Christ, God has come to abide in humanity and humanity has been accepted into God. Put simply, God abides in us. When we offer our silence to our neighbor, we are offering it to a person in whom God abides and thus we are offering it to God. Second, Jesus bears the excess trust necessary to offer our silence. It would make no sense to risk ourselves by

---

7 The connection between silence before God and silence between persons does not precisely parallel the connection between love of God and love of neighbor, for there does not appear to be the same kind of necessity at work with silence. In Rahner's theology and spirituality, there is no way to love God apart from other persons. However, there does seem to be a possibility of being silent before God in solitude. The structure of his system supports the idea that every offering of silence to God is also an offering to another person, but it does not happen out of the same level and type of necessity as with love.

being so open to another human being. No human being, aside from
Jesus, can warrant such a leap of faith. We properly have the right of
extravagance to be so open to another only in relation to Jesus Christ.
Yet this right of extravagance can be extended to those who are included in the affirmation of Jesus Christ. Standing surety for both parties,
Jesus is the ground of the open offering of silence, and as such he too is
given silence whenever we give it to another human person.

Someone who views Rahner as an unrepentant modernist might
see this as yet another articulation of the logic of the same. A faithful
person ought to listen to the other, precisely *as other*, risking her own
transformation in the hearing. Yet the reasoning behind this opening to otherness is that all persons are really the same (loved by God)
and there is one single narrative (of Jesus Christ) that explains this
identity. Surely here, on the topic of listening to the other, Rahner's
Christocentric anthropology is highly problematic. In contrast, I have
argued above against reading Rahner simply as a modernist, and sug-
gested the possibility of a Christian apophatic anthropology. This has
been funded by reading Rahner in a non-foundationalist way: not as
grounded in a neutral philosophical explication of human nature, but
rather as a theological interpretation of human existence in relation to
God in light of Christian faith.

The picture of listening to the other that results from this interpretation of Rahner is not one in which the Christian should step
outside of her faith identity in order to encounter the other on neutral
or secular ground. Rather, the Christian offers silence to the other in a
kind of listening that is enabled by faith. Such listening, which opens
the self to the unknown other and risks real transformation, enacts the
faith that the mystery permeating human life is meaningful, that the
void beyond our comprehension shelters us in love. There is paradox
and tension here: a person who has faith in the love of God enacts,
in listening, an openness to the other that may well change how she
understands divine love. Faith is enabled by grace to risk itself in love.
Faith that fails to do this is something less than faith.

A Rahnerian gloss on silence and listening contributes to the current conversation a sense that this open listening is precisely an act of
faith. It is difficult, risky, enabled by grace, and an integral part of what
it is to say "yes" to God. We say "yes" to God as other— as one whom

we cannot control or possess—when we give our silence to God. We wait, in prayer and faith, to hear God's word, creating room in our lives where God's voice can be heard. One way that our offering silence to God is realized concretely and historically is in offering silence to our neighbor. This does not mean that everything our neighbor says is the word of God. We will ultimately contest and reject many words uttered in response to our silence. Yet the disposition of openness to the other, of risking transformation by encountering difference, is a fundamental part of faith. In this way, offering silence to the other has a mystical, as well as political, element.

Such an articulation of the unity between offering silence to God and listening to neighbor might well resonate (in Rahnerian fashion) with Christians who experience a connection between the silence of prayer and worship and the political and mystical act of listening to the concrete human other. Each act draws upon, and contributes to, a disposition of self-possessing openness to the other, a disposition that then funds other acts of silence before both God and the human other.

Viewing listening as part of Christian faith has the further benefit of exhorting those who have privilege and power to offer silence to the oppressed and marginalized. In so doing, it repeats Rahner's bias of writing for those who speak more than for those who are silenced. Such a focus becomes problematic if it leaves power primarily in the hands of the privileged as both speakers and those who enable the speech of others. Rahner's emphasis on openness to the other cuts against this somewhat, but such concerns are more directly addressed by the work of Ada María Isasi-Díaz.

A mujerista theologian, Isasi-Díaz writes explicitly about the struggle to find her own voice and the role of listening (1994, 77). She is careful to discuss the enabling power of listening in a way that does not take power away from the oppressed who speak, or imply that the speech of the oppressed is dependent on the good-will and understanding of the privileged. Isasi-Díaz writes about the audience Rahner appears to assume: those who have voice and privilege. She states, "the oppressors who are willing to listen and to be questioned by the oppressed begin to cease being oppressors—they become 'friends' of the oppressed"

(82).[8] She acknowledges that "[t]he response of the 'friends' is one of the enabling forces which help the oppressed to become agents of their own history" (83). At the same time, the response of the "friends" and the voice that is gained through it can become problematic if focus and power is shifted away from the oppressed.

Isasi-Díaz asserts that in freely listening, these "friends" open themselves up to transformation that is empowered by the oppressed:

> This word uttered by the oppressed divests those who allow themselves to be questioned by it of whatever they have totally appropriated. This word carries in its very weakness the power to judge the desire for wealth and power. It also is able to signify effectively the real possibility of liberation for those oppressors who allow themselves to be questioned. The leap the oppressors must take in order to be questioned is also made possible by the efficacious word uttered by the oppressed. … This word also makes it possible for the "friends" to question and judge the oppressive structures which they support and from which they benefit, and to become cocreators with the oppressed of new liberating structures. (83)

Isasi-Díaz thus advocates a relationship of mutuality between the oppressed and the friends (81-82). This emphasis on mutuality can help guard against some of the problematic dynamics that could be fostered by Rahner's focus on those who have the power of speech. Furthermore, Isasi-Díaz discussion of mutuality might be useful in addressing the lack of self-protective norms in Rahner's theology of love.

This brief discussion suggests ways that Rahner's use of silence can be brought into current conversations among feminist, womanist, and mujerista theologians about silence and listening. Rahner's theology, especially his use of silence and his work on love, contributes a theological framework in which Christian faith is enacted in self-possessing openness to the unknown other. Continuing Rahnerian theology can also benefit from struggles within this conversation to advocate

---

8 She notes, "I have based this section about the relationship between the oppressor and the 'friend' on Juan Carlos Scannone, *Teología de la Liberación y Praxis Popular* (Salamanca: Ediciones Sigueme, 1976), Scannone uses the word brother. I have used friend in translating into English in order to avoid a sexist term" (n. 25, 86, 87).

listening within a norm of mutuality that limits the power of the privileged.[9]

Emerging from such conversation between the work of Rahner and that of feminist, womanist, and mujerista theologians is an analysis of sinful silencing and an appreciation that listening can help to empower the voices of others. Such empowering listening has particular characteristics. It is open to the other *as other*, instead of hearing her only insofar as she affirms the worldview of the listener. It risks the transformation of the listener and of the relationship between both parties. It is part of a posture of faith, of openness to the other and trust in mystery. Therefore it is connected to the silence of worship and liturgy, such that worshipful silence and transformative listening are mutually enabling. Finally, such listening—as faith, happening within grace—is an encounter with the Divine.

## LOVE AND DEATH

In Chapter Three I elaborated Rahner's theology of love, parts of which have been recounted once again above. I have also noted the ways in which Rahner's theology has created space in which some liberation theologies operate, both through his claims that each person can know God and in his assertions that we say "yes" to God by loving our neighbor. Without repeating all of that, here I mention that Rahner's theology of love, in conjunction with his reflections on death,[10] are a particular kind of resource for social justice work in postmodern times. Specifically, his theology is a resource for political action that is resistant to failure.

A student of modern history knows a litany of struggles for social justice that have, to some degree or another, failed. In recent times in the United States, the Civil Rights Movement affected some changes but failed to fully stem the ongoing tide of racial inequality, injustice, and hatred. The Women's Liberation Movement made some progress, but did not disarm the oppressive forces of patriarchy. When these movements are touted as simple successes, it is a deception that un-

---

9 See also Díaz (2001, 136-137).

10 Mannion notes, "Rahner often speaks movingly about both love and death—indeed his thoughts on one are, more often than not, bound up with and illuminated by those on the other" (2004, 167).

dermines resistance, fosters complacency, and masks current injustice. An international focus, and a longer memory, multiplies the instances of failure exponentially.

Also, such a student's awareness of herself and her actions in the world are increasingly complicated by the various analyses of postmodernism, postcolonialism, globalization, and climate change. She learns that her ways of thinking replicate oppressive patterns of thought, so deeply ingrained in her that she cannot think otherwise. She analyzes her location within the Western center of epistemic power as participating in the damage done to colonized cultures. How she sees and speaks the world is inextricably bound with the oppression of others. The clothes she buys for herself and her children are made in *maquiladoras*, south of the border, in deplorable conditions, by children younger than her own. She can go online and calculate how much $CO_2$ she is emitting in her daily life, how quickly she is contributing to the destruction of the planet, with the only bitter comfort offered being the grim reality that the poor in underdeveloped countries will pay the first, and most brutal, cost for her participation in excess.

Both the fragmentation and the unification of postmodern worldviews can make action for social justice seem futile and impossible. How can we tell a common story, rally behind a common cause, understand ourselves as a stable group? Even if we managed to do so, in a globalized world the interwoven systems of injustice are too encompassing to dismantle.

Such tensions are not merely an effect of postmodern discourse. They are also inherent in liberation and political theologies that are deeply committed to social justice. These theologies demand sustained analysis of the realities of oppression and injustice. Furthermore, they examine the structural and systemic nature of sin and evil. This leads to acknowledgement of the depth and breadth of the problem, and to a sense of the difficulty of enacting change. How then, are the hope and energy necessary for social justice work sustained?

Feminist and liberation theologian Letty Russell, as a teacher, performs her response to such questions in two ways that emphasize the importance of community. In many classes, a student will ask her how one finds continuing motivation for social justice efforts. Sometimes Russell responds by acknowledging that the task is immense and progress is slow. But, she asserts, small steps towards justice can be made through communities of struggle. Russell says that while any given social movement will not succeed in eradicating injustice, a community can make "chickee steps." By this, Russell means that the small changes made by group struggle can have lasting effects and liberating influence. When Russell describes "chickee steps," she also performs them, taking one tiny step, then another, and another, and another. Students see their august and revered professor stepping away from the podium to perform a silly chickee dance in front of the class, and they laugh. The whole class laughs, out loud, together. In that moment, a collection of individual students—worn down by awareness of sin and evil—becomes a whole: a community joined together in laughter that dispels despair. It is this experience of community, more than any simple assertion of slow progress through small steps, that embodies Russell's understanding of hope and motivation.[11]

This communal hope is also performatively produced in the "shalom meals" with which Russell concludes her classes. After a demanding semester in which students analyze oppression and recognize their own complicity in unjust social structures, the class comes together at Russell's home to eat, drink, sing, pray, laugh, act out skits, and create impromptu rituals of Christian hope and resistance. Serene Jones and Margaret Farley write about how students come to recognize themselves, in the midst of this celebration, as a community formed over the months of learning and struggle (1999, vii). Jones and Farley recall that Russell "reminds her students in the midst of the party, [that] what they are experiencing is just a brief glimpse of God's gift of shalom to all creation. The joyous meal offers a preview of the New Creation that God, in Jesus Christ, has promised to all. Her parties are thus a small but powerful enactment of the 'liberating eschaton' that stretches before all humanity" (viii).

In both the shared laughter that follows her "chickee steps" and the group celebration of "shalom meals," Russell creates communities of struggle and solidarity in which her students experience, "proleptically," the communal liberation of the New Creation.[12] Such experiences

11   In describing this, Russell states, "You need a lot of chickees." Personal conversation, May 24, 2007.

12   See Russell (1974, 41-42).

are Russell's response to questions about how to sustain motivation to work for social justice, given the entrenched, systemic realities of sin and oppression.

While the theologies of Rahner and Russell differ in many important regards, there are fruitful connections on this particular issue of sustaining motivation for social justice work. In both of their theologies, present work for social justice can be understood in terms of communal eschatology.

Unlike Russell, Rahner does not analyze interlocking systems of oppression such as racism, sexism, and classism. However, he does offer an abstract but unflinching depiction of human life as a difficult and bitter reality. He further claims that Christian faith does not permit one to gloss over the brutalities of life, but rather requires squarely facing them. He writes that

> Christian life is the acceptance of human existence as such, as opposed to a final protest against it. But this means that a Christian sees reality as it is. Christianity does not oblige him to see the reality of the world of his experience and the reality of his historical experience of life in an optimistic light. On the contrary, it obliges him to see this existence as dark and bitter and hard, and as an unfathomable and radical risk. (1982, 403)

Rahner famously advocates a kind of Christian pessimism that sees clearly the limitations, hardships, and horrors of human life (403-404; 1991b, 155-162). He calls for preaching of this pessimism, against the "euphoric belief in progress" (157), and regrets that *Gaudium et Spes*, a document of Vatican II,

> does not insist enough on the fact that all human endeavors, with all their sagacity and good will, often end up in blind alleys; that in questions of morality, when we really face the whole of reality, we get lost in obscurities which no moral formula can wholly remove. In short, as Scripture says, the world is in a bad way and it will stay that way, even if, as we are obliged to do, we fight against evil to the death. (158)

We participate in the ills of the world through our own sinfulness and through our every act of freedom. Rahner writes:

> "this very exercise of freedom—being that of a creature, depending on pre-requisites, as the freedom of a material, inter-personal

and communicative being—is at once a restriction of the space of another's freedom, essentially and inevitably. No one can act freely without impinging on the sphere of another's freedom without his previous consent—without doing 'violence' to him..." (1966g, 396).

This bleak view does not mean that Christians should accept evil passively, resign ourselves to injustice, or use the moral complexities of human life as an excuse for inaction.[13] While, according to Rahner's theology, attempts to create a just social order in history will never fully succeed due to the realities of sin and finitude, this does not mean that Christians ought not participate in such efforts. On the contrary, struggling for social justice is a profound act of faith. We know God, become who we are called to be, experience the indwelling of the Holy Spirit, and say "yes" to God in love of neighbor. This love has significant implications for social action.[14] If we embrace this element of Rahner's theology, then Christian faith includes, but is not limited to, work for social justice.

Furthermore, in loving neighbor we shape our own eternity, as this "yes" to God is granted eternal validity and significance. In the love of neighbor that takes place in work for social justice, the Christian opens herself to a future with God by anticipating that future in history. Rahner says "that the creation of a humane future is not something optional for the Christian, but is the means by which he prepares himself, in actuality and not merely in theory, for God's absolute future" (1972b, 201).[15]

Thus Rahner's theology affirms the deep, abiding, and eternal significance of work for social justice in a way that is not dependent on historical success. This is not simply a move away from the historical to the eternal, but rather a claim that when someone manages to love her neighbor, thus saying "yes" to God, she participates in eternity

---

13   See Rahner (1991b, 158 and 1966g). Also, in what I take to be an allusion to the moral quandaries of *The Brothers Karamazov*, Rahner states that "We have neither the possibility nor the right to give back our admission ticket to existence, a ticket which is still used and not allowed to expire even when someone tries to annihilate himself in a suicide attempt" (1982, 106).

14   See Rahner (1986b, 135, 202-203), (1991, 63), and (1972b, 189).

15   See also Rahner (1982, 447).

within history.[16] Rahner asserts that "in a radical affirmation of love for another person, something eternal has taken place" (1982, 439).

The eternity which comes to be in history is fundamentally a communal reality. Rahner emphasizes a vision of a communally sanctified humanity in eternal communion with God. Within Rahner's theology, each Christian hopes for herself and her own salvation only within a larger hope for humanity as a whole.[17] Thus the love in which something eternal takes place is necessarily interpersonal and is part of a larger intercommunion of humanity and God.

Such love can participate in eternity within history because it also goes through death, the death that happens throughout human life. This affirmation of the significance of love, and therefore of work for social justice, in the context of a Christian pessimism is Christological. Recall that for Rahner, when someone loves another person who dies, there is a loss of self, a death within the self of the surviving lover. Love risks death. To live lovingly is then to live "a dying life" with Christ (Rahner 1997c, 147).

Commitment to social justice, even when such efforts appear to fail, is similarly a love that risks death, that entails a loss of self, and that is, ultimately, a dying life. Christianity—as lived faith in the life, death, and resurrection of Jesus Christ—claims that dying life is eternally meaningful. Rahner writes:

> Presupposing that a Christian faces death, every struggle for existence and every inner-worldly hope in the future is legitimate—indeed it is imposed upon him. But he is a Christian only if he believes that everything positive and beautiful and everything which blossoms has to pass through what we call death. Christianity is the religion which recognizes a man who was nailed to a cross and on it died a violent death as a sign of victory and as a realistic expression of human life. (1982, 404)

Living a dying life with Christ is both a lonely, individual commitment and an intensely relational, communal way of being. The limited, conditioned, and profoundly impinged-upon freedom of the human person demands that a choice be made. While one may attempt to analyze this freedom out of existence by tracing the determining fac-

---

16   For a discussion of this, see Mannion (2004, 174).

17   See Rahner (1972b, 189; 1975b, 176-178, 183).

tors of human life, within a person's own day-to-day reality, she cannot abdicate the responsibility of disposing of herself in relation to other persons and to God. No one else can shoulder this burden. Thus her decision is a lonely one. At the same time, this decision is deeply relational and communal in three ways. First, without embarking on extended Trinitarian reflections, it is clear that saying "yes" involves self-committing surrender into the mystery of the incomprehensible God, it is made possible by Jesus Christ, and it is an experience of the Holy Spirit. Second, saying "yes" takes place concretely in loving the human neighbor. Third, saying "yes" both anticipates and participates in eternity, in the eternal intercommunion of humanity with God. Put more bluntly, an individual's act of Christian faith takes place within the love of a Triune God, in a concrete human community, and within the communion of saints. While being Christian requires individual self-commitment, it cannot be done alone.

A Rahnerian impetus for social justice work is not for the faint of heart. It describes love in conjunction with death and warns against "euphoric belief in progress" (Rahner 1991b, 157).While our struggle will not create a perfect world in history, in our efforts we are living the history whose mature fruit is the eternal intercommunion of humanity and God. Thus Rahner writes, "as Christians, we have the sacred duty, for which we will be held accountable before God, to fight for this very history of ours joyfully, courageously, confidently. We also have the duty to bring about a foretaste of God's eternal reign through our solidarity, unselfishness, willingness to share, and love of peace" (160).

Rahner and Russell are similar in holding an eschatological view of human community in relation to God. This communal future funds efforts to shape a humane and just present. Even more, present love and work for justice actually participate, to some degree, in this eschatological communion. Russell, writing in a Protestant theological framework, describes the New Creation as "the future (*adventus*) which comes toward us from God as a *promise*" (Russell 1974, 42). Christians are called to live now *as if* God's future were already fully present (42, 46). Christians anticipate this future proleptically by "participating in the action of God on behalf of human liberation," thus "establish[ing] signs of hope, horizons of the future, in the midst of the present" (41-46).

Rahner's depiction of love of neighbor as participating in eternity relies on his understanding of eternity as the mature fruit of time, of saying "yes" to God, and of dying with Christ. This sober account of Christian love as dying with Christ can be a theological support for social justice work that continually acknowledges apparent failure. Indeed, the metaphor assumes that the criteria of success are often beyond human calculation and understanding, The crucifixion appeared to be the end of a new community. And yet, in Christ's death and resurrection humanity says "yes" to God and God accepts this "yes," securing the eternal intercommunion of humanity with God. Similarly, Christian work for justice often fails in its aims, and yet it is a "yes" to God, participating in this eternal intercommunion.

Rahner's reflections lack the buoyant communal hope of Russell's "chickee steps" and "shalom meals." However, I believe they are complementary insights. Alongside experiences of community and solidarity, work for justice also includes isolation and the necessity of individual commitment when support networks are not obvious. Rahner's theology acknowledges such moments of loneliness and apparent failure, while affirming them—as dying with Christ and participating in eternal communion—as elements of saying "yes" to God. Indeed, Rahner asserts that it is the "situation of death," in which our own possibilities are at end, which "constitutes precisely the prior condition which makes hope in the strictly theological sense possible" (Rahner 1975b, 181).

Both Rahner and Russell describe Christian hope as funded by grace, rather than assurance of human capabilities for progress. Russell notes, "hope comes not from foolproof plans or illusions, doctrines or traditions, mythologies or ideologies, but from confidence in God's promise of liberation" (33-34). Recall that Rahner similarly rejects equating what is hoped for in faith with "that which is planned, that which is undertaken as the outcome of neutral speculation" (1975b, 177). In contrast, he describes hope as "the free and trustful commitment of love to the 'impossible', i.e. to that which can no longer be constructed from materials already present to the individual himself and at his disposal" (177). Given this, it follows that "what is hoped for is present to us only within the hope itself, and is otherwise not even present as really conceivable" (178).

Rahner thus articulates a view of hope as a "paradoxical unity" of human creative commitment and Divine gift (178). Within this unity, inside the act of hoping, one can imagine new possibilities that are, rationally speaking, impossible to construct from the world as it is. This sense of hope echoes profoundly with Russell's performative creation of communities of hope. In such communities, people creatively commit to the future of liberation that is the gift of God.

For Rahner, criticism of the structures of this world is "one of the concrete forms of Christian hope" (Rahner 1977, 258. Emphasis removed.). Both theologians assert that hope exposes such structures as "provisional" (Rahner 1977, 258; Russell 1974, 45). In active hope for our communal future with God, new possibilities can be conceived and lived into.

## CONCLUSION

This book, as a reflection on saying "yes" to God in Rahner's theology, has focused on silence, love, and death. This unusual lens, along with a non-foundationalist interpretation of Rahner, fosters a generous reading of his theology and brings his work into current conversations. Rahner's theology has been characterized as one of "rescue" rather than "criticism," as he attempted to find continuing value in traditional Christian doctrine.[18] I have attempted to imitate this aspect of his approach by seeking the elements and interpretations of Rahner that might be useful today. This practice illumines an abundance of resources in Rahner's work, of which this coda gestures towards only a few. Rahner's theology, which portrays Christian faithfulness and the human person as self-possessing openness to the other, is itself open to multiple other uses, deployments, and dialogues.

---

18  Vorgrimler (1986, 21) refers to J. B. Metz's characterization in *Den Glauben lernen und lehren. Dank an Karl Rahner*, Munich 1984, 14; and *Unterbrechungen. Theologisch-politische Perspektiven und Profile*, Gütersloh 1981, 44.

# WORKS CITED

Abraham, Susan. 2004. The Caress of the Doer of the Word: A Post-colonial Critique of Miguel Díaz's *On Being Human*. *Philosophy and Theology* 16: 115-121.

Adams, Nicholas. 2005. Rahner's Reception in Twentieth Century Protestant Theology. In *The Cambridge Companion to Karl Rahner*, ed. Declan Marmion and Mary E. Hines, 211-224. New York: Cambridge University Press.

Austin, J. L. 1975. *How To Do Things With Words*. 2nd edition, ed. J.O. Urmson and Marina Sbisà. Cambridge, MA: Harvard University Press.

Berryman, Phillip. 1987. *Liberation Theology: Essential Facts about the Revolutionary Movement in Latin America—and Beyond*. New York: Pantheon Books.

Beste, Jennifer. 2003a. Receiving and Responding to God's Grace: A Re-examination in Light of Trauma Theory. *Journal of the Society of Christian Ethics* 23 (1): 3-20.

———. 2003b. Trauma, Relationality, and Freedom before God. Ph.D. diss., Yale University.

Bell, Catherine. 2005. Constraints on the Theological Absorption of Plurality. In *Rahner Beyond Rahner: A Great Theologian Encounters the Pacific Rim*, ed. Paul G. Crowley, 39-49. Lanham, MD: Rowman & Littlefield.

Boros, Ladislaus. 1965. *The Mystery of Death*. Trans. Gregory Bainbridge. New York: Herder and Herder.

Brinkman, Bruno. 1984. Theology Present to Itself: A Tribute to Karl Rahner. *The Heythrop Journal* 25 (3): 257-259.

Burke, Patrick. 2002. *Reinterpreting Rahner: A Critical Study of His Major Themes*. New York: Fordham University Press.

Butler, Judith. 1990. *Gender Trouble: Feminism and the Subversion of Identity*. New York: Routledge.

Cannon, Katie G. and Carter Heyward. 1994. Can We Be Different But Not Alienated? An Exchange of Letters. In *Feminist

*Theological Ethics: A Reader,* ed. Lois K. Daly, 59-76. Louisville, KY: Westminster/John Knox Press.

Caponi, Francis J. 2007. A Speechless Grace: Karl Rahner on Religious Language. *International Journal of Systematic Theology* 9 (2): 200-221.

Chauvet, Louis-Marie. 1995. *Symbol and Sacrament: A Sacramental Reinterpretation of Christian Existence.* Trans. Patrick Madigan and Madeleine Beaumont. Collegeville, MN: Liturgical Press.

Chopp, Rebecca. 1989. *The Power to Speak: Feminism, Language, and God.* New York: Crossroad.

Coffey, David. 2001. The Spirit of Christ as Entelechy. *Philosophy and Theology* 13 (2): 363-398.

———. 2004. The Whole Rahner on the Supernatural Existential. *Theological Studies* 65 (1) 95-118.

Conway, Eamonn. 1993. *The Anonymous Christian—A Relativised Christianity? An Evaluation of Hans Urs von Balthasar's Criticisms of Karl Rahner's Theory of the Anonymous Christian.* New York: Peter Lang.

Dallavalle, Nancy A. 2005. Feminist Theologies. In *The Cambridge Companion to Karl Rahner,* eds. Declan Marmion and Mary E. Hines, 264-277. New York: Cambridge University Press.

Derrida, Jacques. 1978. Structure, Sign, and Play in the Discourse of the Human Sciences. In *Writing and Difference,* trans. Alan Bass, 278-93. Chicago: University of Chicago Press.

———. 1992. How to Avoid Speaking: Denials. In *Derrida and Negative Theology,* ed. Harold Coward and Toby Foshay, and trans. Ken Frieden, 73-142. Albany, NY: State University of New York Press. Essay reprinted from *Languages of the Unsayable: The Play of Negativity in Literature and Literary Theory,* eds. Sanford Budick and Wolfgang Eiser (New York: Columbia University Press, 1989).

Descartes, René. 1999. *Discourse on Method and Related Writings.* Trans. Desmond Clarke. New York: Penguin Books.

Díaz, Miguel. 2001. *On Being Human: U.S. Hispanic and Rahnerian Perspectives.* Maryknoll, NY: Orbis Books.

Dych, William V. 1992. *Karl Rahner.* New York: Continuum.

Egan, Harvey D. 1980. "The Devout Christian of the Future Will...Be a 'Mystic.'" Mysticism and Karl Rahner's Theology. In *Theology and Discovery: Essays in Honor of Karl Rahner, S.J.*, ed. William J. Kelly, 139-158. Milwaukee, WI: Marquette University Press.

———. 1998. *Karl Rahner: Mystic of Everyday Life*. New York: Crossroad.

Endean, Philip. 1996. Rahner, Christology, and Grace. *The Heythrop Journal* 37 (3): 284-97.

———. 2001. *Karl Rahner and Ignatian Spirituality*. New York: Oxford University Press.

Eugene, Toinette M., Ada María Isasi-Díaz, Kwok Pui-Lan, Judith Plaskow, Mary E. Hunt, Emilie M. Townes, and Ellen Umansky. 1994. Appropriation and Reciprocity in Womanist/Mujerista/Feminist Work. In *Feminist Theological Ethics: A Reader*, ed. Lois K. Daly, 88-117. Louisville, KY: Westminster/John Knox Press.

Farley, Margaret. 1992. Feminism and Universal Morality. In *Prospects for a Common Morality*, eds. Gene Outka, John P. Reeder, Jr., 170-190. Princeton: Princeton University Press.

Fields, Stephen. 2000. *Being as Symbol: On the Origins and Development of Karl Rahner's Metaphysics*. Washington, D.C.: Georgetown University Press.

Fiorenza, Elisabeth Schüssler. 1996. Breaking the Silence—Becoming Visible. In *The Power of Naming: A Concilium Reader in Feminist and Liberation Theology*, ed. Elisabeth Schüssler Fiorenza, 161-174. Maryknoll, NY: Orbis Books.

Fletcher, Jeannine Hill. 2005. Rahner and Religious Diversity. In *The Cambridge Companion to Karl Rahner*, eds. Declan Marmion and Mary E. Hines, 235-248. New York: Cambridge University Press.

Govinden, Betty. 1994. No Time for Silence: Women, Church, and Liberation in Southern Africa. In *Feminist Theology from the Third World: A Reader*, ed. Ursula King, 283-302. Maryknoll, NY: Orbis Books.

Goldstein, Valerie Saiving. 1960. The Human Situation: A Feminine View. *Journal of Religion*, 40 (2): 100-112.

Grant, Jacquelyn. 1993. The Sin of Servanthood and the Deliverance of Discipleship. In *A Troubling in my Soul: Womanist Perspectives on Evil and Suffering*, ed. Emilie M. Townes, 199-218. Maryknoll, NY: Orbis Books.

Guenther, Titus F. 1994. *Rahner and Metz: Transcendental Theology as Political Theology*. Lanham, MD: University Press of America.

Hampson, Daphne. 1990. Luther on the self: A feminist critique. In *Feminist Theology: A Reader*, ed. Ann Loades, 215-224. Louisville, KY: Westminster/John Knox Press.

Healy, Nicholas. 1992. Indirect methods in theology: Karl Rahner as an ad hoc apologist. *The Thomist* 56: 613-34.

Heidegger, Martin. 1968. Identité et Différence. In *Question I*, trans. A. Préau. Paris: Gallimard, 1968. Quoted in Louis-Marie Chauvet, *Symbol and Sacrament: A Sacramental Reinterpretation of Christian Existence*, trans. Patrick Madigan and Madeleine Beaumont (Collegeville, MN: Liturgical Press, 1995), 27.

Hogan, Kevin. 1998. Entering into Otherness: The Postmodern Critique of the Subject and Karl Rahner's Theological Anthropology. *Horizons* 25 (2): 181-202.

Isasi-Díaz, Ada María. 1994. Solidarity: Love of Neighbor in the 1980s. In *Feminist Theological Ethics: A Reader*, ed. Lois K. Daly, 77-87. Louisville, KY: Westminster/John Knox Press.

Irigaray, Luce. 1985. *Speculum of the Other Woman*. Trans. Gillian C. Gill. Ithaca, NY: Cornell University Press.

———. 1993. *An Ethics of Sexual Difference*. Trans. Carolyn Burke and Gillian C. Gill. Ithaca, NY: Cornell University Press.

Jones, Serene. 1997. Women's Experience between a Rock and a Hard Place: Feminist, Womanist, and *Mujerista* Theologies in North America. In *Horizons in Feminist Theology: Identity, Tradition, and Norms*, eds. Rebecca Chopp and Sheila Greeve Davaney, 33-53. Minneapolis: Fortress Press.

———. 2000. *Feminist Theory and Christian Theology: Cartographies of Grace*. Minneapolis: Fortress Press.

Jones, Serene, and Margaret Farley. 1999. Introduction. In *Liberating Eschatology: Essays in Honor of Letty M. Russell*, eds. Margaret

Farley and Serene Jones, vii-xv. Louisville, KY: Westminster/ John Knox Press.

Kelly, Brian. 1984. Aspects of the Theology of Death. *The Irish Theological Quarterly* 50: 233-238.

Kelly, Geffrey B. 1992. Introduction. In *Karl Rahner: Theologian of the Graced Search for Meaning*, ed. Geffrey B. Kelly, 1-62. Minneapolis: Fortress Press.

Kelsey, David. 1997. Two Theologies of Death: Anthropological Gleanings. *Modern Theology* 13 (3): 347-70.

Kerr, Fergus. 1997a. [1986] *Theology after Wittgenstein*, 2nd edition. New York: Blackwell.

———. 1997b. *Immortal Longings: Versions of Transcending Humanity*. Notre Dame, IN: University of Notre Dame Press.

———. 2007. *Twentieth-Century Catholic Theologians: From Neoscholasticism to Nuptial Mysticism*. Malden, MA: Blackwell.

Kilby, Karen. 2004. *Karl Rahner: Theology and Philosophy*. New York: Routledge.

Kress, Robert. 1982. *A Rahner Handbook*. Atlanta: John Knox Press.

Lash, Nicholas. 1988. *Easter in Ordinary: Reflections on Human Experience and the Knowledge of God*. Charlottesville: University Press of Virginia.

Lindbeck, George. 1984. *The Nature of Doctrine: Religion and Theology in a Postliberal Age*. Philadelphia: Westminster Press.

Loades, Anne. 1990. Introduction. *Feminist Theology: A Reader*, ed. Anne Loades, 1-11. Louisville, KY: Westminster John Knox.

Malcom, Lois. 2005. Rahner's Theology of the Cross. In *Rahner Beyond Rahner: A Great Theologian Encounters the Pacific Rim*, ed. Paul G. Crowley, 115-131. Lanham, MD: Rowman & Littlefield.

Mannion, Gerard. 2004. The End of the Beginning: Discerning Fundamental Themes in Rahner's Theology of Death. *Louvain Studies* 29 (2): 166-86.

Marmion, Declan. 1998. *A Spirituality of Everyday Faith : A Theological Investigation of the Notion of Spirituality in Karl Rahner*. Louvain: Peeters Press.

———. 2003. Rahner and His Critics: Revisiting the Dialogue. *Irish Theological Quarterly* 68 (3): 195-212.

Martinez, Gaspar. 2001. *Confronting the Mystery of God: Political, Liberation, and Public Theologies.* New York: Continuum.

Metz, Johannes Baptist. 1980. An Identity Crisis in Christianity? Transcendental and Political Responses. In *Theology and Discovery: Essays in Honor of Karl Rahner, S.J.*, ed. William J. Kelly, 169-178. Milwaukee: Marquette University Press.

———. 1998. *A Passion for God: The Mystical-Political Dimension of Christianity.* Trans. J. Matthew Ashley. New York: Paulist Press.

Milbank, John. 1990. *Theology and Social Theory: Beyond Secular Reason.* Oxford: Blackwell.

Morton, Nelle. 1985. *The Journey Is Home.* Boston: Beacon Press.

Muers, Rachel. 2004. *Keeping God's Silence: Towards a Theological Ethics of Communication.* Malden, MA: Blackwell.

———. 1989. *Beyond Servanthood: Christianity and the Liberation of Women.* Lanham, MD: University Press of America.

Nelson Dunfee, Susan. 1982. The Sin of Hiding: A Feminist Critique of Reinhold Neibuhr's Account of the Sin of Pride. *Soundings* 65 (3): 316-27.

Ochs, Robert. 1969. *The Death in Every Now.* New York: Sheed and Ward.

———. 1973. Death as Act: An Interpretation of Karl Rahner. In *The Mystery of Suffering and Death*, ed. Michael J. Taylor, 119-138. New York: Alba House.

Phan, Peter C. 1988. *Eternity in Time: A Study of Karl Rahner's Eschatology.* Selinsgrove, PA: Susquehanna University Press.

———. 2005. Eschatology. In *The Cambridge Companion to Karl Rahner*, eds. Declan Marmion and Mary E. Hines, 174-192. New York: Cambridge University Press.

Pineda-Madrid, Nancy. 2005. Guadalupe's Challenge to Rahner's Theology of Symbol. In *Rahner Beyond Rahner: A Great Theologian Encounters the Pacific Rim*, ed. Paul G. Crowley, 73-85. Lanham, MD: Rowman & Littlefield.

Plaskow, Judith. 1980. *Sex, Sin, and Grace: Women's Experience in the Theologies of Reinhold Niebuhr and Paul Tillich.* Washington: University Press of America.

Purcell, Michael. 1998. *Mystery and Method: The Other in Rahner and Levinas*. Milwaukee: Marquette University Press.

———. 2005. Rahner Amid Modernity and Post-Modernity. In *The Cambridge Companion to Karl Rahner*, eds. Declan Marmion and Mary E. Hines, 195-210. New York: Cambridge University Press.

Rahner, Karl. 1960. *Theos im Neuen Testament*. In *Schriften Zur Theologie*, vol. 1. Einsiedeln: Benziger.

———. 1961a. Concerning the Relationship between Nature and Grace. In *Theological Investigations*, vol. 1, trans. Cornelius Ernst, 297-317. New York: Crossroad.

———. 1961b. Theological Reflections on Monogenism. In *Theological Investigations*, vol. 1, trans. Cornelius Ernst, 229-296. New York: Crossroad.

———. 1961c. The Immaculate Conception. In *Theological Investigations*, vol. 1, trans. Cornelius Ernst, 201-214. New York: Crossroad.

———. 1964. *On the Theology of Death*. Trans. Charles H. Henkey. London: Burns & Oates.

———. 1966a. Christianity and the Non-Christian Religions. In *Theological Investigations*, vol. 5, trans. Karl-H. Kruger, 115-134. Baltimore: Helicon Press.

———. 1966b. The "Commandment" of Love in Relation to the Other Commandments. In *Theological Investigations*, vol. 5, trans. Karl-H. Kruger, 439-459. Baltimore: Helicon Press.

———. 1966c. The Concept of Mystery in Catholic Theology. In *Theological Investigations*, vol. 4, trans. Kevin Smyth, 36-73. Baltimore: Helicon Press.

———. 1966d. The Hermeneutics of Eschatological Assertions. In *Theological Investigations*, vol. 4, trans. Kevin Smyth, 323-346. Baltimore: Helicon Press.

———. 1966e. The Life of the Dead. In *Theological Investigations*, vol. 4, trans. Kevin Smyth, 347-354. Baltimore: Helicon Press.

———. 1966f. The Theology of the Symbol. In *Theological Investigations*, vol. 4, trans. Kevin Smyth, 221-252. Baltimore: Helicon Press.

―――. 1966g. Theology of Power. In *Theological Investigations*, vol. 4, trans. Kevin Smyth, 391-409. Baltimore: Helicon Press.

―――. 1967a. "Behold This Heart!": Preliminaries to a Theology of Devotion to the Sacred Heart. In *Theological Investigations*, vol. 3, trans. Karl-H. Kruger and Boniface Kruger, 321-330. Baltimore: Helicon Press.

―――. 1967b. Priest and Poet. In *Theological Investigations*, vol. 3, trans. Karl-H. Kruger and Boniface Kruger, 294-317. Baltimore: Helicon Press.

―――. 1967c. The Comfort of Time. In *Theological Investigations*, vol. 3, trans. Karl-H. Kruger and Boniface Kruger, 141-157. Baltimore: Helicon Press.

―――. 1967d. The Consecration of the Layman to the Care of Souls. In *Theological Investigations*, vol. 3, trans. Karl-H. Kruger and Boniface Kruger, 263-276. Baltimore: Helicon Press.

―――. 1967e. Thoughts on the Theology of Christmas. In *Theological Investigations*, vol. 3, trans. Karl-H. Kruger and Boniface Kruger, 24-34. Baltimore: Helicon Press.

―――. 1968. *Everyday Faith*. Trans. W.J. O'Hara. New York: Herder and Herder.

―――. 1969a. Anonymous Christians. In *Theological Investigations*, vol. 6, trans. Karl-H. Kruger and Boniface Kruger, 390-398. Baltimore: Helicon Press.

―――. 1969b. *Grace in Freedom*. Trans. Hilda Graef. New York: Herder and Herder.

―――. 1969c. Philosophy and Theology. In *Theological Investigations*, vol. 6, trans. Karl-H. Kruger and Boniface Kruger, 71-81. Baltimore: Helicon Press.

―――. 1969d. Reflections on the Unity of the Love of Neighbour and the Love of God. In *Theological Investigations*, vol. 6, trans. Karl-H. Kruger and Boniface Kruger, 231-249. Baltimore: Helicon Press.

―――. 1971a. Christian Living Formerly and Today. In *Theological Investigations*, vol. 7, trans. David Bourke, 3-24. New York: Seabury Press.

―――. 1971b. On Christian Dying. In *Theological Investigations*, vol. 7, trans. David Bourke, 285-293. New York: Seabury Press.

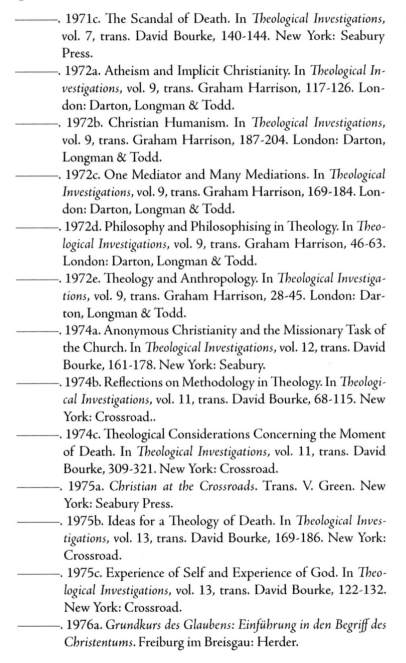

———. 1971c. The Scandal of Death. In *Theological Investigations*, vol. 7, trans. David Bourke, 140-144. New York: Seabury Press.

———. 1972a. Atheism and Implicit Christianity. In *Theological Investigations*, vol. 9, trans. Graham Harrison, 117-126. London: Darton, Longman & Todd.

———. 1972b. Christian Humanism. In *Theological Investigations*, vol. 9, trans. Graham Harrison, 187-204. London: Darton, Longman & Todd.

———. 1972c. One Mediator and Many Mediations. In *Theological Investigations*, vol. 9, trans. Graham Harrison, 169-184. London: Darton, Longman & Todd.

———. 1972d. Philosophy and Philosophising in Theology. In *Theological Investigations*, vol. 9, trans. Graham Harrison, 46-63. London: Darton, Longman & Todd.

———. 1972e. Theology and Anthropology. In *Theological Investigations*, vol. 9, trans. Graham Harrison, 28-45. London: Darton, Longman & Todd.

———. 1974a. Anonymous Christianity and the Missionary Task of the Church. In *Theological Investigations*, vol. 12, trans. David Bourke, 161-178. New York: Seabury.

———. 1974b. Reflections on Methodology in Theology. In *Theological Investigations*, vol. 11, trans. David Bourke, 68-115. New York: Crossroad..

———. 1974c. Theological Considerations Concerning the Moment of Death. In *Theological Investigations*, vol. 11, trans. David Bourke, 309-321. New York: Crossroad.

———. 1975a. *Christian at the Crossroads*. Trans. V. Green. New York: Seabury Press.

———. 1975b. Ideas for a Theology of Death. In *Theological Investigations*, vol. 13, trans. David Bourke, 169-186. New York: Crossroad.

———. 1975c. Experience of Self and Experience of God. In *Theological Investigations*, vol. 13, trans. David Bourke, 122-132. New York: Crossroad.

———. 1976a. *Grundkurs des Glaubens: Einführung in den Begriff des Christentums*. Freiburg im Breisgau: Herder.

————. 1976b. Observations on the Problem of the "Anonymous Christian." In *Theological Investigations*, vol. 14, trans. David Bourke, 280-294. New York: Seabury.

————. 1977. On the Theology of Hope. In *Theological Investigations*, vol. 10, trans. David Bourke, 242-259. New York: Seabury.

————. 1978a. Ignatius of Loyola Speaks to a Modern Jesuit. In *Ignatius of Loyola*, ed. Paul Imhof and trans. Rosaleen Ockenden, 9-46. London: Collins.

————. 1978b. *Meditations on Freedom and the Spirit*. Trans. Rosaleen Ockenden, David Smith and Cecily Bennet. New York: Seabury Press.

————. 1979. Modern Piety and the Experience of Retreats. In *Theological Investigations*, vol. 16, trans. David Morland, 135-155. London: Darton, Longman & Todd.

————. 1979b. Enthusiasm and Grace. In *Theological Investigations*, vol. 16, trans. David Morland, 35-52. London: Darton, Longman & Todd.

————. 1979c. The One Christ and the Universality of Salvation. In *Theological Investigations* vol. 16, trans. David Morland, 199-224. London: Darton, Longman & Todd.

————. 1981a. "The Intermediate State." In *Theological Investigations*, vol. 17, trans. Margaret Kohl, 114-124. London: Darton, Longman & Todd.

————. 1981b. How to Receive a Sacrament and Mean It. In *The Sacraments: Readings in Contemporary Sacramental Theology*, ed. Michael J. Taylor, 71-80. New York: Alba House.

————. 1981c. The Body in the Order of Salvation. In *Theological Investigations*, vol. 17, trans. Margaret Kohl, 71-89. London: Darton, Longman & Todd.

————. 1981d. The Abiding Significance of the Second Vatican Council. In *Theological Investigations*, vol. 20, trans. Edward Quinn, 77-89. New York: Crossroad.

————. 1982. *Foundations of Christian Faith: An Introduction to the Idea of Christianity*. Trans. William V. Dych. New York: Crossroad.

————. 1983a. Christian Dying. In *Theological Investigations*, vol. 18, trans. Edward Quinn, 226-256. New York: Crossroad.

————. 1983b. The Human Question of Meaning in the Face of the Absolute Mystery of God. In *Theological Investigations*, vol. 18, trans. Edward Quinn, 89-104. New York: Crossroad.

————. 1983c. Experience of the Holy Spirit. In *Theological Investigations*, vol. 18, trans. Edward Quinn, 189-210. New York: Crossroad.

————. 1983d. On the Importance of Non-Christian Religions for Salvation. In *Theological Investigations*, vol. 18, trans. Edward Quinn, 288-295. New York: Crossroad.

————. 1983e. Purgatory. In *Theological Investigations*, vol. 19, trans. Edward Quinn, 181-193. New York: Crossroad.

————. 1983f. *The Love of Jesus and the Love of Neighbor*. Trans. Robert Barr. New York: Crossroad.

————. 1983g. Mary and the Christian Image of Women. In *Theological Investigations*, vol. 19, trans. Edward Quinn, 211-217. New York: Crossroad.

————. 1985. *I Remember : An Autobiographical Interview with Meinold Krauss*. Trans. Harvey D. Egan. New York: Crossroad.

————. 1986a. *Politische Dimensionen Des Christentums: Ausgewahlte Texte Zu Fragen Der Zeit*. Ed. Herbert Vorgrimler. Munich: Kösel.

————. 1986b. *Karl Rahner in Dialogue: Conversations and Interviews 1965-1982*. Translation ed. Harvey Egan and ed. Paul Imhof and Hubert Biallowons. New York: Crossroad.

————. 1988. A Theology that We Can Live With. In *Theological Investigations*, vol. 21, trans. Hugh M. Riley, 99-112. New York: Crossroad.

————. 1990. Letter to Cardinal Juan Landazuri Ricketts of Lima, Peru, 16 March 1984. In *Liberation Theology: A Documentary History*, ed. and trans. Alfred T. Hennelly. Maryknoll, New York: Orbis Books.

————. 1991. *Faith in a Wintry Season: Conversations and Interviews with Karl Rahner in the Last Years of His Life*. Trans. Harvey Egan and ed. Paul Imhof and Hubert Biallowons. New York: Crossroad.

————. 1991b. Christian Pessimism. In *Theological Investigations*, vol. 22, trans. Joseph Donceel, 155-162. New York: Crossroad.

————. 1992a. Experiencing the Spirit. In *The Practice of Faith: A Handbook of Contemporary Spirituality*, eds. Karl Lehmann and Albert Raffelt, 77-83. New York: Crossroad.

————. 1992b. The Social Dimension of Hope. In *The Practice of Faith: A Handbook of Contemporary Spirituality*, eds. Karl Lehmann and Albert Raffelt, 257-259. New York: Crossroad.

————. 1993a. *The Great Church Year: The Best of Karl Rahner's Homilies, Sermons, and Meditations*. Trans. Harvey Egan and ed. Albert Raffelt. New York: Crossroad.

————. 1993b. The Birth of the Lord. In *The Content of Faith: The Best of Karl Rahner's Theological Writings*, eds. Karl Lehmann and Albert Raffelt, trans. ed. Harvey Egan, trans. Kenneth Baker, 286-289. New York: Crossroad.

————. 1997a. Before God. In *Prayers for a Lifetime*, ed. Albert Raffelt, trans. Rosaleen Brennan, 4-8. New York: Crossroad.

————. 1997b. God of Knowledge. In *Prayers for a Lifetime*, ed. Albert Raffelt, trans. James M. Demske, 14-20. New York: Crossroad.

————. 1997c. God of the Living. In *Prayers for a Lifetime*, ed. Albert Raffelt, trans. James M. Demske, 144-149. New York: Crossroad.

————. 1997d. The Seven Last Words. In *Prayers for a Lifetime*, ed. Albert Raffelt, trans. William V. Dych, 48-59. New York: Crossroad.

————. 1997e. Meeting Jesus. In *Prayers for a Lifetime*, ed. Albert Raffelt, trans. Renate Craine, 81-82. New York: Crossroad.

————. 1997f. The Life of Grace. In *Prayers for a Lifetime*, ed. Albert Raffelt, trans. Rosaleen Brennan, 95-97. New York: Crossroad.

————. 1997g. The Sacrament of the Altar. In *Prayers for a Lifetime*, ed. Albert Raffelt, trans. Rosaleen Brennan, 127-129. New York: Crossroad.

————. 1999. *Encounters with Silence*. Trans. James M. Demske. South Bend, IN: St. Augustine's Press.

————. 2005. *The Trinity*. Trans. Joseph Donceel, with Introduction, Index and Glossary by Catherine Mowry LaCugna. New York: Crossroad.

Rahner, Karl, and Herbert Vorgrimler. 1965. *Theological Dictionary*. Trans. Richard Strachan and ed. Cornelius Ernst. New York: Herder and Herder.

————. 1981. *Dictionary of Theology*. Trans. Richard Strachan, David Smith, Robert Nowell and Sarah O'Brien Twohig. 2nd ed. New York: Crossroad.

Raueiser, Stefan. 1996. *Schweigemuster: Uber die Rede vom Heiligen Schweigen*. Frankfurt am Main: Peter Lang.

Reno, Russell R. 1995. *The Ordinary Transformed: Karl Rahner and the Christian Vision of Transcendence*. Grand Rapids: William B. Eerdmans Publishing Company.

Russell, Letty M. 1974. *Human Liberation in a Feminist Perspective— A Theology*. Philadelphia: Westminster.

Scanlon, Michael J. 1999. A Deconstruction of Religion: On Derrida and Rahner. In *God, the Gift, and Postmodernism*, ed. John D. Caputo and Michael J. Scanlon, 223-228. Bloomington: Indiana University Press.

Schwerdtfeger, Nikolaus. 1982. *Gnade und Welt : Zum Grundgefüge von Karl Rahners Theorie der "anonymen Christen."* Freiburg: Herder.

Tallon, Andrew. 1982. *Personal Becoming: In Honor of Karl Rahner at 75*. Milwaukee: Marquette University Press.

Taylor, Mark Lloyd. 1986. *God Is Love: A Study in the Theology of Karl Rahner*. Atlanta: Scholars Press.

Tracy, David. 1994. Theology and the Many Faces of Postmodernity. *Theology Today* 51 (1): 104-14.

Turner, Denys. 1995. *The Darkness of God: Negativity in Christian Mysticism*. Cambridge: Cambridge University Press.

Vorgrimler, Herbert. 1966. *Karl Rahner: His Life, Thought and Works*. Trans. Edward Quinn. Glen Rock, N.J.: Deus Books.

————. 1986. *Understanding Karl Rahner: An Introduction to His Life and Thought*. Trans. John Bowden. New York: Crossroad.

# INDEX

## A

Abraham, Susan 93, 181, 233
Adams, Nicholas 7, 23, 32, 63, 197, 233
All-Cosmic Soul 145-149
Anonymous Christianity 96, 103-106, 108, 195
Apocatastasis 140
Apologetics 14, 16, 33, 60, 72, 176, 177, 179, 195
Apophatic 11, 73, 213, 221
Austin, J. L. 67, 233

## B

Bell, Catherine 32, 233
Berryman, Phillip 114, 233
Beste, Jennifer 170, 171, 186, 192, 233
Body/Soul Relation 12, 13, 36, 49, 67, 75, 83, 122, 123, 137, 144, 145, 147, 148, 157, 159, 188
Boros, Ladislaus 127, 233
Brinkman, Bruno 37, 200, 233
Burke, Patrick 14, 233, 236
Butler, Judith 166, 233

## C

Cannon, Katie 218, 233
Caponi, Francis 31, 64, 234
Carr, Anne 181, 184
Categorical 22, 24, 25, 27, 55, 58, 73, 86, 99, 185, 203

Chauvet, Louis-Marie 158, 159, 161, 162, 234, 236
Chopp, Rebecca 214, 218, 234, 236
Christology 29, 83, 93, 102, 146, 198, 200, 235
Church 32, 47, 61, 63, 97-99, 101, 104, 105-107, 109, 112, 116, 118, 134, 175, 176, 180, 195-198, 216
Coffey, David 30, 44, 100, 103, 234
Communion of Saints 112, 146, 149, 230
Community 8, 10, 11, 15, 36, 40, 52, 63, 76, 101, 106, 109-114, 116-119, 122, 137, 150, 160, 167, 168, 172, 178, 179, 183, 187, 209, 213, 214, 225-227, 229-232
and the individual 12, 13, 113, 119, 120, 137, 150, 213
Constructivism 168, 193-195
Conway, Eamonn 96, 97, 234
Creation 11, 25, 29, 30, 35, 42, 45, 69, 75, 92, 116, 131, 145, 163, 172, 182, 183, 187, 198, 200, 203, 226, 228, 232

## D

Dallavalle, Nancy A. 181, 234
Damnation 85, 97, 123, 136
Death 10-13, 34, 36, 39, 48, 49, 50, 52, 53, 58, 75, 79, 81, 101, 114, 122-136, 138-140, 142-146, 148, 150-153, 159, 198,

201, 202, 205, 211-215, 220,
224, 227, 229-232
and dying in sin 128
and immortality 12, 13, 123, 128,
144, 152
and the finality of our freedom
25, 125, 128, 129, 135, 138,
140, 142, 143, 152, 202, 212,
228
as act 126, 127
as passive 124, 132, 133, 149,
151, 193
Derrida, Jacques 55, 59, 158, 163-
165, 202, 234, 245
Descartes, René 13, 17, 32, 62,
156-160, 166, 175, 176, 185,
206, 234
Despair 35, 47, 80, 123, 125, 127,
139, 152, 202, 206, 212, 226
Divine/Human Dialogue 42, 121,
214, 216
Dych, William V. 16, 29, 65, 177,
234, 242, 244

**E**

Egan, Harvey D. 14, 31, 34, 60, 235,
243, 244
Endean, Philip 14, 17, 29, 30, 32,
33, 44, 59, 62, 71, 72, 115,
130, 135, 176, 180, 181, 197,
198, 200, 235
Epistemology 12, 17, 51, 81, 145,
157, 160, 166, 167, 203, 225
and *a posteriori* knowledge 24
and unthematic experience 22, 24,
25, 58, 86, 112
immediate knowledge 30
infinite horizon as condition of
knowledge 24, 33, 80, 204

mediated knowledge 24, 25, 65,
86, 99, 118, 120, 145, 148,
194, 195, 217
Eschatology 12, 112, 122, 131, 136,
138, 142, 147, 194, 195, 198,
227, 230
Essentialism 9, 163, 165, 168, 169,
181, 183, 184, 192-195, 209
eschatological 194, 195
strategic 194
Eternity 11, 36, 49, 50, 88, 125, 127,
128, 131, 139, 141, 144, 147,
148, 150, 151, 199, 228-231
Existentialism 11, 117, 168, 176
Experience 14, 15, 18-26, 30-34,
41-45, 47, 48, 53-55, 58-64,
66, 68-72, 74, 75, 77, 87, 92,
93, 95, 100, 101, 103, 106,
108-110, 115, 116, 118, 126,
128, 138, 151, 152, 161,
167-170, 174-177, 179-181,
183, 189, 194, 196, 197, 200,
203, 206, 207, 208, 211, 212,
222, 226-228, 230
immediate 24, 25, 28, 30, 61, 63,
65, 86, 99, 118, 120, 128,
145, 148, 166, 176, 194, 195,
203, 217
of the everyday 9, 31, 197
thematic 23, 31, 117
unthematic 22, 25, 58, 86

**F**

Faith 9, 10, 14-16, 18, 19, 31-33,
40, 42, 44, 46, 49-52, 62, 71,
72, 79, 86, 89, 91, 94, 97, 98,
102, 105-107, 110, 112, 115,
117, 120, 126, 127, 132-136,
139, 146, 150-153, 155, 171,

180, 184, 198-202, 204, 207, 209-212, 221-224, 227-231
Farley, Margaret 7, 214, 226, 235, 236
Feminism 12, 13, 95, 162, 167, 180, 181, 211, 214-216, 218, 223, 224, 236
Fields, Stephen 67, 235
Finality 125, 128, 129, 142, 143, 202
Finitude 11, 21-23, 25, 46, 54, 174, 228
Fiorenza, Elizabeth Schüssler 214, 235
Fletcher, Jeannine Hill 109, 235
Foundationalism 14, 15, 17-19, 59, 64, 111, 166, 174, 177, 197
Freedom 10, 11, 13, 20-22, 25-29, 35, 36, 40, 42, 51-54, 57, 64, 65, 69, 75, 78, 79, 81-83, 86, 91, 92, 94, 96, 101-103, 112, 113, 115, 117-132, 135-143, 147-150, 152, 153, 155, 160, 168-171, 175-177, 179, 182, 185-196, 201-203, 209, 210, 212, 215, 217, 227, 229, 231
and finality in death 125, 128, 129, 142, 143, 202

G

God
and holy mystery 25, 59, 60, 207, 217
and the term of transcendence 40, 48, 54, 57, 58
and transcendental knowledge 25, 203
as infinite horizon 22, 24, 25, 28, 35, 40, 59, 73, 103, 166, 204, 212

as personal 27
knowledge of 24, 25, 54, 60, 61, 71, 73, 80, 86, 173, 203
self-communication of 28, 29, 30, 31, 35, 44, 52, 60, 82, 96, 100, 102, 103, 112, 121, 129, 136, 139, 155, 178, 181, 183, 191, 198, 209, 212
Goldstein, Valerie Saiving 95, 235
Govinden, Betty 214, 235
Grace 8, 13, 16, 24, 27-32, 36, 41-43, 47, 49, 52, 53, 61, 70, 71, 74, 77, 85, 86, 89, 90, 92-94, 96, 97, 100, 102-109, 116-119, 121, 123, 128, 137, 138, 140, 141, 146, 151, 168, 169, 171, 176, 177, 182, 183, 187, 191, 193, 194, 197, 198, 200, 201, 211, 217, 220, 221, 224, 231
as unexacted 29
sanctification 13, 140, 150
Grant, Jacquelyn 95, 236
Guenther, Titus F. 111, 114, 236

H

Hampson, Daphne 95, 236
Healy, Nicholas 14, 17, 33, 236
Heaven 97, 136, 138-142, 149
Heidegger, Martin 158, 159, 175, 176, 196, 236
Hell 34, 36, 89, 124, 138-140, 142, 149
Heyward, Carter 218, 233
Historicity 26, 27, 118, 183, 189, 194
History 15, 16, 19, 20, 25-27, 31, 36, 41, 43, 57, 67, 71, 73, 74, 97-99, 101, 102, 106, 107, 109, 112-116, 118, 121, 125,

128-131, 137, 138, 141-143,
147, 149, 158, 162, 164, 165,
168, 169, 171-173, 175, 179,
183, 184, 186, 187, 189, 191,
192, 194-200, 203, 209, 211,
212, 215, 223, 224, 227-230
Hogan, Kevin 71, 196, 200, 236
Holy Spirit 10, 32, 60, 86, 116, 145,
149, 176, 204, 207
Hope 31, 42, 44, 75, 81, 98, 109,
115, 126, 132, 133, 135, 136,
139, 180, 199, 208, 212, 225,
226, 229, 231, 232
Humanity
corporate nature of 14, 136, 150
Human Nature 27, 29, 43, 44, 45,
52, 96, 173, 181, 182, 187,
194, 195, 221
Hypostatic Union 43, 44, 45, 53, 90

**I**

Immortality 12, 13, 123, 128, 144,
152
Incarnation 29, 43-45, 83, 88, 89,
220
Intersubjectivity 111, 167, 178, 197
Irigaray, Luce 82, 158, 162, 163, 236
Isasi-Díaz, Ada María 222, 223,
235, 236

**J**

Jesus Christ
and incarnation 29, 43, 44, 45, 83,
88, 89, 220
death of 129
Johnson, Elizabeth A. 181
Jones, Serene 7, 168, 180, 181, 193,
216, 226, 236
Judgment 84

**K**

Kelly, Geffrey B. 17, 60
Kelsey, David 7, 169, 182, 237
Kerr, Fergus 17, 29, 62, 63, 105,
166, 167, 176, 177, 181, 237
Kilby, Karen 13, 18, 19, 23, 30, 32,
33, 72, 106, 181, 202, 237
Kress, Robert 66, 237

**L**

LaCugna, Catherine M. 181, 245
Language 54, 56, 58, 59, 62-64,
70-73, 161-163, 193, 203,
209, 214
and binary oppositions 162
and negative theology 59, 73, 74
and pre-linguistic knowledge/ex-
perience 59, 60, 62, 71, 161
utility words 68
Lash, Nicholas 72, 77, 237
Liberation Theology 113, 115-117,
174
Lindbeck, George 63, 170, 237
Loades, Anne 214, 236, 237
Love 10-13, 18, 22, 24, 25, 30, 31,
34-36, 39, 40, 43, 44, 46, 47,
49-51, 65, 69, 71, 75, 76,
78-96, 98, 101, 103, 105,
109, 111-115, 117-122, 124,
126,-132, 134, 135, 137-
139, 141, 149-153, 167-170,
178, 185, 186, 188, 192, 195,
200-202, 205-207, 209, 211,
212, 213, 214, 215, 216, 217,
220, 221, 223, 224, 228-232
absolute 90
and mystery 91
and self-abnegation 94
commandment of 111

of God 35, 80, 82-87, 90-93, 127,
137, 139, 178, 188, 192, 200,
202, 212, 220, 221
of neighbor 11, 83-88, 90-93,
111-115, 117, 118, 120, 121,
167, 202, 220, 228, 231
unconditional 11, 89, 90, 152
unity of love of God and love of
neighbor 85, 87, 93, 119,
202

**M**

Malcom, Lois 237
Mannion, Gerard 134, 146, 224,
229, 237
Marmion, Declan 20, 31, 63, 110,
207, 233-235, 237-239
Martinez, Gaspar 113, 238
Metaphysics 67, 73, 158, 159, 161,
165
Method 9, 14, 16-20, 23, 60, 118,
157, 166, 169, 171, 173, 174,
177, 179, 183, 191, 196
Metz, Johann Baptist 113, 114, 118,
171-173, 196, 198, 208, 232,
236, 238
Milbank, John 118, 173, 174, 179,
196-198, 238
Modernity 10-13, 17, 23, 32, 33, 56,
60, 64, 70, 75, 80, 105, 109,
117, 148, 155-163, 165-167,
169, 173-179, 184, 185,
198-200, 202-209, 211, 212,
224
and certainty 56, 88, 157, 159,
164, 167, 178, 203, 205-207,
209
and the sacred/secular 11, 196
Morton, Nelle 216, 218, 238
Muers, Rachel 75, 238

Mystery 9-12, 18, 24, 28, 30, 33-35,
40-43, 45, 48, 50, 52, 54, 56,
58, 68, 71, 73, 74, 76, 80, 82,
91, 92, 94, 96, 101, 102, 113,
114, 116, 119, 120, 121, 126,
128, 133-135, 139, 141, 142,
153, 182, 185, 195, 199, 200,
202-204, 206-209, 212, 213,
215-217, 220, 221, 224, 230
holy mystery 25, 59, 60, 207, 217
Mysticism 10-12, 23, 31, 61, 79, 93,
113, 114, 117-119, 135, 196,
208, 222

**N**

Negative Theology 59, 73, 74
Nelson Dunfee, Susan 95, 238
Nonfoundational 18, 19, 32, 58

**O**

Obediential Potency 30, 44, 197
Ochs, Robert 34, 124-128, 153, 238
Ontology 9, 28, 30, 56, 87, 120, 145,
146, 158, 195
Ontotheology 158, 161, 162, 165,
207, 208
Openness 10, 12, 22, 23, 25, 37, 40,
54, 77, 79, 92, 93, 95, 96,
109, 110, 112, 113, 119-122,
134, 135, 141, 153, 169, 170,
178, 180, 184, 190, 201-203,
206, 207, 209, 212, 213,
215-218, 220-224

**P**

Personhood 9, 10, 12, 13, 19, 20,
22-27, 29, 30, 32, 35, 37,
43-45, 52, 54, 56, 62, 70,
76, 77, 86, 96, 99, 103, 105,

110-112, 117, 118, 120, 122, 124, 127, 128, 133, 142, 143, 146, 157, 161, 166, 168, 169, 173, 178, 181-185, 187, 189, 190, 192-197, 201, 204, 206, 209, 211-214, 221, 229
and intersubjectivity 14, 75, 76, 81, 94, 110-112, 121, 122, 135, 137, 149, 150, 167, 170, 193, 214, 220, 229
Phan, Peter C. 16, 122, 138, 140-142, 147, 148, 238
Philosophy 10, 13, 15, 18-20, 23, 52, 62, 67, 73, 76, 156, 164, 167, 175, 176, 208
Pineda-Madrid, Nancy 179, 238
Plaskow, Judith 95, 235, 238
Political Theology 114
Postmodernism 9, 12, 13, 15, 17, 56, 70, 75, 109, 155, 156, 161-163, 165, 172-175, 180, 193, 196, 198, 200, 208-211, 224, 225
Prayer 43, 44, 46, 48, 50-52, 76, 139, 150, 151, 188, 206, 222
Purcell, Michael 76, 110, 200, 203, 239
Purgatory 138, 142-146, 148, 191

**R**

Raueiser, Stefan 39, 245
Reason 15, 23, 54, 65, 80, 161, 191, 204, 205, 209
as secular reason 173, 174, 179, 196
Reno, Russell R. 16, 177, 245
Responsibility 25-27, 36, 61, 95, 108, 112, 113, 137, 189, 230

Resurrection 16, 45, 107, 130, 131, 136, 143, 145, 147-149, 171, 198, 229, 231
Russell, Letty M. 7, 16, 225-227, 230-232, 236, 245

**S**

Salvation 9, 11, 23, 36, 85, 86, 97-100, 104, 106-109, 115, 116, 118, 121, 123, 126, 129-131, 135-141, 146, 150, 170, 171, 174, 183, 188, 189, 195, 201, 202, 208, 229
and God's universal salvific will 36, 98, 99, 110, 140, 183
corporate character 98, 130, 131, 136, 139, 141, 150
individual character 136, 137
Sanctification 13, 140, 150
Scanlon, Michael J. 17, 202, 245
Schwerdtfeger, Nikolaus 30, 245
Secular Humanism 84
Silence 8, 10-13, 24, 27, 28, 36, 39-42, 45-56, 58-60, 62, 70, 71, 73-77, 79, 81, 91, 92, 109, 112, 119-121, 126, 127, 135, 145, 150-153, 201, 202, 204, 207, 208, 211-224, 232
Sin 26, 27, 95, 102, 128, 129, 132, 149, 150, 188, 189, 199, 220, 225-228
original sin 27, 128, 149, 188
Social Construction 12, 166, 169, 182, 184, 187, 193-196, 200, 209, 210
Speech 39, 47, 48, 49, 51, 54, 56, 59, 72, 74, 75, 76, 215, 216, 218, 219, 220, 222, 223
Supernatural Existential 17, 18, 23, 27-30, 32-35, 44, 54, 60, 70,

71, 93, 98, 100-103, 118,
120, 130, 167, 171, 173, 182,
184, 197, 217
Symbol 66-68, 71, 73, 75, 102, 106,
186

**T**

Tallon, Andrew 7, 76, 110, 186, 200,
245
Taylor, Mark Lloyd 95, 111, 167,
178, 200, 201, 238, 242, 245
Theological Anthropology 9, 11, 12,
19, 44, 56, 77, 85-87, 93, 98,
110, 119, 122, 123, 127, 136,
142, 146, 155, 156, 169, 170,
172, 179, 184, 191, 194, 196,
208, 210, 213, 214
Time 24, 26, 122, 123, 125, 128,
131, 139, 142, 143, 147, 172,
215, 231
Townes, Emilie 218-220, 235, 236
Tracy, David 7, 113, 157, 158, 175,
200, 245
Trust 11, 81, 88, 125-127, 134, 197,
212, 220, 224
Truth 15, 18, 19, 51, 52, 55, 63, 70,
80, 95, 108, 109, 123, 128,
139, 152, 157, 159, 160, 162,
165, 177, 195, 197, 202, 209,
213, 214
Turner, Denys 7, 23, 213, 245

**U**

Universalism 19, 27, 36, 60, 63, 86,
98, 99, 102, 106, 110, 123,
126, 140, 141, 165, 167, 168,
183, 194, 195, 197, 203

**V**

Vorgrimler, Herbert 13, 73, 74, 140,
141, 175, 181, 232, 243, 245

**W**

Wildung Harrison, Beverly 180,
241
Williams, Delores 95, 218